W9-BSI-447

Convertible
Arbitrage

Convertible
Arbitrage

Insights and Techniques
for Successful Hedging

NICK P. CALAMOS

WILEY

John Wiley & Sons, Inc.

Published by John Wiley & Sons, Inc., Hoboken, New Jersey
Published simultaneously in Canada

For general information on our other products and services, or technical support,
please contact our Customer Care Department within the United States at 800-
762-2974, outside the United States at 317-572-3993 or fax 317-572-4002.

Wiley also publishes its books in a variety of electronic formats. Some content that
appears in print may not be available in electronic books.

For more information about Wiley products, visit our Web site at www.wiley.com.

Library of Congress Cataloging-in-Publication Data

Calamos, Nick, P. 1961–
    Convertible arbitrage: insights and techniques for successful hedging/Nick P.
Calamos.
        p.   cm.   — (Wiley finance series)
    Includes index.
        ISBN 0-471-42361-0 (CLOTH)
    1. Hedging (Finance) 2. Arbitrage. I. Title. II. Series.
    HG6024.A3C345 2003
    332.64′5—dc21
    2003000580

Printed in the United States of America
10 9 8 7 6 5 4 3 2 1

To my wife Kim, my parents Joan and Angelo,
and my children, Zach, Katie, Kristie, and Cole

Acknowledgments

This book's target audience includes beginner and intermediate convertible specialists, hedge fund consultants, and convertible securities traders. It should also be a useful handbook for retirement and endowment plan sponsors that invest in hedge funds and individual investors who would like to understand more about what their convertible hedge manager is doing and what the risks may be.

I want to thank John Calamos, Sr. for the opportunity he provided me 20 years ago to join Calamos Asset Management, which was then a small specialist convertible securities investment shop managing $35 million in client assets. Today, the firm has grown to become Calamos Investments, one of the largest convertible managers in the country as well as a respected growth-equity, convertible-arbitrage, and high-yield manager with more than $13 billion in assets under management. Over the years John has been a mentor and consultant to me in business as well as in my personal life. He has offered me many opportunities and challenges to grow professionally and his commitment to constant improvement and lifetime learning has been an example that I hope to pass on to my children. Put simply, John's guidance has been instrumental in my career and provided the foundation for this book.

I also want to thank my wife Kim, as in all things over the past 22 years, for her love, patience, and support during the many weekends, evenings, and vacations spent in my office writing this book.

A number of colleagues at Calamos Investments have had a hand in the completion of this book. I want to thank Jeff Kelley who spent many hours editing and improving my rough draft. His hard work and talent allowed this book to progress quickly and provided much better flow than would otherwise have been the case. I also want to thank Marilyn Dale, who coordinated most of the communication and scheduling with the publisher, and kept me on schedule. Finally, I want to thank Tony Onorati and Chris Hartman who helped with many of the graphs and charts in the book and Jeff Scudieri who reviewed drafts and provided valuable feedback.

Contents

CHAPTER 1

Convertible Arbitrage: An Overview

There was a time when the word "arbitrage" brought to mind a picture of a mysterious realm in finance which few people seemed to be inclined or at least to have the knowledge to discuss. I knew in a general way that profits depended upon price differences, but I believed that it was with lightning speed at a nerve-racking pace that computations, purchases, and sales must be executed in order to reap a profit.

—Meyer H. Weinstein, *Arbitrage in Securities*

CONVERTIBLE ARBITRAGE: A BRIEF HISTORY

The practice of convertible arbitrage includes the traditional purchase of a convertible while shorting its underlying stock, but also includes warrant hedging, reverse hedging, capital structure arbitrage, and various other techniques that exploit the unique nature of the global convertible and warrant marketplace. While the quantitative modeling, arcane mathematics, and hedge fund strategies affiliated with such techniques may make the practice seem a symbol of the latest in financial innovation, it has actually been around for more than a century, practically since the launch of convertible securities. Convertible securities came into being as a way to make securities more attractive to investors. Convertible bonds are not new; issuers and investors have been using them since the 1800s. During the nineteenth century, the United States was what we would now classify as an emerging market. It was not easy to gain access to capital in a rapidly growing country. The convertible clause was added first to mortgage bonds to entice investors to finance the building of the railroads. The Chicago, Milwaukee & St. Paul Railway, for example, used many convertible issues for financing between

1860 and 1880. In 1896, that company had 12 separate convertible issues outstanding, most bearing a 7 percent coupon.

Convertible securities are relatively simple in concept: A convertible bond is a regular corporate bond that has the added feature of being converted into a fixed number of shares of common stock. Conversion terms and conditions are defined by the issuing corporation at issuance. (A convertible security may also be preferred stock, but convertibles are best understood by studying convertible bonds.) The actual terms can vary significantly, but the traditional convertible bond pays a fixed interest rate and has a fixed maturity date. The issuing company guarantees to pay the specified coupon interest, usually semiannually, and the par value, usually $1,000 per bond, upon maturity. Like other nonconvertible bonds, a corporation's failure to pay interest or principal when due results in the first step toward company bankruptcy. Therefore, convertible bonds share with nonconvertible bonds the feature that bond investors consider most precious: principal protection. Convertibles are senior to common stock but may be junior to other long-term debt instruments. Convertibles have one important feature that other corporate bonds do not have: At the holder's option, the bond can be exchanged for the underlying common stock of the company. This feature completely changes the investment characteristics of the bond, and is one of the characteristics that make convertible arbitrage possible.

Meyer Weinstein's 1931 book, cited above, notes that with the advent of rights, warrant options, and convertible securities that began during the 1860s railroad consolidation, arbitrage in equivalent securities was born. By the 1920s, the practices and techniques established became the focus of Weinstein's book; while rudimentary, they were effective. Most of the convertible, warrant, and rights arbitrage positions depicted in the book either offered discounts to parity at conversion, or were passive hedges without mathematical precision. Although lacking the exactitude required today, these hedges were driven by the same premise: to successfully exploit the non-linear relationship of the convertible with respect to the underlying stock:

> If the price of the stock and the convertible security of a company are not rising and falling together, there is an opportunity for the arbitrageur to take a long position in the convertible security, and a short position in the stock into which the convertible security is convertible. When the convertible security is selling at a price close to its investment value, and the price of the stock into which it is convertible is not at a great discount, the arbitrageur may buy the convertible security and sell one-half of the stock short, leaving himself in a position of being theoretically long and short at the same time. In this form of arbitrage he is hedged against either a rise or

> a fall of the stock, and any rise in the convertible security will be a
> profit. (Weinstein, *Arbitrage in Securities*, p. 151)

Weinstein is describing a classic convertible "market-neutral" hedge, still a
cornerstone of contemporary convertible arbitrage practices. Without the
benefit of option pricing models or financial calculators, however, the early
years of arbitrage resembled more art than science. The author does not attempt to quantify investment values (fixed income components), and most
hedging is based on shorting simply "one-quarter," "one-half," or "three-
quarters" of the stock against the long convertible position. Since the same
limits of precision applied to the whole marketplace, presumably greater inefficiencies still left room for successful arbitrage. Despite the simpler nature
of the hedging described in this book written more than 70 years ago, it remains remarkably relevant to convertible arbitrage practiced today. The
book ventured into some of the pitfalls and basic necessities, including margin, short interest rebates, trading, merger arbitrage, and even international
securities arbitrage.

In 1967, Edward O. Thorp's and Sheen T. Kassouf's book, *Beat the
Market*, became a must read for the convertible and warrant arbitrage community. This may be the first book that approached the convertible arbitrage
market in a mathematical format. (Thorp had already made a name for himself as a master of quantitative systems a few years earlier, when his best-
selling book, *Beat the Dealer*, introduced card counting to players of Black
Jack.) The authors advanced the concept of breaking down convertibles into
two components, bond and warrant, and quantifying each separately in order
to identify hedging opportunities. Using their approach, they sought to identify a convertible when priced close to its value strictly as a fixed-income instrument (its investment value), while also selling close to its equity value
(conversion value). Issues with these attributes tend to be undervalued and
offer good downside protection (being priced close to their bond "floor"),
along with a high degree of upside participation should the stock price rally.
Not content with the returns of a market-neutral strategy, Thorp and Kassouf
also looked for the opposite hedge opportunity by identifying overpriced issues
and applying a ratio hedge (a strategy to be discussed in Chapter 9). The authors' portrayals of their successes in ratio and reverse hedging thus promoted
using mathematical formats well beyond Weinstein's less precise market neutral hedges, and signaled the beginnings of the complex quantitative modeling
techniques that make up the toolbox of the modern convertible arbitrageur.

John Calamos' book, *Convertible Securities*, 1985, was the first complete
book on convertibles and included option price theory applied to convertible
valuation as well as many convertible hedging techniques.

Moving from the conceptual breakthrough of separately valuing a convertible's bond and option components to the current state of convertible

arbitrage, the range of opportunities is clearly wider than at any time in the past, due largely to the rapid growth in the global convertible market, augmented by improvements in technology, financial models, innovative derivative products, and global information flows. With this unprecedented breadth in the opportunity set comes unprecedented complexity, competition, and even new kinds of risks. During this same period, hedge funds have both benefited from and contributed to the growth of convertible arbitrage: As the benefits of the asset class have become more apparent to issuers and to investors, issuance and liquidity have grown exponentially, with hedge funds providing a large role in demand. Typically, most investors who gain access to the convertible arbitrage arena do so through hedge funds.

Although A.W. Jones founded the first hedge fund in 1949, the concept remained virtually unknown until 1966, when *Fortune* magazine highlighted Jones's investment feats. The hedge fund "industry" sprouted up in the next few years as a number of investors (including Warren Buffett) delved into hedging techniques. (The timing of this first wave of hedge funds corresponds with the publication of *Beat the Market*, and is another example of the emergence of quantitative analysis, which began its dramatic, ongoing influence on the investment community.) During the 1970s, the macro investment hedge funds popularized by George Soros made large bets regarding currency, bond, equity, and commodity markets across the globe. These funds were not necessarily hedged nor were they considered market neutral. The bull market of the 1980s and 1990s helped fuel the hedge fund industry's growth as investors looked for even better returns or non-correlated return profiles.

The 1990s produced the hedge fund industry's greatest growth, as it moved from the margins to the mainstream, at least among high-net-worth circles. The globalization of the marketplace, combined with the tremendous wealth creation and technological progress during that decade, all fed the growth of the hedge fund industry. The hedge fund industry today includes funds that specialize in one hedge strategy as well as funds of funds that include a full spectrum of hedge fund strategies. According to Hedge Fund Research Inc., the hedge fund universe was estimated to include less than 200 funds with approximately $20 billion in assets in 1990; by 2000, over 4,500 funds existed with nearly $500 billion in assets—not including leverage. The assets employed in convertible arbitrage strategies have also grown dramatically. According to Tremont Advisors, assets in convertible arbitrage have increased 25-fold over the past nine years. See Figure 1.1.

The hedge fund universe can be roughly divided into two camps: directional strategies that participate in market movements, and non-directional strategies, whose returns are for the most part unaffected by broad market moves. Convertible arbitrage is placed in this second group, along with

Tremont Advisers, Inc.
555 Theodore Fremd Ave.
Rye, New York 10580
T 914 925 1140

Total Asset History
December 1994 – December 2002

U.S. dollars in millions

	Dec-94	Dec-95	Dec-96	Dec-97	Dec-98	Dec-99	Dec-00	Dec-01	Dec-02
Total assets	$798	$1,232	$2,727	$5,276	$6,861	$8,486	$11,912	$20,725	$25,647
Asset flows	$14	$240	$1,188	$1,952	$1,268	$307	$1,698	$7,100	$3,150
% change	0.0%	1614.3%	395.0%	64.3%	−35.0%	−75.8%	453.1%	318.1%	−55.6%

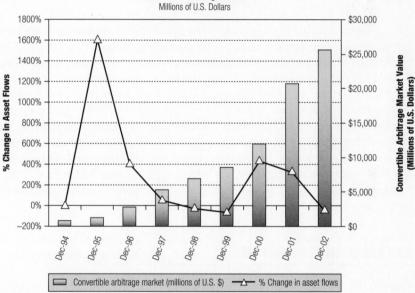

**Convertible Arbitrage Market Value
From Dec-94 through Dec-02**
Millions of U.S. Dollars

Source: Tremont Advisers, Inc, used with permission.

FIGURE 1.1   Convertible Arbitrage Market Value.

other arbitrage practices that tend to gain more investor attention during sideways or declining markets. For example, during the corporate-scandal-ridden second quarter of 2002, more than half of all new hedge fund inflows went to either equity or convertible arbitrage strategies, according to Tremont Advisors Research. The following list contains the various hedge fund strategies common in the hedge fund universe, divided according to directional and non-directional strategies.

Directional Strategies

1. Global macro—invests in global markets emphasizing macroeconomic changes.
2. Equity (non-hedged)—long only equity with manager's specialty focus including value stocks, growth stocks, or sector/industry.
3. Short only—short sells equity for companies that are overvalued.
4. Emerging market—invest in global emerging market countries' debt and/or equity securities.
5. Distressed security—invest in companies that are bankrupt or undergoing reorganization.

Non-Directional Strategies

6. Convertible arbitrage—purchases long convertible securities and shorts the underlying stock with very low equity exposure.
7. Merger arbitrage—generally invests long in the stocks of companies that are being acquired while shorting the stock of the acquiring company.
8. Equity market neutral—long equity and short equity with total net exposure of near zero.
9. Fixed-income arbitrage—includes arbitrage in fixed-income securities, including corporate bonds, government bonds, mortgage-backed bonds, futures, and options. The hedging includes yield curve arbitrage, relative value trades, and swaps.
10. Relative value arbitrage—arbitrage in related securities that temporarily diverge from their expected value or relationship.

WHY HEDGE WITH CONVERTIBLES?

Convertible securities are hybrid issues that have fixed-income and equity characteristics. Convertible arbitrage is popular because of the relatively predictable hedge that can be established between the underlying common stock and the convertible. Convertible arbitrage is often considered a relative-value strategy because convertible arbitrage funds often establish a market-neutral profile with very little correlation to the equity markets. The profit potential is largely a function of relative price inefficiencies between the convertible and common stock along with the series of cash flows derived from the hedge. However, many other techniques are employed that not only rely on the predictability of the relationship between the convertible and its underlying stock but also exploit the convexity of the security as well as the arbitrageur's other expertise. In fact, convertible hedging should be considered a relative-value strategy on the downside because the hedge is less precise and the price inefficiencies are greater, but the value of the short stock and long convertible positions are dependent on each other to varying degrees. While on the upside (when the convertible price is greater than 120 percent of par), the strategy should be considered convergence hedging because of the clear convergence of the convertible and underlying stock.

CONVERTIBLE ARBITRAGE PERFORMANCE

As shown in the list above, the success and dramatic growth in hedge funds over the past decade have been mirrored in the convertible-hedge fund field, and many hedge funds utilize convertible arbitrage techniques. The popularity of convertible arbitrage is attributable to its high risk-adjusted returns with a low degree of equity risk and low correlation to both equity and bond markets.

The performance histories of three well-known convertible arbitrage indexes, each of which includes various managers employing various degrees of leverage and hedging techniques, illustrate the benefits of the strategy. See Table 1.1. The indexes (HFR, CSFB/Tremont, and Hennessee) demonstrate a much lower volatility level (3.5 percent–5.2 percent annual standard deviation) than the global equity index MSCI World (14.1 percent) or the S&P 500 (13.7 percent). More importantly, the Sharpe ratio indicates a much better risk-reward trade-off than the equity markets: HFR's index posts a Sharpe ratio of 1.96, while the Hennessee index comes in at 1.36. Both of these compare very favorably to the 0.48 Sharpe ratios for the MSCI World index, and the 0.97 for the S&P 500. Furthermore, the convertible arbitrage indexes showed more consistent returns with a smoother wealth-creating process. The equity markets posted negative returns in 32 percent to 36 percent of the months over the 124-month period, while the convertible arbitrage indexes posted negative returns in only 13 percent to 18 percent of the months.

The convertible arbitrage indexes show remarkably low equity sensitivity (Beta) and equity correlations. See Table 1.2. The betas compared to the MSCI World index are only in the range of 0.04 to 0.09, meaning that only 4 percent to 9 percent of the volatility in returns of the hedge indexes can be explained by the changes in the world equity markets. The return distribution has a slight negative skew and the positive kurtosis indicates that the distribution also demonstrates a high degree of peakedness relative to a normal distribution and therefore a tighter distribution of returns is present. The low beta and correlation indicate that the source of returns in convertible arbitrage investing is not a function of taking equity market risks. Obviously, the positive alphas generated by the convertible arbitrage indexes are desirable,

TABLE 1.1 Convertible Arbitrage Risk and Return

	# of Monthly Returns	Annual Returns (%)	Volatility Annual (%)	Sharpe Ratio	Worst 1-Month Return (%)	Negative Months	Worst 1-Year Return (%)
S&P 500 (total return)	124	18.3	13.7	0.97	−14.5	32	−3.1
MSCI World (total return)	124	11.7	14.1	0.48	−13.3	36	−16.5
MSCI Europe (total return)	124	13.5	14.7	0.58	−12.6	34	−12.1
HFRI Convertible Arbitrage Index	124	11.9	3.5	1.96	−3.2	13	−3.8
Hennessee HF Index—Convertible Arbitrage	88	10.1	3.7	1.36	−3.3	14	−7.1
CSFB/Tremont Convertible Arbitrage Index	76	9.3	5.2	0.83	−4.7	18	−9.0

Source: HFR, Hennessee, CSFB/Tremont, Datastream, UBS Warburg calculations, period ending April 2000.

TABLE 1.2 Statistical Analysis of Convertible Arbitrage Returns

	Alpha to MSCI World	Beta to MSCI World	Skew	Excess Kurtosis	Correlation MSCI World	Correlation JPM Global Bonds
HFRI Convertible Arbitrage Index	0.86	0.08	−1.52	3.54	0.330	−0.004
Hennessee HF Index—Convertible Arbitrage	0.68	0.09	−1.23	3.17	0.308	−0.058
CSFB/Tremont Convertible Arbitrage	0.71	0.06	−1.66	4.08	0.146	−0.252
EACM Relative-value Convertible Hedge	0.82	0.04	−1.56	4.46	0.183	−0.457

Source: HFR, Hennessee, CSFB/Tremont, Evaluation Assoc., Datastream, UBS Warburg calculations, period ending April 2000.

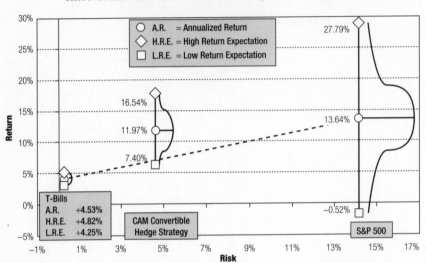

FIGURE 1.2 Capital Market Line (CML) and Potential Return Distributions.

but the low beta, low correlation to the debt and equity markets, along with the high Sharpe ratio makes the case very compelling. In fact, the returns are equity-like while the volatility levels are below that of the bond market. It is clear why convertible arbitrage has grown so dramatically in the past decade.

The Capital Market Line (CML) in Figure 1.2 indicates in yet another way the attractive risk-reward tradeoff produced by convertible hedge investing over the 1990s. The CML is used to demonstrate the risk premium assumed in the Capital Asset Pricing Model, or CAPM, and illustrates the expected rates of return of a particular investment based on its beta and in relation to the risk-free rate of return. Here, we see not only the dramatically lower risk than that of the equity market, but also that the annualized returns are well above the expected return implied by the risk premium. In fact, a full 85 percent of the range of distribution lies above the CML. Clearly, over the long term convertible arbitrage has offered an exceptional financial market investment opportunity.

Our experience at Calamos Investments, with convertible arbitrage can be seen in Figures 1.3 and 1.4. The low correlation with the stock and bond markets produces a significant reduction in overall portfolio risk—without sacrificing any return. In fact, this non-levered convertible arbitrage fund has produced returns that have beat the equity market since 1995 with nearly one-quarter of the volatility. The annual returns can also be seen with the

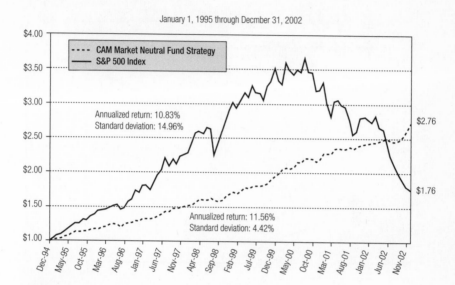

FIGURE 1.3   Growth of $1.00: Calamos Market Neutral Fund Strategy versus the S&P 500 Index.

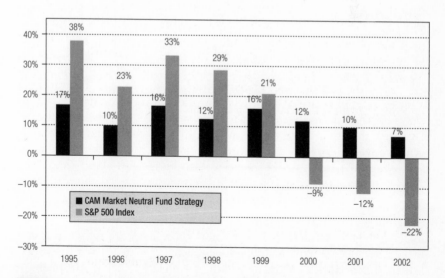

FIGURE 1.4   Distribution Comparison of Annual Calendar Returns: Calamos Market Neutral Fund Strategy versus the S&P 500 Index.

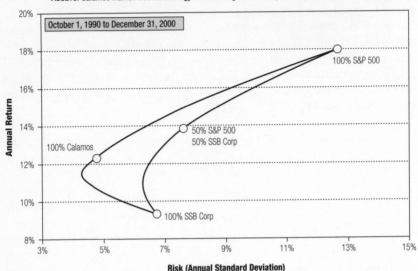

ASSETS: Calamos Market-Neutral Strategy with SSB High-Grade Corporate Bonds & S&P 500 Stock Index

FIGURE 1.5 Risk versus Reward.

bar chart once again indicating a consistent return profile. See Figure 1.4. The smoother wealth creation process created by blending convertible arbitrage into the asset mix moves investors into the coveted northwest quadrant of the risk-return spectrum. Another reason for the surge in convertible arbitrage in the hedge fund products can be seen by the positive shift in the efficient frontier that has occurred from including convertible arbitrage funds into the asset mix as demonstrated in Figure 1.5.

WHAT ABOUT RISKS?

Calling convertible arbitrage a "low-risk" strategy is calling it a low-volatility one, but it should not suggest that the strategy does not encounter *types of* risk; indeed, the strategy is immersed in risk. It could be said that convertible arbitrage is actually defined by how those risks are recognized, controlled, avoided, or exploited. Investment hedging is an attempt to avoid or lessen a financial risk or loss by making a counterbalancing investment. In practice, hedging techniques create a tradeoff between acceptable and unacceptable risks by managing or attempting to eliminate specific unacceptable risks. The hedge or counterbalancing position often introduces a new, arguably controlled, risk to the position. Of course the objective would be to control the risks that are predictable or acceptable while retaining risks that are not significant or are very unlikely. In this respect, convertible arbitrage is no different than other hedging practices, as many types of risks and profit opportunities exist. Chapter 3 will further investigate the types of macro risk factors and the convertible arbitrageur's methods of controlling them, briefly listed here:

1. *Equity Market Risk*—Convertible arbitrageurs control equity volatility by shorting the underlying stock against the long convertible position, producing a very low beta risk and if properly hedged, a market neutral position.
2. *Interest Rate Risk*—Like all corporate bonds, prices of convertible bonds move inversely to interest rate changes. The degree of sensitivity to a change in rates varies, and is a function of how closely the issue trades in relation to the fixed income value of the security. The short stock position provides a degree of hedging against rising interest rates because such a change often precipitates declining stock prices. Also, unlike its fixed income value, a convertible's embedded option value instead moves in tandem with rate changes and provides some additional interest rate protection. In general, convertible arbitrageurs hedge interest rate risk with treasury futures or interest rate swaps.
3. *Credit Risk*—Convertible arbitrage is exposed to credit risk through the long convertible position. To some extent, the short stock position will hedge a portion of the credit-spread risk because as spreads widen, stock prices generally decline. But to eliminate most of the credit-spread risk with a short stock position, the arbitrageur would need to short considerably more stock than a neutral hedge profile would call for, placing the position at considerable risk should spreads not widen and stock prices appreciate. Convertible arbitrageurs typically hedge credit-spread risk with the use of credit default swaps or by shorting a straight bond or another convertible bond from the same issuer against the long convertible position.
4. *Liquidity Risk*—Convertible arbitrage is subject to various liquidity risks, including the long convertible position not trading well and bid-ask spreads widening, the short stock borrow being called in, or a short squeeze occurring. Lower credit quality convertibles face additional liquidity risks if they fall out of favor during certain market environments. Also, liquidity risk can occur due simply to the size of an issue when issued by small companies or in small amounts. Since hedging liquidity risk is not possible, the arbitrageur must utilize the listed options market, eq-

uity market, and straight corporate market to provide additional protection against the difficult liquidation of a long, or the calling in of a short.

5. *Legal Provision and Prospectus Risks*—The prospectus provides many degrees of potential risks for issues such as early call, take-over protection, special dividends, last interest rate payment in the event of call, and so forth. Convertible arbitrageurs can best protect against these risks by being aware of the potential pitfalls and by adjusting the hedge or type of hedge to address any such risks.

6. *Currency Risks*—Convertible arbitrage opportunities often cross many borders, exposing positions to currency risks. In some convertible structures, multiple currency risks are present. Arbitrageurs generally employ currency futures or forward contracts to hedge this risk.

7. *Leverage Risk*—Financial leverage is one of the major macro risks that exist in the hedge world. Leverage magnifies returns—and mistakes. It is important to understand the degree of leverage employed in the convertible hedge marketplace as well as the entire hedge universe. Shocks to the system often cause a huge exodus out of a particular market or asset type, a situation made all the more severe if leverage is excessive. When short interest rates rise and increase the cost of carry for hedge funds, de-leveraging can have a disruptive market impact. Although arbitrageurs can avoid this problem by hedging against short interest rates, in general all of the above macro risks need to be further hedged if a highly levered market is disrupted.

Another important facet of the convertible market that attracts hedge funds is the ability to establish hedged positions that earn a levered yield while offsetting any equity risk in the underlying stock. In fact, the levered yield hedge profile—in certain interest rate environments with convertibles trading in the money—offers the nearly perfect hedge (this hedge, and the application of leverage in general, is explained further in Chapter 5).

Not all convertible arbitrageurs seek to master all of the above risk opportunities and pitfalls: Convertible-hedge funds will often establish positions that have a fundamental or credit bias as well as an interest-rate bias to take advantage of the skill set or expertise of the particular arbitrage firm, in effect determining which risks to isolate and exploit. Prospective investors should determine which of the macro risks a given hedge fund seeks to manage. Proper disclosure from the convertible arbitrage fund should provide some clarity regarding these macro risks and their approach to them. In addition to their awareness of these macro risk issues, arbitrageurs also analyze the more issue-specific "greek" risks (discussed in detail in Chapter 3) and portfolio level risks (discussed in Chapter 10).

BASICS OF CONVERTIBLE SECURITIES

A primer on convertible bonds may be necessary before jumping into some of the more complex valuation and hedging discussions. The concept promoted by Thorp and Kassouf back in 1967 still provides a foundation for such a primer: Convertible bonds can be thought of as fixed-income securities with an embedded equity option. See Figure 1.6. The convertible security has characteristics of both securities and as a result offers an asymmetrical risk and return profile.

The convertible feature allows a convertible holder to convert the bond into a predetermined number of shares of common stock (known as the conversion ratio, this number is set at a bond's issuance).

Conversion Ratio = Par Value/Conversion Price

Conversion Price = Par Value/Conversion Ratio

Like traditional fixed-income securities, the convertible bond has a par value and pays coupon interest (usually semiannually for U.S. issues and annually for European issues). Because the convertible bond offers a stream of cash flows and par value at maturity, it is also sensitive to changes in interest rates and credit-quality assessments, as are other fixed-income vehicles. The convertible bonds embedded option or warrant changes the nature of the security, though, making the convertible's price movements also sensitive to changes in the underlying equity value. Thus, this unique security is sensitive to both equity and fixed-income factors to varying degrees throughout the life of the security. The convertible's unique structure contributes to the non-linear relationship between it and its underlying security, making it especially suitable for hedging.

Figure 1.7 illustrates the convertible's structure and risk/reward trade-off: The horizontal axis represents the underlying stock's price range for the convertible, while the vertical axis represents the convertible bond's price range. The horizontal line labeled investment value (*IV*) represents the fixed-

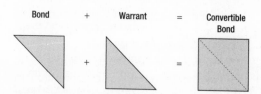

Bond   +   Warrant   =   Convertible Bond

FIGURE 1.6 The Convertible Bond.

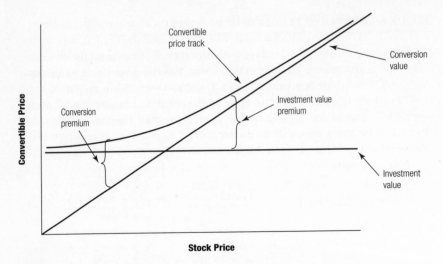

FIGURE 1.7   Convertible Structure and Risk-Reward Tradeoff.

income value of the convertible. The investment value is equal to the present value of the coupon interest payments plus the principal value discounted at the appropriate credit-adjusted rate, where:

$$IV = \sum_{t=1}^{n} CPN/(1 + k)^t + par/(1 + k)^n$$

CPN = coupon, par = par value, k = credit adjusted discount rate, n = number of periods to maturity, t = current time.

The fixed-income value (investment value) will rise or fall in accordance to changes in either interest rates or credit-quality ratings. Of course, the investment value approaches par value as maturity nears, so it increases in value each year, if all other factors were held constant.

Since each convertible can be converted into a predetermined number of shares of common stock, we can represent this equity value on the graph as a 45-degree line. As the stock price increases, the equity value (conversion value) of the convertible also increases. The investment value and the conversion value become minimum values for the convertible price and represent boundary conditions for convertible valuation. This occurs because if the value of the convertible breaches either of these boundaries, theoretically a risk-free arbitrage would exist with speculators quickly correcting such an inefficiency. In reality, slight discounts to conversion value do occur. Discounts to the investment value may also occur, but only rarely in the investment-grade universe. In the below-investment-grade convertible universe, where bond valuation is more a matter of supply and demand as well as an art form, many opportunities present themselves. But to maintain the simplicity of this discussion, the conversion value and the investment value represent hard boundary conditions. In fact, convertibles normally trade at a premium to these values because they represent the combination of these components. The investment value premium represents the amount that the convertible is trading above its investment value or fixed-income component expressed as a percentage. The higher the investment value premium, the more equity sensitive the issue.

$$\text{Investment Value Premium} = \frac{(\text{Convertible Price} - \text{Investment Value})}{\text{Investment Value}}$$

The premium above conversion value represents the percentage premium that the convertible is trading above its equity value component. The higher the conversion premium, the lower the equity sensitivity, and the lower the conversion premium, the more equity sensitive the issue. The conversion value is also known as parity value in the convertible marketplace.

$$\text{Conversion Value Premium} = \frac{(\text{Convertible Price} - \text{Parity})}{\text{Parity}}$$

Figure 1.7 also depicts the investment value, investment value premium, conversion value, and conversion premium, and finally the theoretical convertible price track. The convertible price track looks similar to a call option price track. The non-linearity of the price track presents convertible buyers and arbitrageurs with a unique risk/reward opportunity. The convertible theoretically has unlimited appreciation potential with limited downside risk.

To understand the basic convertible terms and premiums, let's start with a hypothetical convertible as seen in Figure 1.7. The convertible is a 5 percent coupon issued by XYZ Corporation with a 10-year maturity and each bond is convertible into 50 shares of stock with a conversion price of $20. The current bond price is 100 percent of par and the stock is priced at $16 per share. The issuing company has an existing straight corporate bond with equivalent seniority trading at 400 basis points over the 10-year treasury bond. Since each bond is convertible into 50 shares of stock, the conversion value of the bond is currently calculated by multiplying the 50 shares by the $16 stock price for a conversion value of $800 per bond. The conversion premium is the difference in percentage terms between the current bond price of $1,000 and the current conversion value of $800 or {($1,000 – $800)/$800} = .25 or 25 percent premium. The investment value can be determined by discounting the present value of the coupon and principal payments (using the formula for investment value discussed at the beginning of this section) at the 400 basis points above the 10-year treasury that is currently yielding 4 percent to maturity. Therefore, discounting the 5 percent bond at 8 percent results in a investment value of $799 per bond. The investment premium is the difference between the current bond price and the investment value or {($1,000 − $799)/799} = 25.2 percent.

RISK-REWARD ANALYSIS

Convertibles make excellent hedge vehicles because of the certainty of convergence in value to parity as the stock price climbs as well as the convergence to fixed-income value as the stock price declines. But they also are an excellent hedge vehicle because of the convexity of the relationship between the stock price moves and the convertible price. This non-linear relationship is the gamma in the convertible that also explains the risk-reward ratio in the investment.

The risk-reward ratio can be determined by moving the stock price up and calculating the convertible's value and total return relative to the underlying stock and then doing the same with a downward stock price move. Chapters 1 and 2 discuss how the convertible's value can be determined. In our XYZ example, if the stock price moves up 20 percent over the next 12 months, the convertible is expected to move up 11 percent and with income the total return should be 16 percent for an upside capture of 16/20 or 80 percent. For a 20 percent stock price decline, the convertible is expected to decline 9 percent and with income be down only 4 percent for a downside capture of only 20 percent. This convertible offers a reward to risk ratio of 4 to 1. Hedging this type of convertible and capturing some of this gamma is explained later in Chapter 6.

METHODS OF VALUATION

Determining the "correct" price track for a convertible involves option pricing models with many variables and assumptions. Valuing the non-traditional convertible becomes even more complex and interesting, as we will discuss in Chapter 2. The Black-Scholes option-pricing model, however, can be used for pricing basic convertible structures. Combining a Black-Scholes model to value a convertible's embedded equity option with a basic bond valuation model offers investors a simple model for convertible valuation. The model needs to be adjusted, however, for factors such as dividend-paying stocks, probability-based call terms, adjusted strike prices (based on the fixed-income value and probability of call), dilution, and European style exercises, to name a few. The basic Black-Scholes call option model determines the call value with the following equation:

$$\text{Call option} = C = N(d_1)Se^{-q(T-t)} - e^{-r(T-t)}N(d_2)K$$

$$d_1 = \frac{\log(S/K) + (r - q + \sigma^2/2)(T - t)}{\sigma\sqrt{T - t}}$$

where:

$d_2 = d_1 - \sigma\sqrt{T - t}$ t = current time

C = call option q = continuous dividend yield

T = expiration date σ = stock volatility

S = stock price r = risk-free rate

K = strike price adjusted

$N(d_1)$ and $N(d_2)$ = the cumulative normal distribution functions for d_1 and d_2

Next, we determine the bond value (*IV*, or investment value), the estimated fixed-income value of the convertible. The bond value is also used to discount the strike price of the convertible. That is because, in effect, the convertible is valued as a straight usable bond with a detachable warrant, and the warrant can only be exercised by surrendering the bond in lieu of cash. Therefore, the convertible strike price is discounted by the amount of the bond value's discount from par. Another complicating factor in this adjustment comes from estimating the probability of call and the appropriate investment value as a result of that probability, along with the probability of non-call and the corresponding investment value and call value.

$$IV = \sum_{t=1}^{n} CPN/(1 + k)^t + par/(1 + k)^n$$

where:

CPN = coupon, par = par value, k = credit-adjusted discount rate, n = number of periods to maturity.
Adjusted strike price = $K = IV/Q$
Embedded convertible equity value = $W = C * Q$
Convertible value = $W + IV$
W = embedded warrant
IV = investment value
Q = conversion ratio

Although the Black-Scholes model with an attached bond is straightforward and calculable on a basic financial calculator, the model does not price the

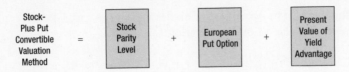

FIGURE 1.8 Convertible Valued as Stock-Plus Put Option.

more complex structures with ease and it simply breaks down in a more dynamic environment.

Stock-Plus Method of Convertible Valuation

Some evaluate convertibles as a combination of the issuer's stock with a relative higher yield, plus a European put option. Instead of viewing a convertible bond as a fixed-income instrument with an embedded option, because of its convertible feature we can think of it as a stock, with a yield greater than its dividend. In adding these two components—the conversion value and the income stream—we still need to account for the fact that the security pays par value at maturity, even if the stock has declined. When valuing a convertible from this viewpoint, the par value's protection against stock declines is effectively a put. See Figure 1.8.

This approach has merit when evaluating some convertible structures. The stock value in this approach is simply the conversion value (stock price multiplied by the conversion ratio) and the put value represents the fixed-income value of the convertible. From this point of assessment, you presume the ability to convert the equity to fixed income or, to state it another way, you have the right to put the equity back to the issuer in exchange for a bond. The exercise price of the put option is the convertible's conversion rate. The valuation also includes the income-stream component, as the present value of the convertible income stream less the underlying stock dividend stream makes up the third component in this pricing technique. The put will not be exercised unless the conversion value of the convertible is below the conversion price at maturity or when called.

$$\text{Parity} = S^*Q$$

$$PV \text{ yield advantage} = (CPN - D)^n$$

where D = stock dividend annual, CPN = annual coupon payment.

$$\text{Put Value} = -N(-d_1)Se^{-q(T-t)} + e^{-r(T-t)}N(-d_2)K$$

Strike = adjusted strike = $K = IV/Q$

In some circumstances, this model will be more intuitive and help frame the hedge and valuation decisions. Convertibles that are deep-in-the-money are the best candidates for this approach because they have a lower probability of maturing and the fixed-income value is significantly below the current price. Therefore, the deep-in-the-money convertibles valuation is derived primarily from its underlying conversion value and the income advantage above the underlying stock yield but some consideration must be assessed to the fixed-income value should the stock price decline precipitously before the call protection expires. This fixed-income value can be modeled and thought of as a put option and valued based on the probability of exercise given the expected stock price volatility over the call protection left on the issue. An example of the use of the stock-plus valuation model may help to understand its usefulness. 3Com Corporation had a convertible with the following terms:

3Com Corporation's 10.25% convertible bond due 11/01/2001.
Stock price: $50.75
Convertible Price: $1,570.00
Conversion ratio: 28.9331
Call protect expires: 281 days

Since the convertible has such a high coupon rate relative to the current interest rate environment, we will evaluate this issue as if the company will redeem the bond as soon as it is available. The first call date is 11/15/1997 and the call price is $1,029.30.

Valuation:

Parity = (stock price * conversion ratio)
= ($50.75 * 28.9331 shares) = $1,468.35

Present value of convertibles yield advantage = (convertible income − stock dividend) discounted over the expected life of the security at the appropriate interest rate. This example = $74.40 = $0.265 per day received for the next 281 days discounted at the cost of money.

Put strike price = (convertible's investment value/conversion ratio)
= ($1,029.3/28.9331) = $35.575

Put value = input option model: strike price $35.575, time to expiration 281 days, stock price $50.75, volatility 38%, European style expiration. This results in a put value = $0.80 and the convertible's imbedded put value is $0.80 multiplied by the conversion ratio (28.9331) for a total put value of $23.15 per bond.

Combine the parts:

Parity	$1,468.35
Plus *PV* of cash flow	$74.40
Plus put value	$23.15
Total convertible value	$1,565.90 as compared to the actual price of $1,570.00.

This stock-plus valuation methodology for deep-in-the-money convertibles may help improve the arbitrageur's understanding of the current valuation and how to set up some possible hedge opportunities.

CONVERTIBLE PROFILE GRAPH

The convertible security in Figure 1.9 offers unlimited appreciation potential because as the stock price increases in value, the conversion option increases along with it. Indeed, many convertible securities have increased 500 percent and even 1000 percent! The graph also indicates that the convertible has limited downside risk; as the stock price declines to near zero, the convertible only trades down to the investment value, as represented by the horizontal line. In reality, if the underlying common-stock price declines and approaches zero, the company's credit is very distressed and the convertible declines to its liquidation value. Figure 1.9 demonstrates this new convert-

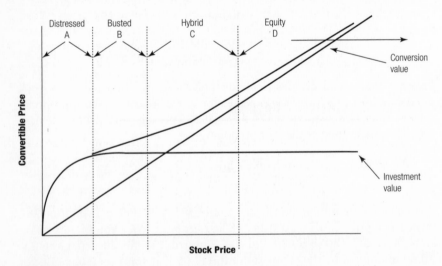

FIGURE 1.9 Degrees of Equity and Fixed-Income Sensitivity.

ible price track that includes the distressed credit range. The convertible arbitrageur must know the credit risk inherent in a position and monitor it closely to avoid the distressed credit zone. There are convertibles, however, that are not subject to the same company credit and equity risks inherent in most convertibles. For instance, some non-traditional convertibles are issued by companies of one credit rating and are convertible into another company's stock with a different credit rating. Because the basis for the credit rating depends on the credit quality of the issuer and not of the company stock, these exchangeable convertibles may avoid some of the distressed-credit risk. Principal-protected convertible structured notes and synthetic convertibles can also reduce this risk. These non-traditional convertible securities will be discussed in Chapter 9.

Figure 1.9 also demonstrates the varying degrees of equity and fixed-income sensitivity as the convertible moves along its price track. The "busted convertible" range means the convertible is out-of-the-money and considerably more sensitive to its fixed-income features than to its equity features. In our XYZ company example, the convertible is exercisable into 50 shares at a price of $20. If the current stock price drops well below this level, say to $5, the convertible trades in the busted range.

The "hybrid range" offers the traditional convertible benefits with both fixed-income and equity sensitivities. The convertible is said to be at-the-money, or the current stock price is very close to its exercise price. In our example, the stock may be plus or minus a few points from the exercise price of $20 exercise or conversion price.

The "equity range" represents the range at which the convertible trades with a high degree of equity sensitivity and either a low degree or no fixed-income sensitivity. The convertible is said to be in-the-money, and in our example any stock price above $30 will trade with a high degree of equity sensitivity. At a $30 stock price, the conversion value is $1,500 per bond.

BASICS OF CONVERTIBLE ARBITRAGE

The traditional convertible arbitrage position entails purchasing long an undervalued convertible bond and selling short the underlying common stock. The amount of stock sold short is a function of the number of shares the bond converts into (conversion ratio), the equity sensitivity of the issue (delta), and the sensitivity of the delta to changes in the stock price (gamma). (The greeks receive scrutiny in Chapter 3.) The objective of the hedge is to produce a risk-return profile that offers an attractive rate of return regardless of the direction the stock moves; it will be discussed in more detail in Chapter 5. The cash flow from the convertible's coupon payment, along

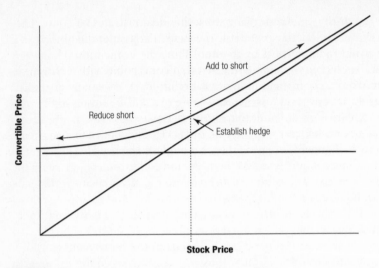

FIGURE 1.10 Traditional Convertible Hedge Profile.

with the short interest credit created from the short stock account, provides a good base return. The hedge will often benefit from movements in the underlying stock and the convertible's non-linear relationship to the stock, offering the arbitrageur additional gains potential. Finally, if the hedge is established when the convertible is undervalued, additional profit potential exists. The traditional convertible hedge profile involves adding to the short stock position as the stock price increases (and the convertible's delta increases), and covering a portion of the short stock position when the stock price declines (and the convertible's delta decreases). See Figure 1.10. As Meyer Weinstein instructed in 1931, the appropriate number of shares to short against the long convertible can determine the hedge's success. Shorting too many shares can cause the hedge to lose money if the stock price increases, and shorting too few shares can cause a loss should the stock price decline. Since each convertible converts into a predetermined number of shares of stock, and a delta can be determined for each convertible, then the appropriate basic hedge ratio is determined by multiplying the delta by the conversion ratio.

Neutral hedge ratio = (Conversion ratio × delta)

In general, convertible arbitrageurs look for convertibles that exhibit the following characteristics:

1. *High volatility*—An underlying stock that demonstrates volatility that is above average. The more volatile the stock, the greater the likelihood of garnering trading profits by re-establishing the hedge ratio.

2. *Low conversion premium*—In general, a convertible with a conversion premium of 25 percent and under is preferred. A lower conversion premium typically means lower interest-rate risk and credit sensitivity, both of which are more difficult to hedge than equity risk. Event risk, such as a merger or takeover, surprise call, or special dividend, can also prompt a conversion premium to collapse and implode the hedge: The lower the conversion premium, the less the premium collapses.

3. *Low or no stock dividend on the underlying shares*—Since the hedge position is short the underlying shares, any dividend on the stock must be paid to the long stockowner, creating negative cash flow in the hedge.

4. *High gamma*—A convertible with high gamma offers dynamic hedging opportunities more frequently, thus offering the possibility of higher returns. High gamma means the delta changes rapidly.

5. *Under-valued convertible*—Since the hedged convertible position is still "long-volatility," the arbitrageur seeks issues that are undervalued or trading at implied volatility levels below the expected norm. The hedge position will provide an additional return if under-valued securities move back to normal pricing.

6. *Liquidity*—The more liquid issues are preferred as a means to quickly establish or close a position.

7. *Below-investment-grade issues with identifiable investment values*—The source of a significant amount of mispricing in the convertible marketplace is due to issues with unclear credit profiles. The arbitrageur must determine the credit quality of an issue to determine the proper hedge ratio. He or she must have a sense of the downside risk in the convertible in order to hedge against a sharply declining stock price.

8. *Stock availability to borrow*—The shorted shares must be available to borrow. Many convertibles that appear undervalued do so because the stock borrow is difficult and the mispricing cannot be easily realized.

9. *Equitable terms and protection*—Many convertible prospectuses offer an array of terms and potential risks. The convertible arbitrageur needs to know the answers to many questions, such as: Upon conversion or put, does the issue pay in stock or cash? Does the issue offer take-over protection? Upon conversion due to a non-voluntary call, will the convertible pay its coupon or dividend? Is the convertible protected against special dividends on the underlying stock? What are the terms of a call or a put option? What is the default status of the issue?

MULTIPLE CONVERTIBLE STRUCTURES

In addition to the traditional convertible bond, many other equity-linked convertible structures exist and more will undoubtedly surface as financial engineering continues to meet the needs of issuers and buyers. The convertible structures range from debt-like to equity-like in their sensitivities. At one end of the spectrum, zero-coupon convertibles and OID convertibles have the most debt-like characteristics at issuance, while mandatory convertibles are issued with the most equity-like characteristics. See Figure 1.11. In the after-market, as equity prices and interest rates change, the characteristics of the various structures can change considerably.

Convertible Preferred Stock

Instead of the traditional convertible structure of a long bond with an embedded equity option, the convertible preferred is structured as a traditional preferred stock with an embedded equity option. In practice, convertible preferred stock behaves similarly to traditional convertible bonds with a long term to maturity. Since preferred stock is lower in the capital structure in regards to claim on assets in the event of default, the credit risk is higher than all other debt holders; only equity holders are lower than preferred holders in this regard. Because of the lower seniority and long term to maturity—if any, the convertible preferred will offer a higher yield than an equivalent convertible bond. The convertible preferred market has tradi-

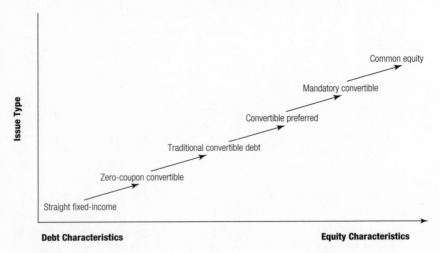

FIGURE 1.11 Convertible Structures—Debt and Equity Characteristics.

tionally been a mainstay in the convertible universe, representing approximately 15 percent to 40 percent of the outstanding market in the previous two decades. In the past, most convertible preferred did not offer an obligation to pay principal value at any time in the future, but many of the new trust-structured convertible preferred now offer a maturity date and principal payment at maturity.

The typical convertible preferred stock pays a quarterly dividend at a fixed rate, while the trust-structure issue pays quarterly interest. Trust-structure preferreds are issued through a subsidiary trust to effectively turn the non-tax deductible dividend issued by the company into a deductible interest payment for the company. Trust-structure preferred are known by numerous acronyms, including: MIPS, TOPrS, QUIPs, TECONS, and BUCS. The purchaser of the trust-structured convertible does not receive the DRD (dividend received deduction) for tax purposes. A trust-structure preferred has a maturity date generally ranging from 20 to 30 years, with a principal payment due.

The flow chart in Figure 1.12 demonstrates how the trust structure is a special purpose vehicle that the issuer guarantees with the sole purpose of changing a preferred dividend payment into a tax-deductible interest payment. The issuer issues a subordinated note to the trust and the trust issues the convertible preferred. The proceeds of the issue flow back through the trust to the issuer. The capital raised is consolidated, and appears as only preferred stock on their balance sheet.

The evaluation of a convertible preferred is similar to valuing a convertible bond, with the exception of long-dated paper with or without principal payment. Convertible arbitrageurs need to address the higher degree of volatility that comes with a longer-term structure with low claims status, but convertible preferred issues are a very active part of the arbitrage marketplace.

Zero-Coupon Convertible Debt

The most bond-like convertible structure is the zero-coupon convertible bond. The zero-coupon bond, as its name implies, does not pay cash interest but instead the bond carries a series of accreting put options. In effect, the

FIGURE 1.12 Trust-Structured Convertible Preferred Securities.

buyer has paid for the series of put options with the coupon stream he forgoes. The issuer can still deduct the phantom interest payment for tax purposes, making the structure more attractive for the issuer. The recent advent of contingent interest convertibles even allows the issuer to deduct their fair straight debt rate, turning the security into a high positive cash-flow vehicle for taxable issuers. That is because the convertible accretes at the lower rate stated in the prospectus and includes the conversion feature, while the issuer deducts interest at the straight-bond equivalent rate that may be 2 percent to 6 percent higher. The zero retains more bond-like features at issue because the put feature provides a bond floor that is close to the current value and this bond floor (put) accretes each year, helping to reduce downside equity risk. The zero-coupon also has a low degree of interest rate risk because of the short-term duration of the series of puts. See Figure 1.13.

Valuation of the zero-coupon convertible must include the series of puts as well as the series of call options that both issuer and buyer can claim as their right. Valuing the zero-coupon convertible as a zero-coupon bond with a call option is partially correct, but the likelihood of putting the bond back to the issuer before a call occurs is also important to proper valuation. The basic long stock plus long put model helps here. Combining the likelihood of the buyer exercising a put with the likelihood of the issuer calling the issue with these two models does a good job at approximating fair value. But, as we will see in Chapter 2, the binomial lattice tree model does a good job of handling these multiple options.

These options are generally not complicated, and arbitrageurs navigate the zero-coupon market quite well. In general, the zero-coupon bond offers better credit ratings and more secure downside hedging for the arbitrage community. But, the lack of income flow, a very important component of total return in the hedge profile, makes these issues less desirable. The series of options embedded in the zero-coupon structure does, however, offer some interesting arbitrage opportunities and hedge profiles, some of which will be discussed in further chapters.

Mandatory Convertible Preferred Issues

Mandatories, the most equity-like of convertible issues, go by the acronyms of DECS, PERCS, PRIDES, ELKS, and so on. Each of these issues is considered a preferred stock whose conversion into common stock is mandatory, usually in three years from issuance. The mandatory convertible offers high dividend yields and a cap or partial cap to upside equity participation. The risk-return profile of a mandatory convertible is very different from the traditional convertible security. Figure 1.14 shows the typical PERCS risk and reward profile. The PERCS security offers a high dividend yield but the up-

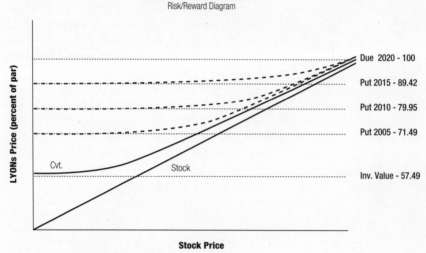

XYZ Inc. 0% Due 2020 (LYONs) Risk/Reward Table

Time	Stock Px % Change	Bond Px % Change	Convertible Participation
1.00 yr	−32.3	−2.1	6.5%
.50 yr	−24.1	−1.4	5.8%
.50 yr	+31.8	+16.2	50.9%
1.00 yr	+47.8	+24.9	52.1%

FIGURE 1.13 XYZ Inc. 0% Due 2020. (LYONS: Liquid Yield Option Notes.)

side participation with equity price moves is capped generally in the 40 percent to 80 percent range. Valuation of a PERCS is relatively simple because it consists of a long stock that it is convertible into and a short of an out-of-the-money European-style call option, plus a yield advantage above the common stock. The short out of the money call option provides the additional yield advantage above the common stock but also caps the upside return. Convertible arbitrageurs may find some hedge opportunities when the embedded short call option is mispriced relative to call options available in the public market, or when the present value of the income stream is not properly discounted.

Another more popular mandatory convertible is the DECS structure. The DECS include multiple options and offer a better risk-reward profile than a PERCS. The DECS structure can be valued as long stock plus short a

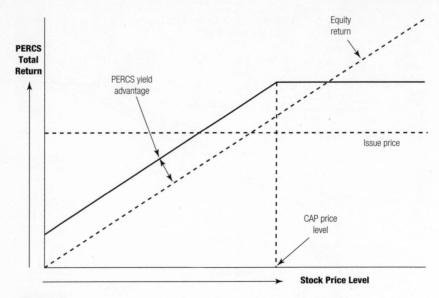

FIGURE 1.14   Mandatory Convertible—PERCS Risk-Reward Profile.

European-style call option at-the-money, plus long a European call option out-of-the-money, plus the present value of the dividend-stream yield advantage. The short European call option is the lower trigger in Figure 1.15 and is usually struck at the current stock price at issue and has a conversion rate equal to one. The second option is a long European call option indicated as the upper trigger and is usually from 15 percent to 30 percent out-of-the-money at issue. The upper trigger has a lower conversion rate than the lower trigger—typically 80 percent of the lower trigger rate. The area between the two triggers is a flat spot or "deck" where the issue does not gain or lose significant values with stock price movement. Below the lower trigger, the security declines one-for-one with the stock, but has a higher dividend yield. The price area greater than the upside trigger provides upside appreciation with the stock price movements but at a lower conversion rate, therefore returning around 80 percent of the stock's upside.

Mandatory convertible securities are popular with equity investors and equity-income funds. They also provide some very good hedge opportunities for the arbitrage community because of price discrepancies that occur and the high degree of certainty at maturity payoff. Chapter 6 will present a detailed discussion about hedging mandatory convertibles with stock or options.

Figure 1.15 shows the DECS risk-reward profile at maturity. Because of the multiple options long and short, it is helpful to see the at maturity payoff structure to understand the dynamics of the security. Figure 1.16 demonstrates

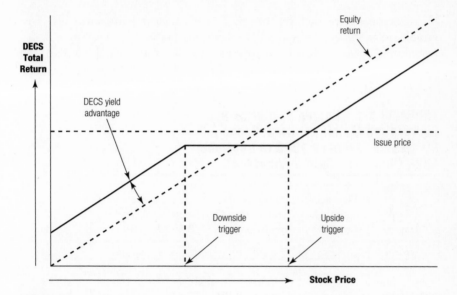

FIGURE 1.15 Mandatory Convertible—DECS Risk-Reward Profile at Maturity.

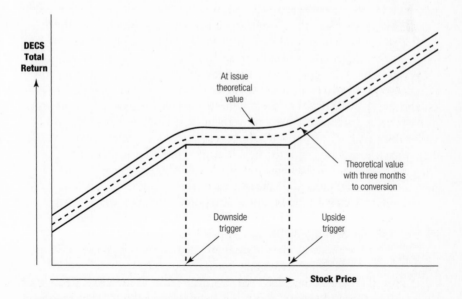

FIGURE 1.16 Mandatory Convertible—DECS Risk-Reward Profile.

the theoretical price track for the DECS at issuance and also with only three months to maturity. As you will see later, profitably hedging a mandatory convertible is not as straightforward as a vanilla convertible because of the volatility and dynamics of the greeks inherent in this structure.

APPENDIX 1.1   Return Statistics and Correlation Matrix to Other Hedge Strategies, January 1990 to December 1999 (Risk-Free Rate Subtracted).

Strategy	Average monthly return	Monthly standard deviation	Correlation to S&P 500	Beta to S&P 500	Alpha
S&P 500	0.8620	3.870	1.000	1.000	0.000
Convertible Arbitrage	0.5159	1.019	0.4027	0.106	0.425
Fixed-Income Arbitrage	0.3609	1.429	−0.0956	−0.037	0.393
MBS Arbitrage	0.4838	1.337	−0.0310	−0.013	0.499
Equity Hedge	1.4256	2.527	0.6453	0.421	1.063
Equity Market Neutral	0.5178	0.973	0.2548	0.064	0.463
Statistical Arbitrage	0.5273	1.088	0.4735	0.133	0.413
Merger Arbitrage	0.6054	1.339	0.5040	00.174	0.456
Relative Value Arbitrage	0.7213	1.191	0.3477	0.107	0.630

Source: From *Market Neutral Investing*, by Joseph G. Nicholas. © 2000. Reprinted by permission of Bloomberg Press.

Correlation Matrix of Market Neutral and Hedge Strategies, 1990–1999.

	Convt. Arb.	Equity Hedge	Equity MN	F.I. Arb.	Merger Arb.	RVA	Stat. Arb.	MBS Arb.	Bonds	Stocks
Convt. Arb.	1.0									
Equity Hedge	0.516	1.0								
Equity MN	0.183	0.466	1.0							
F.I. Arb.	0.124	0.036	0.0067	1.0						
Merger Arb.	0.482	0.473	0.149	−0.082	1.0					
RVA	0.552	0.518	0.201	0.308	0.392	1.0				
Stat. Arb.	0.187	0.252	0.577	0.096	0.244	0.200	1.0			
MBS Arb.	0.360	0.138	0.234	0.658	0.089	0.331	0.116	1.0		
Bonds	0.230	0.137	0.184	−0.274	0.114	0.042	0.427	0.111	1.0	
Stocks	0.398	0.642	0.246	−0.100	0.499	0.345	0.483	−0.033	0.395	1.0

CHAPTER 2

Valuation

Everything should be made as simple as possible, but not simpler.

—Albert Einstein

CONVERTIBLE VALUATION MODELS

The most theoretically accurate convertible model will not ensure your success as a convertible arbitrageur any more than having the most expensive golf clubs will ensure your golf handicap. Because theoretical valuation is as much art as science, a good convertible valuation model is a necessary tool for the arbitrageur's trade—but it is only a tool. Valuation models without understanding offer no competitive advantage, while the combination of modeling with understanding and experience provides the precision often needed to orchestrate a profitable position as opposed to an unprofitable one. Models add value only if their user understands factors such as market biases and supply and demand, and can foresee shifts in both volatility and market preferences.

Convertible arbitrage existed well before the advent of option models, but the models allow for more complex structures and in the end they have kept the relative opportunities the same. The model used should be simple enough to navigate and just sufficiently complex enough to get the job done. As convertibles and their derivatives have become more complex, so too have the requirements for useful models.

BINOMIAL OPTION MODEL

In this new age of financial engineering that is reshaping the convertible marketplace, the increased complexity of convertibles and equity-linked issues calls for a more robust convertible valuation model, as new wrinkles make derivations of the Black-Scholes option models potentially cumbersome. As an alternative, the binomial options pricing model offers additional flexibility and ease in adjustments to model the ongoing innovations in the convertible market. Indeed, a trinomial model with stochastic interest rates capability is even one step better. This chapter will focus on the basics of the binomial model to enhance the readers understanding of this tool and to demonstrate its flexibility.

The binomial option model uses a lattice or tree approach to value an option. This approach allows for easier mathematical adjustments to the more complex convertible structures than does the closed-form-solution Black-Scholes model. A well-constructed, flexible convertible valuation model needs to allow for non-Brownian (non-continuous) motions in stock price movements, stochastic interest rates and volatility levels, and credit spreads that both vary stochastically and are correlated to the underlying stock. (Black-Scholes assumes a Brownian motion for stock price changes.) These allowances are necessary for a convertible model in most cases today, and given the emerging complexity among new issues, models will need to address other adjustments as well. For example, models may now need to take into account step-up coupon payments, dual or triple options on the same security, multiple security conversions, reset features, ratchet clauses, coupon- and premium-make-whole provisions, and a host of contingency clauses. As will be seen below, the lattice method of the binomial model makes it much easier for the arbitrageur to factor in such complexities.

The binomial model can be best understood from Figure 2.1, a two-step binomial tree diagram. Each node represents a different stock price. The tree begins with the initial date (today) and ends at the maturity date of the option. At each node of the tree, the stock price can either move up or down from the current time period to the next. Between each node, the time interval, up/down ratio, and probability remain constant. The intrinsic option value is then indicated at each node. The stock's price movements thus follow a geometric motion, not an absolute dollar change.

Before determining option values, the model needs to establish the range of possible stock prices for the time frame. For simplicity, a two-period binomial option model will be described first. See Figure 2.1. Here, "S" represents the current stock price. During the first period, the stock price can either go up to Su or down to Sd. We will assume here that each occurrence—an up or down movement in price—has an equal probability. If the stock price goes up in the first period, then during the second period the stock can either move up to Su^2 or down to Sd^2. This process is continued over the entire valuation period to determine all possible stock price

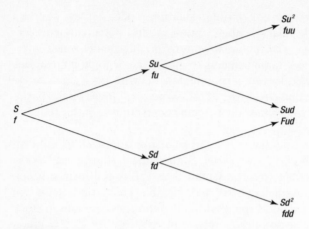

FIGURE 2.1   Binomial Tree.

movements up to and including the time of expiration. The model then computes the terminal option value for each of the range of possible stock prices at expiration (*fuu*, *fud*, etc.). Then, the model moves back step by step along each branch from the expiration time to determine the current option price (*f*).

If we assume the risk-free interest rate is *r* and the time period between each step in the tree is Δt years, then the value of the option at a current stock price of *S* can be solved with the following equation:

$$f = e^{-2r\Delta t} \left[p^2\, fuu + 2p(1-p)\, fud + (1-p)^2\, fdd \right]$$

The variables p^2, $2p(1-p)$ and $(1-p)^2$ represent the probabilities that each of the nodes is reached. The option value is equal to the expected payoff discounted at the risk-free interest rate.

Because it uses discrete time periods, the binomial model offers simplicity and a level of flexibility in pricing options that is unavailable within Black-Scholes models, which are underpinned by continuous time (Brownian) assumptions. For example, the continuous time model requires a constant volatility level for all time periods throughout the life of the option, while the binomial model can be adapted to allow for different volatility assumptions. Evidence shows that stock volatility increases with lower stock prices and decreases at higher stock prices. One possible adjustment, for example, is that during periods of abnormally high (low) volatility for a long dated option, warrant, or convertible, the volatility input into the binomial model can vary: For current and near-term periods, the model can use the higher (lower) volatility, while for periods further out, the volatility can be set to regress to the longer-term expected mean volatility.

The effectiveness and adaptability of the discrete-time-period versus continuous-time models can be further demonstrated as we trace the construction of a basic binomial convertible model, then adjust for various factors in the following example.

The convertible is a 5-year bond (*n*) paying 6 percent interest (I) annually. The issue cannot be called for two years and is convertible into 16 shares (cr) of common stock. The stock's annual volatility is 30 percent (σ) and the current price (*S*) is $50 per share. The 5-year treasury currently yields 7 percent (*r*) with a flat yield curve. The company's cost of credit (k) is 400 basis points above the treasury curve.

First, we build a stock price tree for all periods ending with the convertible's maturity date. The model can be broken up into as many periods as one desires. For simplicity, we will work with a five-period model, even though the tree may be subject to some minor error due to the large gaps between stock price nodes: In practice, a tree with several hundred periods is often used. To determine the stock price movements, a stock volatility (σ), a time interval, and the risk-free interest rate (*r*) must be used. The stock price tree should be constructed with the risk-neutral profile in mind. This is accomplished by calculating transition probability growth rates that are equal to the risk-free rate, as indicated in the transition probability calculation below.

The risk-neutral binomial tree satisfies the arbitrage-free assumption but also allows for a normal-shaped yield curve to be built into the model. The Black-Scholes model assumes a flat yield curve.

If the underlying stock pays a dividend, it can also be built into the tree diagram at this point. The least complex way to adjust the stock price tree for stock dividends is to assume a constant dividend yield, but of course this is not appropriate in almost every case.

To build the stock price tree, the up transition multiplier (*u*) and down transition multiplier (*d*) must be determined from the stock's volatility (σ) and the time (*t*) between each period using the following equation.

$$u = e^{\sigma \sqrt{t}} \quad u = e^{.3\sqrt{1}} = 1.3499 \quad\quad d = 1/u \quad d = .7408$$

Therefore the up transition probability is

$$p = (e^{r\Delta t} - d)/(u - d) \quad p = (e^{.07} - 0.7408)/(1.3499 - 0.7408) \quad p = .5446$$

Down transition probability = $1 - p = .4554$

Start with the current stock price. Multiply it by the up transition and then again multiply the current price by the down transition to get the next two nodes of the tree. Continue this process at each node until the desired number of steps is reached. See Figure 2.2

Once the entire stock price tree is built for the range of stock values over the time to maturity of the convertible, the convertible price tree can be constructed. Unlike the stock price tree, the convertible tree is constructed using backward induction *starting with the maturity date* of the issue and working back to the current time and stock price. The convertible tree can be built to include the issuing company's call feature and almost any other unique twist.

The convertible value at each node is divided into the hybrid's two components. The first component is the value if the convertible ends up as equity, and the second component is the value if the convertible ends up as debt or matures. The probability of conversion to equity at each node must be assigned by overlaying a conversion probability tree. At each node, the security at maturity is worth the maximum of the conversion value or par value plus any coupon payment due.

$$\text{Convertible value} = \text{Max}(S * cr, \text{par value} + I) \text{ where}$$
$$S = \text{stock price}, cr = \text{conversion ratio}, I = \text{coupon payment}.$$

The convertible at maturity will have a series of nodes that determine the tree's final time period, and it is the starting point of the binomial convertible valuation tree.

Using the stock tree in Figure 2.2, the 5-period convertible tree begins with the final maturity nodes and is constructed by multiplying the final stock price by the conversion ratio of 16. If the conversion value is at or below that of the par value plus coupon due, then the conversion probability is 0 and the latter replaces the conversion value. See Table 2.1.

Current	Year 1	Year 2	Year 3	Year 4	Year 5
					224.12
				166.03	
			122.99		122.99
		91.11		91.11	
	67.50		67.50		67.50
50.00		50.00		50.00	
	37.04		37.04		37.04
		27.44		27.44	
			20.33		20.33
				15.06	
					11.16

FIGURE 2.2 Binomial Stock Price Tree.

TABLE 2.1 Conversion Value

Node Location	Final Convertible Value	Conversion Probability
5,5	$3585.90	1.0
5,4	$1967.90	1.0
5,3	$1079.90	1.0
5,2	$1060.00	0.0
5,1	$1060.00	0.0
5,0	$1060.00	0.0

If conversion to equity is optimal, the node is assigned a 1.0 conversion probability; otherwise it is assigned 0.0. The conversion probability tree can now be calculated for the remaining nodes by backward induction, applying the following process: Multiply the up transition probability by the value of the previous up-node plus the down transition probability, multiplied by the previous down-node value. For example, for the node marked (4, 2), the previous up-node has a conversion probability of 1.0 and the up transition probability is equal to .5446, while the previous down-node has a conversion probability of 0.00 and the transition probability is equal to .4554. Node (4, 2) is therefore assigned a conversion probability of .5446.

$$\text{Conversion probability } (q) = (p * Nu - 1) + ((1 - p) * Nd - 1)$$
where Nu = previous up node, Nd = previous down node.

$$q = (.5446 * 1.0) + (.4554 * 0.0) = .5446$$

This process continues for each time period until the current period is reached. The complete tree can be seen below in Figure 2.3

Current /Node	Year 1 /Node	Year 2 /Node	Year 3 /Node	Year 4 /Node	Year 5 /Node
					1.00 (5,5)
				1.00 (4,4)	
			1.00 (3,3)		1.00 (5,4)
		0.91 (2,2)		1.00 (4,3)	
	0.75 (1,1)		0.79 (3,2)		1.00 (5,3)
0.58 (0,0)		0.57 (2,1)		0.54 (4,2)	
	0.38 (1,0)		0.30 (3,1)		0.00 (5,2)
		0.16 (2,0)		0.00 (4,1)	
			0.00 (3,0)		0.00 (5,1)
				0.00 (4,0)	
					0.00 (5,0)

FIGURE 2.3 Conversion Probability Tree.

The conversion probability values will be used to determine the discount rate for the node. The proper interest rate to discount the fixed-income value of the convertible is dependent upon the likelihood of conversion to equity. The discount rate should reflect the risk-free interest rate over the expected time period for nodes that are deep-in-the-money and assigned a conversion probability of 1.0. This is because the investor will convert to stock with no risk of default. Stock price nodes that are well out-of-the-money should reflect the appropriate credit spread above the risk-free rate considering the credit quality of the issue.

Formula to determine credit discount rate:

$$\text{Credit discount rate} = ((1 + rf) * q) + ((1 + k) * (1 - q))$$

Where q = conversion probability,
k = credit spread adjusted discount rate.

At extremely low stock valuations, a distressed credit spread can also be used to reflect the high possibility of credit impairment. This credit impairment valuation reflects the possibility of bankruptcy. Credit-risk assessment is extremely critical in the valuation process for convertibles. The binomial model allows for stock-price correlated credit spreads as well as stochastic credit spreads in the convertible valuation process.

The convertible graph in Figure 2.4 demonstrates how the binomial model allows for the range of credit discount rates in conjunction with the convertible's credit risk. The no-credit-risk portion of the convertible curve has a discount rate equal to the risk-free rate of 7 percent. Here, the convertible is deep in the money and in effect the risk of default is zero. On the other end of the spectrum, the credit-impaired discount rate of 19 percent can be found at very low stock prices with the convertible well out of the money and the risk of default at a very high level. The hybrid portion of the convertible curve, or the portion between the two extremes, represents a weighted probability of these polar scenarios. The flexibility of the binomial model allows for the range of credit assumptions linked to the company's stock price. The credit models and equity linked credit spread tools are discussed further in Chapter 4.

The credit-adjusted discount rate assumptions indicated in Figure 2.4 are appropriate for traditional convertible securities, but should not be used for exchangeable issues, structured notes, and synthetic convertibles. That is because the basic assumption built into the sliding-scale discount rate is that the debt issuer and the underlying stock are highly correlated or come from the same company. At low stock prices, the credit becomes questionable, as the equity market values the company at very low levels. At higher prices, the equity market values the business at a high market value and the issue is

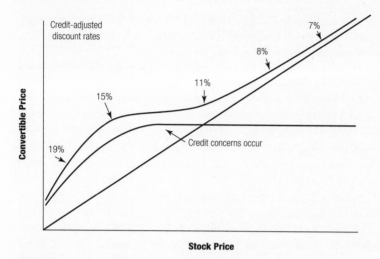

FIGURE 2.4 Allowing for Discount Rates and Convertible Credit Risk.

deep-in-the-money with little risk of default. However, with an exchangeable convertible or structured note, the convertible is backed by one company's credit and is exchangeable into another company's stock. The low stock price in this case has no bearing on the issuer's credit and, likewise, a high stock price may not reflect low default risk because conversion to equity or the cash value of the equity may be subject to credit issues unrelated to the equity.

With the maturity value of the convertible calculated and the conversion probability tree complete, the remainder of the convertible tree can be determined. Moving backward to the next time period, each node is calculated by multiplying the previous up-node value by the up-node transition rate and discounting it at the appropriate credit spread and conversion probability. We then add to this discounted up-node value the discounted down-node value, following the same process.

$$CV = p(Nu - 1/1 + q) + 1 - p(Nd - 1/1 + q) + cpn$$

Where q = credit adjusted discount rate, cpn = coupon payment,
$Nu - 1$ = previous up-node value, p = probability transition value.
$Nd - 1$ = previous down-node value.

At each node, the price should be at least equal to the conversion value. Also, at each node the optimal issuer call and the convertible holder's options or actions must be considered. (Later examples will expand on this point.) The probability of conversion is calculated at each node, along with the fixed-income value discounted at the appropriate credit spread. The convertible value at each node is then calculated by combining the conversion-to-equity value with the probability of conversion with the debt value and the probability of holding or redeeming the issue.

For example, in Figure 2.5 the convertible value at node A with a stock price of $224.12 is determined by comparing the conversion value of $3,585.9 (224.12 × 16.0) and the conversion probability of 1.0 to the maturity value of $1,000 plus the $60 coupon payment. Since the conversion probability is 1.0, the value of the convertible at this node is $3,585.90. At node B, the conversion value is only $178.56 while the maturity value is $1,060. The conversion probability is 0.0, so the value of the convertible at this node is $1,060. At the node marked C, with a stock price of $67.50, the convertible value is $126.92. The convertible value is arrived at by multiplying the credit-adjusted discount value of the previous up-node value of 152.12 by the up transition rate probability of .5446, then adding to this the credit-adjusted discount value of the previous down-node value of 104.4 multiplied by the down transition probability. Finally, the 6 percent coupon is added in, assuming it is paid at the end of this time period.

The credit-adjusted discount rate for this node is

$$(1.07 \times .79) + (1.11 \times (1 - .79)) = 1.0784 \text{ or } 7.84 \text{ percent}$$

The convertible value at node D is

$$(.5446 \times (152.12/1.0784)) + ((.4554 \times (104.4/1.0784))$$
$$= 120.92 \text{ plus 6 percent coupon payment} = 126.92$$

This process continues for each node until the current time period and stock price is reached. See Figure 2.6.

Since the issuer also retains the option to call the issue, the probability of issuer redemption must be considered. This includes redeeming the bond because the coupon interest rate carried on the convertible is higher than the rate at which the company would be able to issue a new convertible, or is close to an interest rate at which straight non-convertible debt could be issued.

In actual application, this basic binomial model would be expanded to cover many more discrete time periods and nodes to accurately determine this standard convertible bond. The robustness of the binomial model makes it easy to incorporate non-traditional convertible structures and terms as well. For example, put features can easily be built into the model by replacing the par value with the put value for the correct node corresponding to the date of the put feature. Likewise, reset features, make-whole clauses, soft-call features, and most other terms can be built into the binomial tree structure. An interest-rate tree can also be constructed to allow for changing interest rates. This allows for stochastic interest rate assumptions.

Current	Year 1	Year 2	Year 3	Year 4	Year 5
					358.59
				265.65	**358.59 (A)**
				272.27	
			196.78		196.79
			209.32		**196.79**
		145.78		145.78	
		165.99		**152.12**	
	108.00		108.00		108.00
	136.68		**126.92 (C)**		**108.00**
80.00		80.00		80.00	
116.89		**111.40**		**104.40**	
	59.26		59.26		59.26
	101.14		**99.87**		**106.00**
		43.90		43.90	
		95.49		**101.50**	
			32.53		32.53
			97.44		**106.00**
				24.10	
				101.50	
					17.86
					106.00 (B)

Upper half of node = parity
Lower half of node= convertible theoretical value

FIGURE 2.5 Parity Tree.

The binomial approach to convertible pricing allows the user easier adjustments to the more complex features we see in the convertible market today. It is also suitable for the early-call events and conversions that convertible holders often face. The binomial stock price tree can also be combined with an interest rate tree to allow for changes in the yield curve over the valuation period.

The convertibles delta and gamma (explained further in Chapter 3) can be determined from the conversion parity lattice tree. The delta is the convertible's sensitivity to changing stock prices or parity level. In this example, the convertible's parity point delta as determined from the parity tree in Figure 2.5 is

$$\text{Delta} = (136.68 - 101.14)/(108 - 59.26) = .73$$

Therefore, a point move in the convertible's parity level should move the convertible price by .73 points. Deltas can also be calculated for a 1 percent move in the stock instead of a point move. The convertible's gamma can also be derived from the above parity and convertible price tree. The gamma is the second derivative of the parity level change in delta and is calculated by the change in delta between the nodes in the first and second years.

$$\text{Upside delta} = (165.99 - 111.40)/(145.78 - 80.00) = .83$$
$$\text{Downside delta} = (111.40 - 95.49)/(80.00 - 43.90) = .44$$

	Current	Year 1	Year 2	Year 3	Year 4	Year 5
						358.59
					272.27	
				209.32		196.79
			165.99		152.12	
		136.68		126.92		108.00
	116.89		111.40		104.40	
		101.14		99.87		106.00
			95.49		101.50	
				97.44		106.00
					101.50	
						106.00
Call Price	N/A	N/A	N/A	104.00	102.00	100.00

FIGURE 2.6 Convertible Pricing Tree.

To determine the parity gamma the change in delta is compared to the change in parity.

$$\text{Parity gamma} = (\text{change in delta/change in parity})$$

$$\text{Parity gamma} = (.83 - .44)/(145.78 - 43.90) = .38$$

The convertible delta will change .38 points for each point change in the parity level. Higher gamma issues exhibit more convexity in the convertible's price track. The other measures of a convertible's sensitivity to changing inputs can also be derived from the lattice tree valuation approach.

Adjusting the Convertible Tree for Unique Security Features

Adapting the binomial convertible model for some of the unique convertible features is relatively easy. Convertibles are often issued with one or more of the following features: put option, provisional (soft) call protection, absolute (hard) call protection, ratchet clauses, resets, step-up coupons, make-whole provisions, and other twists. Starting with the basic five-period tree previously discussed, and then blending in one or more of these features, provides an example of the flexibility of the binomial convertible model. Let's assume the convertible has a put feature in year 3 at 115 percent of par and a soft call after year 3 at 150 percent of par. To include the put feature in year 3, simply add the put value for the calculations for all year 3 nodes. See Figure 2.7. In the convertible valuation, the conversion probability is adjusted for the likelihood of exercising the put option based upon the conversion value at each node. To include the soft call feature in year 3 at 150 percent, the probability of conversion for all nodes that have a conversion value in excess of 150 percent of par are awarded a probability of 1.0. The convertible at this point actually has two years of hard call and a third year of provisional call with a put in year 3.

	Current	Year 1	Year 2	Year 3	Year 4	Year 5
						358.59
					272.27	
				209.32		196.79
			165.99		152.12	
		139.35		126.92		108.00
	122.11		117.74		104.40	
		110.42		115.00		106.00
			110.21		101.50	
				115.00		106.00
					101.50	
						106.00
Put Option				115.00		
Call Price	N/A	N/A	N/A	104.00	102.00	100.00

FIGURE 2.7 Convertible Pricing Tree.

The convertible tree can also be modified for reset features by adjusting the conversion price at the appropriate nodes. In fact, most other adjustments to the model are relatively straightforward.

For those not inclined to develop a proprietary system of their own design, many exceptional convertible models can be purchased with financial modeling software packages. Bloomberg also offers a very good convertible tool set and various convertible valuation models.

Non-quantitative Factors Impacting Convertible Valuation—Relative Risk-Reward, Relative Industry Opportunities, and Supply and Demand

Despite all of the factors that a binomial model can address, there are many significant factors that have an impact on convertible valuation that are difficult to model or may call for an understanding of various models to understand valuation. Obviously, differing assumptions regarding an issuer's credit quality and forward-looking volatility assumptions keep the markets relatively inefficient. But, with a wide range of investors participating in the convertible marketplace, many investment styles and valuation models converge. The convertible arbitrage community is often at odds with the traditional long convertible buyer. Many issues at first glance look like an excellent hedge opportunity, but an understanding of what drives valuation outside of the theoretical world will readily foresee the weakness of the hedge in a real-world application. In many instances, a long convertible buyer is less concerned about short-term valuation but very concerned with an issues such as gamma or the long-term risk-reward advantage. Because the long buyer also has a longer holding period, he or she is focused on longer-term credit issues and a longer-term mean volatility. For the arbitrageur, the convergence to theoretical valuation may be a long and painful process.

Recognize What Attracts Each Type of Investor to the Asset Class   The many investors that participate in the convertible marketplace each have a slightly different approach to the asset class. It is important to know how much of a presence the various participants have, and what their unique biases are when looking for one's own purchase and sales opportunities. Often, issues look significantly mispriced from a convertible arbitrage viewpoint, but not so from an outright long buyer perspective. Good examples of this occur in the zero-coupon convertible marketplace in which valuations swing wider than models would expect; the traditional busted high-yield buyer is slow to purchase a busted zero, while traditional long buyers receive no risk-reward advantage. As a result, the busted zero-coupon convertible issue often needs to become severely undervalued to represent an attractive purchase opportunity to either buyer. Many crossover high-yield investors scorn zero-coupon issues unless the yield to put or maturity is especially attractive.

Relative Risk-Reward Investing   Companies with multiple issues available or industry groups with a wide range of security options also are subject to wider security valuation swings. For example, if one of a company's three outstanding convertible issues offers outright long buyers much better gamma, the other issues would be sold and the position offering a better risk-reward would be purchased. This may occur until the lower gamma issues get pushed down in price significantly enough to offer a gamma similar to the original high gamma position that is now less attractive on a relative basis. The original high gamma position is often pushed up to a price that looks overvalued, while the other issues are pushed down in price and look significantly undervalued. But importantly enough to the long buyer, all three issues now offer similar risk-reward profiles. The convertible arbitrageur must take this relative risk-reward valuation into consideration before a hedge is established. These mispriced issues may represent good hedge opportunities, but an understanding of why they may be theoretically priced wrong but still rationally valued from some buyers' perspective is necessary. The arbitrageur may need to determine at what point the valuation convergence occurs to still feel comfortable with hedging these issues.

Regression Equations and Historical Price Tracks—Understanding Behavioral Stability

Convertible arbitrageurs also arm themselves with actual trading data that aids in understanding and adjusting the convertible's expected price track. Theoretical valuation is important, but a reality check must also be performed. In some instances, a neutral hedge condition is not present and therefore the option model's "fair valuation" is not proper. These conditions

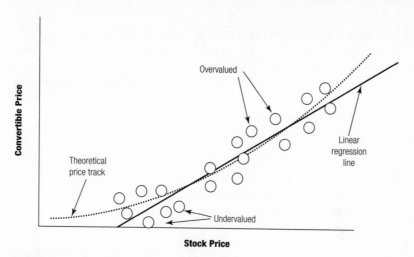

FIGURE 2.8   Regression—Convertible Price Track.

include the lack of stock borrow for a short position to be established or, as in some countries, shorting stock is not easy or even legal. Temporary supply and demand shifts also wreak havoc on the valuation models. One can quickly observe the stability of the convertible and stock relationship over time and adjust the risk of errors accordingly. Plotting historical price graphs of the convertible compared to the common stock price over various time frames improves one's understanding of the way to set up the hedge. Figure 2.8 shows the historical price points of the convertible and stock as well as the theoretical price track. A linear regression line can also be calculated to estimate the recent trading delta and identify issues that are not only undervalued theoretically but also based on the short-term trading delta.

The historical price information combined with the theoretical price track and a simple linear regression analysis can reduce hedge errors if properly employed, but a few cautions must be noted. Historical price tracks that go back far enough to capture yield curve shifts and time decay may not be relevant for the current environment. If the interest rate environment, market volatility, or passage of time are significantly different, do not compare the data to today's. Instead, compare the historical data with the theoretical curves established at that time to get an understanding of the stability of the relationship. Using the regression analysis is helpful for trading moves but not valid for large price jumps in the common stock because the non-linear relationship of the convertible will appear and the analysis will be incorrect. The Bloomberg Terminal offers historical price charts with color-coded time intervals to help a person understand the relationship over time.

CHAPTER 3

The Greeks

It looks just a little more mathematical and regular than it is; its exactitude is obvious, but its inexactitude is hidden; its wildness lies in wait.

—G.K. Chesterton, English essayist

MEASURES OF RISK

Convertible arbitrageurs employ models as their tools of the trade. Convertible valuation models provide the framework to seek opportunities, and the "greeks" they produce contribute to a more complete understanding of the risks and sensitivities of the convertible in a dynamic environment. Dynamic convertible arbitrage calls for an arbitrageur to predetermine a maximum or minimum exposure to the convertible greeks and to rebalance periodically to ensure that the proper risk posture is maintained. The elimination of all risks ensures very little return, or as academic theory would hold, only the risk-free rate of return could be captured if all risks are eliminated. Therefore, the experienced arbitrageur manages risks at the portfolio level on an active basis, often trading off one measure of risk for another. To promote further understanding, the Black-Scholes formulas that can be used to solve for the various risks are also provided.

DELTA (Δ)

The first greek to understand is the delta. The convertible's delta measures the change in the convertible's price (CV) with respect to the change in the underlying common-stock price (S).

$$\text{Delta} = \partial CV/\partial S$$

$$\Delta = e^{-q(T-t)}N(d_1)$$

The convertible's delta is an estimation tool used by arbitrageurs to determine the number of shares of stock to short against the long position to establish a neutral hedge. At each point along the convertible price track, a delta can be calculated. The delta measures the convertible's equity sensitivity for very small stock-price changes. A convertible price track will have a different delta for each infinitely small move in the stock price. A simple way to visualize the delta (Figure 3.1) is to draw a line (A) tangent to the convertible price track for the given stock price. The slope of the line measures the delta. Now change the stock price and draw a tangent line again (B) and compare that to the first. The difference between the slopes indicates how much the delta changes (gamma).

Theoretically speaking, the convertible price track contains thousands of deltas. The convertible's delta approaches 1.0 as the convertible moves deep-in-the-money (line C) because a convertible behaves more like the underlying stock price as the stock price moves above the conversion price. A delta of 1.0 implies that the convertible will move up or down by a percentage equivalent to that of the common stock. The convertible security behaves more like fixed income as the common stock drops below the conversion price. Therefore, the delta approaches 0.0 as the common-stock price declines and the convertible reaches its fixed-income value. However, this is not always true and represents some additional risks for hedging, as ex-

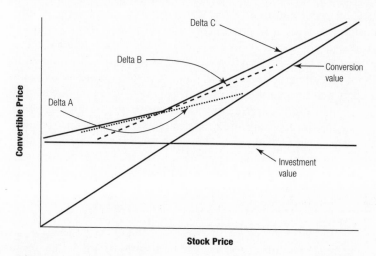

FIGURE 3.1   Visualizing Delta.

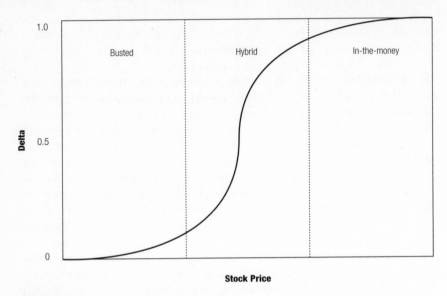

FIGURE 3.2   Delta Change with Underlying Stock Price Changes.

plained later in this chapter. As indicated in Figure 3.2, the delta increases with increasing stock prices and decreases with decreasing stock prices.

Many hedging textbooks and articles highlight the delta as an important risk measure and a significant tool. However, the delta measure assumes that hedging occurs in continuous time, when, in reality, continuous time hedging does not occur and most arbitrageurs are not concerned with infinitely small changes in the stock price. Therefore, seasoned arbitrageurs are not concerned with the theoretically correct continuous-time finance delta. In practice, the delta measure should also incorporate some of the other important greeks, including the gamma and possibly vega. A more useful delta measure is calculated by determining the upward movement and downward movement in the stock price over an expected time period or relevant price range. For example, the arbitrageur expects to rebalance the hedge for each 5-percent move in the underlying stock. He determines the convertible value for a 5-percent upward move and a 5-percent downward move and then calculates a discrete or modified delta.

$$\text{Modified delta} = \tfrac{1}{2} \left(\partial\ CV\!/\!-\partial S + \partial CV\!/ + \partial S \right)$$

Where CV = convertible price, S = stock price.

The new modified delta is now dependent on the arbitrageur's determination of the range of stock-price moves or time interval. Since volatility is also a function of time, the arbitrageur may estimate how often the hedge is rebalanced based on weekly volatility and then back into the expected stock-price moves over a week to calculate the modified delta.

Although the modified delta does not measure the "pure" continuous-time delta, it is much improved. The discrete or modified delta actually is "impure" because other greeks have bled into the calculation, but this is also why it is better. The modified delta incorporates the gamma and vega and may also include theta. In practice, the modified delta can best capture the total hedge risks and opportunities. The continuous-time delta measure does not adequately measure the assumption of the frequency of hedge adjustments. It also assumes that the equity-sensitivity risk of two issues with identical deltas is the same. However, a convertible with a delta of .70 and a gamma of .35 does not have the same risk as a convertible with a delta of .70 and a gamma of .15. The modified delta helps to better distinguish the total risk in the position.

Delta is not a complete measure of risk, although the modified delta improves this measure. Arbitrageurs measure the other greeks as a means to better understand how the hedge position will respond. A dynamic delta hedge must rebalance for each move in the stock price, and as the stock price changes, the delta also changes. Dynamic hedging stresses the need for understanding the convertible's gamma, vega, rho, and theta along with the delta.

GAMMA (Γ)

The change in delta with respect to changes in the common-stock price is called gamma. Gamma is a second-order partial derivative of the convertible price with respect to changes in the underlying common stock. Gamma measures the convexity of the convertible price track.

$$\text{Gamma} = \partial^2 \, CV/\partial \, S^2$$

$$\Gamma = N'(d_1)e^{-q(T-t)}/S\sigma\sqrt{T-t}$$

Determining the gamma in a dynamic hedge helps in understanding the delta and how it will change with regard to changing stock prices or volatility. Gamma measures need to be associated with a range of stock-price changes. In convertible hedging, the arbitrageur selects the expected range before a rebalance occurs by taking into consideration the stock's volatility, trading spread, and technical sentiment. The spot gamma may also help him select an appropriate stock-price range. The higher the convertible's gamma measure, the more often the hedge needs to be rebalanced.

Convertible hedging to capture gamma is a means of taking advantage of the change in delta for rising stock prices as compared to a smaller change in delta for declining stock prices. Figure 3.3 depicts how the gamma of a convertible changes for the full range of stock prices. Convertibles that are deep-in-the-money have a low gamma, as do convertibles that are far-out-of-the-money. Convertibles that are at-the-money have higher gammas. Chapter 6 discusses convertible gamma hedging.)

Hedging convertibles to capture the risk/reward advantage often entails high-gamma convertibles. But more importantly, one gamma measure can be determined for stock-price movements that are upward and another gamma measure for downward stock-price moves. The upside gamma is best determined by calculating the convertible's fair value and delta and then moving the stock price upward and recalculating the delta. The change in the deltas is the upside gamma.

Upside gamma = the change in delta with a specific upward move in the underlying stock.

Downside gamma = the change in delta with a specific downward move in the underlying stock.

The downside gamma is calculated in the same manner. The significance of the upside gamma and the downside gamma for convertible hedging is obvious. The convertible hedge position can be hedged with a lower hedge ratio than the delta calls for if the downside gamma is smaller than the upside gamma. The lower downside gamma allows the arbitrageur the opportunity

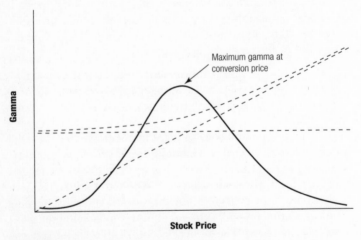

FIGURE 3.3 Maximum Gamma at Conversion Price.

to capture additional profits if the stock price increases without any additional risk of loss. The gamma hedge is more fully discussed in Chapter 6.

The change in gamma with respect to changes in volatility is another important tool in the arbitrageur's tool kit. The long-volatility gamma hedge is often established with a convertible that is trading at an implied volatility that is lower than the arbitrageur assumes is correct. The convertible is trading undervalued, and as the volatility increases, the delta and gamma will change. Since the greeks are moving, the overall risk/return profile of the hedge may change significantly. One method used to avoid unpleasant surprises or poorly balanced hedges is to calculate the upside gamma and downside gamma with the current implied volatility and then again with the expected future volatility. The "second gamma" calculation becomes an expected scenario along with the no-change-in-volatility scenario.

The Risks of Negative Gamma

Measuring delta mathematically is easy, but theoretical accuracy must be supported by fundamental and credit analysis for the issue in question. The graph in Figure 3.4 demonstrates how the delta for a convertible increases

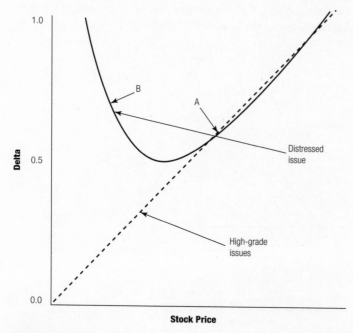

FIGURE 3.4 Delta Curve.

as the stock price increases and decreases with declining stock prices. In fact, the portion of the delta curve labeled "high-grade issues" is only accurate theoretically or in the case of exchangeable issues or principal-protected convertible notes. These issues can in fact have a delta that declines and approaches zero as the underlying stock price approaches zero. Typical convertibles issued by a company and convertible into the same company's common stock exhibit a much different delta graph for lower stock prices. As the common-stock price approaches zero, the convertible begins to break down toward liquidation value while the delta again starts to rise and the gamma moves into negative territory, as depicted in Figure 3.5. Investment-grade credits should demonstrate a much higher threshold before the delta decline reverses, while low-grade credits may be impacted with a small decline in equity values. The solid line depicts the low-grade delta curve and the delta reversal at low equity prices.

The delta reversal is extremely meaningful when considering a neutral hedge. The initial hedge at point A on the graph calls for a 60 percent hedge. If the stock price declines through the point that a perceived credit impairment is implied and the credit spread widens, the delta on the convertible increases. The convertible at point B now has a delta of 70 percent. Unfortunately, the original hedge set up with a 60 delta is now losing money.

Figure 3.5 shows the actual gamma curve for the range of stock prices. Gamma is at its maximum at the conversion price and decays slowly as the

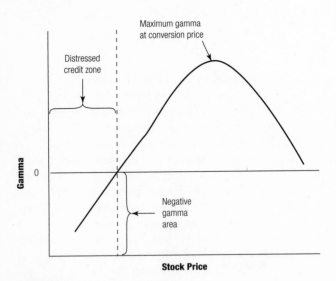

FIGURE 3.5   Actual Gamma Curve.

stock price increases. On the downside, the gamma declines as the stock price declines, but if the credit on the convertible is distressed or is expected to be impaired, the gamma moves negatively as a result of the delta moving back up. Obviously, this presents a real risk for convertible arbitrage and demonstrates the importance of understanding the credit quality of the convertible issue. (The negative gamma problem with convertible hedging will be discussed later in Chapter 9.)

Convertible hedge-fund shops with a credit bias have a distinct advantage in hedging low-grade convertible paper. Many issues trade into the distressed-credit zone and have negative gamma. However, many of these issues move out of the trouble area, and large profits are possible when this occurs. The movement of the convertible out of the distressed negative gamma zone occurs as a result of improved credit assessment by the investment community. The convertible will increase in value rapidly and may have a delta equal to 1.0 and, in some cases, the convertible's delta can exceed 1.0 as it emerges from the distressed depths!

VEGA (v)

Changes in a convertible's implied volatility could have dramatic effects on the convertible-hedge return profile. The vega measures the sensitivity of the convertible's price to changes in implied volatility.

$$\text{Vega} = \partial\ CV/\partial\sigma$$

$$v = S\sqrt{T - t} * N'(d_1)e^{-q(T-t)}$$

Increases in volatility increase the value of a convertible while decreases in volatility decrease the value of a convertible (see Figure 3.6). Since many stock-hedge profiles are dependent on or enhanced by purchasing undervalued convertibles, the vega risk in a position is very important. In general, an undervalued convertible trades with an implied volatility that is below the volatility expected by the arbitrageur. The vega risk measure quickly indicates the upside capture from a move in the volatility back to the expected level or the reverse. The arbitrageur needs to determine the correct volatility to use in pricing the convertible. Since the correct answer can only be determined through hindsight, many trading opportunities exist. Volatility is mean reverting, but the mean may not be stable and the reversion time is not consistent.

The arbitrageur has at his disposal historical volatility for the underlying stock over various time periods, along with the history of the convertible's

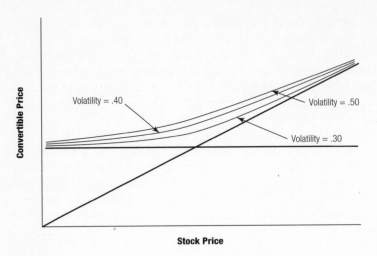

FIGURE 3.6   Volatility Price Tracks.

implied volatility levels. If stock options exist on the underlying stock, this information is also helpful; the options market is at least forward looking in regard to implied volatility levels for various time periods. Historical volatility can be a guide but it can also be a trap when trying to understand future volatility. The historical volatility does not reflect the company's recent capital structure change, the new tax law that may impact the company's profitability, or other new and relevant information that the market knows. The use of the options market helps the arbitrageur understand the "term structure" of future implied volatility as well as the volatility of the volatility. The arbitrageur enters a hedge with an expected holding period and an expected volatility level to approximate the holding period. The vega is the guide to understanding the risk and opportunity if the implied volatility changes.

Convertibles that are trading in the "hybrid" range or near the conversion price demonstrate the highest degree of sensitivity to changes in volatility, and thus the vega is the highest. The vega curve is similar to the gamma curve in that convertibles in-the-money or out-of-the-money demonstrate lower vegas. Convertible arbitrageurs need to be aware of a position's vega because market sentiment and volatility shifts occur very quickly. See Figure 3.7.

Convertible arbitrage is considered a long-volatility strategy and the vega measure is a key portfolio risk management tool. Vega risk can be reduced by hedging the portfolio with put options on an index or industry

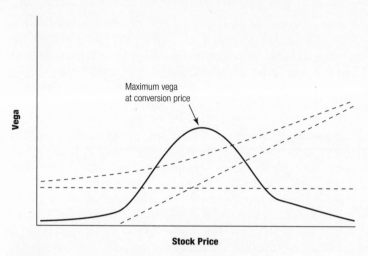

FIGURE 3.7   Maximum Vega at Conversion Price.

group. Generally, the market declines as volatility declines, making the put option more valuable as the long convertibles decline in value.

THETA (ϑ)

A convertible's theta measures the change in the convertible's price with respect to changes in time. The time-premium decay of a convertible is complicated to some degree by the realization that the option portion of the convertible is subject not only to a maturity date but also to variations in call probabilities. Like an option, convertibles nearing maturity or the end of their call protection trade with a higher degree of theta risk. Unlike an option, a convertible that is slightly out-of-the-money with no call protection remaining but with a low coupon payment on the issue will most likely remain outstanding. However, a reduction in interest rates to levels that may make the convertible's issuer likely to call the issue in order to refinance at a lower rate has the effect of increasing the theta risk of the issue.

$$\text{Theta} = \partial CV/\partial t$$

$$\vartheta = \left[-SN'(d_1)\sigma e^{-q(T-t)} \setminus 2\sqrt{T-t}\right] - rKe^{-r(T-t)}N(d_2) + qSN(d_1)e^{-q(T-t)}$$

Theta risk or time-premium decay can eat away a hedged position if not monitored. Theta should also be looked at in regard to volatility; if the implied volatility changes for a position, the theta should also be recalculated. Convertible hedge positions are often established when the implied volatility levels are lower than the arbitrageur's expectation for volatility. The theta should be calculated under both assumptions to discern the change in theta.

Figure 3.8 demonstrates the impact of time on various convertibles. The out-of-the-money issue has very little theta sensitivity until the push to par value at maturity drives the bond up toward par. The at-the-money issue carries the highest theta risk, as the conversion premium is large and the price is above the call price or par value. Eventually, keeping all other factors constant except for time, the at-the-money issue loses all of its conversion premium and drops to conversion value or par value, whichever is highest. The convertible's theta risk accelerates in the last 3 to 6 months before maturity. Of course this may also occur with an issue that has a very high relative coupon payment and its absolute call protection is running out, making a call very likely, and the issue's theta risk increases. The in-the-money issue has less conversion premium to lose and therefore is less sensitive to changes in time. But any conversion premium left with an in-the-money issue will evaporate in the last few months as indicated in Figure 3.8.

Figure 3.9 shows the relationship of the convertible price track to changes in absolute call protection. For example, a convertible issued with 2 years of absolute call protection would trade on the convertible track

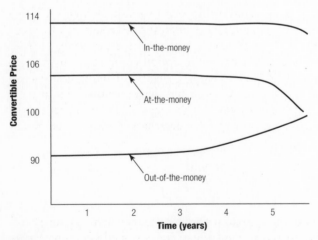

FIGURE 3.8   Theta-Time Decay for Various Convertibles.

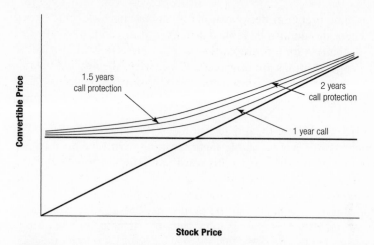

FIGURE 3.9 Convertible Price Track Changes in Absolute Call Protection.

indicating 2 years call protection. If the issue only had 1.5 years or 1.0 years call protection, the convertible curve is lower than the issue with the longer-term call protection. At any stock-price point, the difference between these convertible price tracks and therefore the actual theoretical convertible prices measures the theta risk in the issue.

RHO (ρ)

Rho measures the change in a convertible security's value with respect to a change in interest rates. In general, higher interest rates result in lower convertible values. Convertibles will have a different interest rate sensitivity than straight corporate bonds because the option component of the convertible moves in tandem with rate changes, slightly offsetting the interest rates' impact on the convertible. Convertibles have negative rho at most points along the convertible price track. The negative rho exists because as interest rates increase, the investment value decreases. A deep-in-the-money convertible will exhibit a rho near zero.

$$\rho = \partial CV / \partial I$$

$$\rho = K(T - t)e^{-r(T-t)}N(d_2)$$

Convertibles maximum interest rate sensitivity occurs when an issue is out-of-the money and the equity option component is valued very low. Figure 3.10 shows the maximum rho occurring with the issue out-of-the money. As

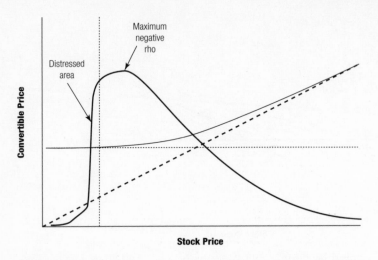

FIGURE 3.10 Rho Sensitivity for Full Convertible Track.

the issue moves in-the-money, it becomes less sensitive to changes in interest rates and more sensitive to equity price moves. The distressed area of the convertible price track will often exhibit very little sensitivity to changes in interest rates; instead, the issue's value is dependent on the individual issue's creditworthiness and probability of bankruptcy occurring. In the distressed zone, macro factors become irrelevant and the business-related factors take complete control of the valuation.

Figure 3.11 shows the change in a convertible's investment value as interest rates rise from 7 percent to 9 percent. The convertible price tracks also shift as indicated. The rho risk is highest for convertibles trading below their conversion price, and the risk decreases as the stock price moves in-the-money. At very high stock prices relative to the conversion price, the rho risk is very low.

A basic rho measure assumes parallel shifts in the yield curve, which is typically not the case in reality. The rho risk for in-the-money convertibles is actually the rho2 that relates to the short end of the yield curve for risk-free government bonds. Rho2 risk is very important at the portfolio level for an arbitrageur's book. Rho1 measures the corporate-yield-curve sensitivity that includes credit-spread widening. Convertible arbitrageurs need to know both measures of interest-rate risk, along with the risk of interest rates on the very short end of the yield curve that relates to their cost of capital, to establish a hedge on margin.

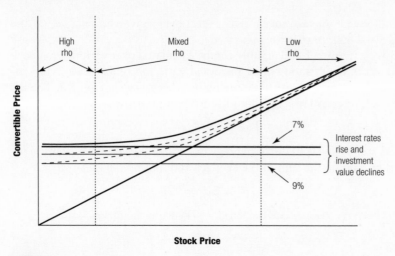

FIGURE 3.11 Rho Risk.

MORE ON VOLATILITY

Understanding volatility, either implied or actual, is critical in the practice of convertible arbitrage. In almost every hedge profile, an estimate of volatility must be made. Volatility is a measure of the amount of fluctuation in an asset or the underlying asset as it relates to convertible securities and options. The more volatile the asset, the more random the returns. Typically, volatility is measured as the annualized standard deviation of returns. Implied volatility is the market's estimate as to future volatility. Historical volatility is often used as an estimate of future volatility, but it is not reliable because it is historically based and it has no knowledge of upcoming events of economic or psychological consequences that impact volatility and risk perceptions. It is for this reason that more complex estimates of volatility, such as arch or garch measures of volatility, still fall short and an override provided by a thinking being must be used to estimate volatility, instead of just making an extrapolation of the past.

Since volatility is said to be mean reverting, some expectation as to a mean and a time frame to revert to the mean should be addressed. The convertible arbitrageur should have a firm expectation regarding the expected future volatility and relate it to his expected holding period to determine if a mean reversion is relevant or not. The volatility of volatility is an important gauge as to what the arbitrageur may expect over a given holding period and the potential margin of error in his hedge profile.

Historical or realized volatility can be calculated over various time horizons to aid in understanding the historical variation of a stock or convertible. The first step is to calculate the day-to-day price change (R_t). The log of the stock price (S_t) moves from the current and previous day (S_{t-1}).

$$R_t = \text{Ln}(S_t/S_{t-1})$$

The next step is to calculate the average price change over the estimation period (n) by finding the sum of the changes and finding the mean (R_m).

$$R_m = \Sigma R_t / n$$

The third step is to calculate the variance (V) from the mean.

$$V = \sqrt{\Sigma(R_t - R_m)^2 / N - 1}$$

Finally, annualize the historical volatility. Multiply the variance by the square root of the time period, in this case 252 days in a year. Table 3.1 shows the calculations to arrive at the annualized 10-day volatility of 50.47 percent. The historical volatility calculation can be easily computed using the functions available on MicroSoft-Excel, and they are also available on Bloomberg.

TABLE 3.1   Calculations to Arrive at Annualized 10-Day Volatility

Day	Stock Price	$R_t = \text{Ln}(S_t/S_{t-1})$	$(R_t)^2$	$(R_t - R_m)^2$
1	25.0000			
2	25.7500	0.029558802	0.000873723	0.000438527
3	24.6250	−0.044672440	0.001995627	0.002839846
4	23.8250	−0.033026738	0.001090765	0.001734265
5	24.5000	0.027937668	0.000780513	0.000373258
6	25.3000	0.032131278	0.001032419	0.000552885
7	26.1250	0.032088315	0.001029660	0.000550866
8	26.7500	0.023641763	0.000558933	0.000225720
9	25.8250	−0.035191458	0.001238439	0.001919248
10	26.0000	0.006753523	0.000045610	0.000003475
11	27.2500	0.046956983	0.002204958	0.001469895
	$R_m =$	0.008617770		
		Sum =	0.010850647	0.010107988
		Variance =	0.031793062	
		10 day vol ann. =	0.504699211	

Implied volatility is an estimate of future volatility given all of the information known at that point in time and an estimate of how it will impact the risk of the asset. It is important to relate fundamental measures of risk to an asset's volatility. High-grade corporate bonds are less volatile than high-yield bonds obviously. Credit deterioration increases the volatility of the stock and credit improvement decreases stock volatility. Volatility is also a function of the price of a stock relative to its capital base. As a stock's price increases, the company's access to capital improves and the cost of equity capital decreases; the debt-to-equity ratio declines and the total capital increases, improving a company's credit standing and further improving the company's cost of debt capital. All of these factors have a stabilizing effect on the stock price and lowers volatility. Decreasing stock prices have the reverse impact. At the extremes, though, this does not hold. A stock trading at a considerable premium to any rational economic value will become more volatile as the momentum begins to slow down.

In fact, volatility is a very complex measure that attempts to gauge the risk inherent in a security, the stability and certainty of a stock's cash flow, balance sheet stability and access to capital, competitive threats, and investor enthusiasm or lack thereof. A convertible arbitrageur needs to rely on the equity and credit assessment of a company in attempting to determine future volatility. It is important to know the answer to questions such as the following. Is the company changing its business strategy? Is it acquiring other companies and raising additional debt to do it? Are patents running out? Has there been a significant change in management? Has a new better-capitalized competitor entered its market space? How have input prices and distribution changed? Any of these factors and many more will impact the volatility of the business and the stock price. Like most other things, the more you know about the company and industry the better job you can do at estimating future volatility.

Volatility cones available from Credit Suisse First Boston also are very good tools to help arbitrageurs understand historical convertible and stock volatility distributions as well as the volatility in the volatility. These volatility cones can be calculated by rolling the various time periods and calculating the minimum, maximum, median, 25th percentile and 75th percentile. See Figure 3.12.

The volatility cones indicate the range of volatility for an equity or convertible for the number of days indicated on the horizontal axis. They also show the mean reversion of volatility over time as the minimum and maximum values regress toward the median level over time, creating the cone shape. Although the mean reversion over time in general is very prevalent, the cones do not necessarily help identify the amount of time it takes for a mean reversion to occur.

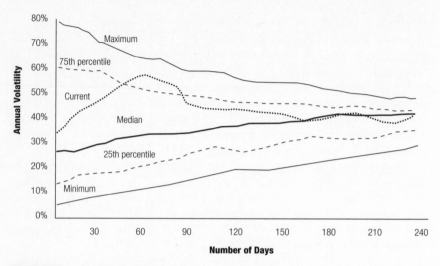

FIGURE 3.12 Historical Volatility Cones for ABC Company.

Figure 3.12 shows that for ABC Company, the 60-day volatility range is very widely distributed over the past 500 days of data ranging from 10 percent to over 70 percent. The current 60-day volatility is indicated at 63 percent, which is above the median of only 33 percent and even above the 75th percentile of 55 percent. Therefore, we can surmise that we would expect the 60-day volatility to be below 55 percent, 75 percent of the time. With a current 60-day volatility at 63 percent, selling volatility at this level should prove profitable over 75 percent of the time. When using the volatility cones with convertible arbitrage, an estimate of the expected holding period of the issue must be determined. Then the cones can help estimate the possible volatility capture available and the statistical pay-off probability of being long volatility at the current volatility level. Volatility is a complex issue that is widely studied and debated, the knowledgeable arbitrageur arms herself or himself with much of this knowledge and relates the quantitative measures to the business risks and balance sheet risks that volatility is attempting to measure.

CHI (χ)

Chi measures the rate of change in the fair value of the convertible security with respect to a change in the spot exchange rate.

$$\partial CV/\partial FX = \chi$$

TABLE 3.2 Convertible Currency Combinations

Convertible Structure	Arbitrageur's Local Currency	Convertible's Principal and Coupon Currency	Underlying Stock Currency
Convertible A	Local	Local	Foreign
Convertible B	Local	Foreign	Foreign
Convertible C	Local	Foreign	Local
Convertible D	Local	Foreign	Other Foreign
Convertible E	Local	Local	Local

Many different convertible currency scenarios exist, with each having a different degree of currency risk. It is important to understand the degree of chi and also what is driving this risk. For local dollar issues that are convertible into foreign currency stock, the parity level is sensitive to currency movements. For foreign pay issues convertible into local stock, the investment value and embedded warrant strike are sensitive to the changes in currency. For foreign issues convertible into foreign stock, the entire investment will be subject to currency changes. For multiple currency or cross currency issues, the security should be bifurcated and the individual risks hedged and, if necessary, cross currency hedged back to local. For the convertible arbitrageur, an understanding of what currency risks are inherent in the foreign security can help in estimating how much of the foreign forward contract to sell. Table 3.2 indicates the various convertible currency combinations.

Because the convertible arbitrageur is short the stock, securities with domestic (USD) pay and convertible into foreign stock need not be hedged for currency exposure because the neutral short stock position takes care of the chi risk. For directional hedges and gamma hedges, the net delta exposure should be hedged. For convertibles with foreign pay and convertible into foreign stock, the currency hedge should be established to hedge the difference between the convertible long value and parity. Convertibles with foreign pay and face value but convertible into domestic (USD) stock should hedge the difference between parity and the fixed-income value with consideration for the impact on the embedded warrant valuation with regard to the changing exercise price.

OMICRON (o)

Omicron measures the change in the fair value of the convertible with respect to a change in credit spread.

$$o = \partial CV / \partial OAS$$

For many low-grade issues, this is an especially telling measure. An out-of-the-money convertible is generally more sensitive to changes in credit spreads than any other variable. Figure 3.13 shows how various convertibles will respond to changes in credit spreads. In general, as credit spreads narrow, a convertible's value increases and, as credit spreads widen, a convertible's value decreases. Convertibles that are deep in-the-money have a very low sensitivity to credit spread changes, while an out-of-the-money convertible will be very sensitive to credit spread changes. Omicron is one of the most important risk measures for convertible arbitrageurs hedging low-grade issues that are trading near or below their exercise price.

The difficulties of hedging low-grade credits and the risks of not evaluating the credit properly can be determined by omicron. In some cases, a rough estimate or a range in credit spread is the best one can access regarding some credits. Knowing the sensitivity of the convertible to changes in credit spreads will help determine the vulnerability of the hedge as well as the potential error in current valuation. Portfolio credit spread hedging can be used as an additional overlay once the overall omicron risk level is determined.

Since some of the most difficult periods for convertible arbitrage investing have occurred during periods of credit spread widening, arbitrageurs must know the portfolio's omicron risk and be aggressive at keeping it in a comfort range. An individual position's omicron is equally important to access because of the dangers of credit deterioration occurring (credit spread

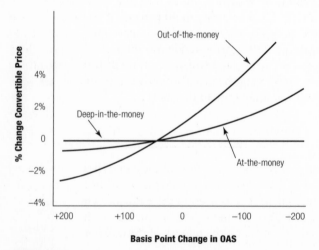

FIGURE 3.13 Sensitivity to Changes in OAS.

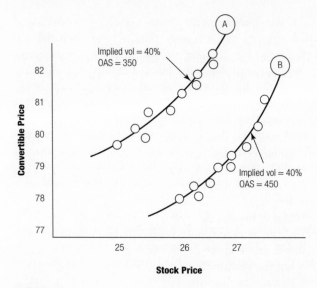

FIGURE 3.14 Change in OAS with Same Implied Volatility.

widens) and a negative gamma occurring, turning a profitable hedge into a quick loss.

The impact of credit spread changes can be seen in Figure 3.14. The historical convertible price track marked A includes prices in the market for XYZ convertible trading with an option adjusted spread (OAS) of 350 basis points and with an implied volatility of 40 percent. Track B is the same security but with the OAS now widening out to 450 due to credit concerns, but again with the same implied volatility of 40 percent. This figure demonstrates the risk of credit spread widening and its impact on a hedged position. For example, with the stock price at $26 on track A, the convertible traded at $82. But as the OAS spread widened, on track B the convertible traded 4 points lower at $78 with the stock still at $26, producing a loss on the long side of the trade and no gain on the short.

UPSILON (υ)

Upsilon measures the change in the fair value of the convertible with respect to a change in the credit recovery rate. The credit recovery rate is an estimation of the principal amount recovered in the event of default on the security. Recovery rates depend on many factors including the seniority of claims on the borrower's assets and the quality of the collateral.

$$\upsilon = \partial CV / \partial RR$$

Since a convertible's value is a function of all possible stock price ranges and corresponding convertible price ranges, it follows that in the credit distressed zone at very low stock levels, the convertible will approach liquidation value. (See Chapter 2 on valuation.) When modeling a convertible, some estimation must be made as to the liquidation value or recovery rate for the security. For convertibles that are trading close to their bond value, this measure becomes more important. Unfortunately, in practice, liquidation value is very difficult to determine, but an approximate range can be estimated with credit analysis and convertible arbitrage shops that specialize in distressed credit because they have an advantage here. Table 3.3 shows the average range of recovery for senior and subordinated convertible debt covering the period 1970 to 2000.

Convertible arbitrageurs typically will not need to focus too much on this measure except for distressed credit hedges. But to understand the downside risk in the hedge and get the convertible valuation correct in the distressed area of the curve, some reasonable approximation of recovery rate must be determined.

To better understand the impact of recovery rate changes and its effect on convertible valuation, see Figure 3.15. The convertible at point A on the price track with a stock price "P1" has a 12- month probability distribution for the stock and corresponding convertible marked **px 1 dist**, while the convertible at point "B" at stock price "P2" has a 12-month probability distribution marked **px 2 dist**. The shift in recovery rate from 40 percent to 20 percent has a much larger impact on convertible valuation at point A because it is trading closer to the distressed zone. A large portion of point A's price distribution is to the left of the vertical X (distressed zone), indicating

TABLE 3.3 Average Defaulted Convertible Bond Prices, 1970–2000.

	Convertible Bonds		
Seniority	Average Price	Standard Deviation	Count
Sr. Secured	$32.78	$8.05	5
Sr. Unsecured	$34.07	$31.19	14
Sr. Subordinated	$27.04	$15.67	21
Subordinated	$28.59	$21.23	225
Jr. Subordinated	$15.37	$25.36	5
All	$28.84	$21.26	276

Source: © Moody's Investor Service Inc. and/or its affiliates. Reprinted with permission. All rights reserved.

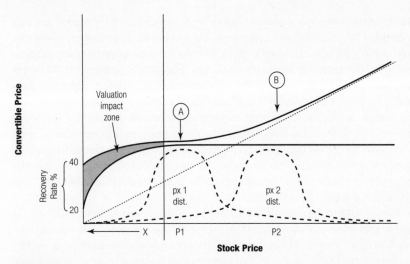

FIGURE 3.15 Impact of Recovery Rate Changes on Convertible Valuation.

a larger probability of credit impairment and therefore the valuation impact zone weighting has a large impact on the convertible valuation as recovery rates change. Convertible B has a small portion of its probability distribution trading to the left of vertical X, indicating a very small probability of distress and the valuation impact zone weighting will have a small impact on valuation as a result of the change in recovery rate. Valuation impact can be seen as the difference between the curves in the valuation impact zone, as denoted by the shaded area.

Upsilon is rarely considered a broad portfolio level risk measure; it is primarily used on an issue-by-issue basis. Hedging the recovery rate risk measure is difficult, but over hedging with short stock does allow for downside protection. It also moves the individual position risk-reward profile out of a neutral profile and into a bear hedge profile. In practice, arbitrageurs will generally close a position that has a high upsilon measure since the arbitrageur has a poor comfort level with the appropriate recovery rate.

PHI (ϕ)

Phi measures the change in the fair value of the convertible with respect to a change in the underlying stock dividend yield.

$$\phi = \partial CV / \partial DIV$$

A convertible's fair value moves inversely to changes in the underlying stock dividend. The valuation of any convertible considers the present value of the convertible's income minus the present value of the underlying stock dividend over the expected life of the security. The option value decreases with higher dividend yields because the option buyer does not receive the dividend. The convertible security typically pays a higher yield than the underlying stock and this cash flow difference is factored into the binomial convertible valuation. But an unanticipated increase in the dividend yield or an increase at a rate higher than estimated will have a negative impact on valuation. The convertible arbitrageur's hedge can be impacted from a lower convertible valuation and at the same time a higher dividend must be paid on the short stock. In practice, this is not a significant risk because most companies do not significantly raise their dividend and most convertible issuers are growth companies that pay little or no dividend but retain their cash flow for growth. Overall risk management for a convertible arbitrage portfolio would generally not consider phi risk, but it can be important for an individual position.

MANDATORY CONVERTIBLE GREEKS

Mandatory convertibles have very different risk profiles from traditional convertibles. See Chapter 1 for an explanation of DECS and mandatory convertibles. The delta (sensitivity to changes in the underlying stock price) of a mandatory at maturity is depicted in Figure 3.16. At issuance, the delta of a mandatory transitions from its high point based on the downside

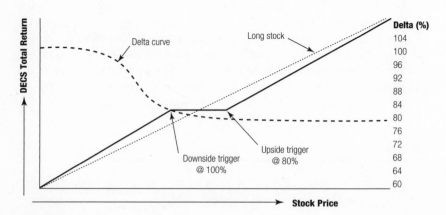

FIGURE 3.16 Mandatory Convertible Delta Profile.

trigger rate to the upside trigger rate and lower delta in a smooth fashion. Because the mandatory is short a call option at the lower trigger or strike price and long a call option at the upper strike price, the delta transitions or reverses at or near these strike prices. As the mandatory approaches maturity, the transition is less smooth and the delta curve exhibits more severe changes in delta. Mandatory convertibles will exhibit a rising delta at stock prices at and below the lower strike price, forcing arbitrageurs to add to the short stock position as the stock price declines. The DECS mandatory will also exhibit a declining delta as the stock price appreciates up to and through the upper strike price. Arbitrageurs must reduce the hedge ratio or purchase stock as the stock price rises. Hedging mandatory issues becomes more difficult as maturity approaches and the delta shifts are more severe.

DECS Gamma

Figure 3.17 depicts a mandatory convertibles gamma profile (sensitivity to changes in delta) near maturity and highlights the big shift in delta that occurs and the swing to negative gamma. Hedging negative gamma is very difficult, especially with mandatory issues, because the gamma will once again rebound into positive territory. As later discussed in this book, hedging mandatory issues with options or short stock and options helps to mitigate some of the difficulties of hedging mandatory issues near maturity. The swing to negative gamma occurs because of the higher downside trigger conversion ratio with the short call option and the theta or option premium decay occurring in the last few months of maturity. The negative gamma territory becomes more severe as time passes and the DECS maturity date is approached.

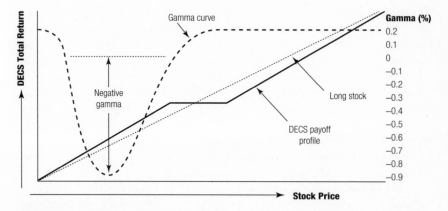

FIGURE 3.17 Mandatory Convertible Gamma Profile—Three Months to Maturity.

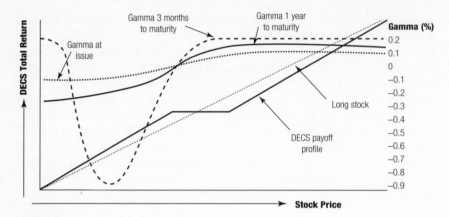

FIGURE 3.18 Mandatory Convertible Gamma Profile—Life of the Security.

Figure 3.18 shows the gamma profile over the life of the security. At issue, the DECS gamma curve is relatively flat. As time passes, the convertible delta becomes more pronounced and therefore the gamma curve shifts also become more pronounced. The negative gamma portion of the curve occurs at stock prices at and below the lower strike price (short call option). With one year to maturity, the DECS gamma curve exhibits a larger area of negative gamma, and just prior to maturity the negative gamma is quite significant.

Mandatory Convertible Vega

The vega profile (sensitivity to changes in volatility) for a DECS structure is also very interesting. The lower strike call option is short, causing the vega to move into negative territory as the stock price moves toward and through the lower strike. The vega swings into positive territory as the stock price increases and moves toward the long option at the upper strike. The vega profile also becomes more pronounced as the DECS moves towards maturity, as Figure 3.19 demonstrates. At issue, the vega curve slopes upward as the stock price increases, but by maturity the vega curve resembles a sign curve. Increases or decreases in implied volatility may be slightly different for the two embedded options in the DECS structure, further complicating the overall vega.

Hedging mandatory convertibles that are trading near the lower strike with negative vega is one means to short volatility during periods of high

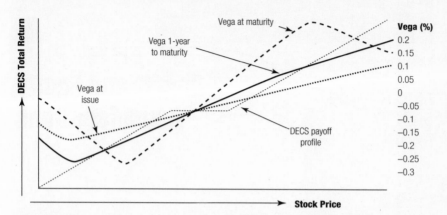

FIGURE 3.19 Mandatory Convertible Vega Profile—Life of the Security.

volatility, with typical convertible arbitrage being long volatility. Other variations of mandatory issues exist, but the DECS structure is the most common. An understanding of the risks inherent in this security will easily be transferred to understanding risks of other mandatory issues.

CHAPTER 4

Credit and Equity Considerations

There are two times in a man's life when he should not speculate: when he can't afford it, and when he can.

—Mark Twain

Pure mathematical hedging techniques generally fail because each discount rate or volatility assumption incorporated into a hedge position requires an accurate, real-world assessment of the business. Securities analysis and credit analyses are thus necessary steps in the convertible arbitrage investment process. Typically, it is only during distressed periods that funds, which lack such research and analysis, reveal this weakness. Convertible arbitrage and hedge funds generally support their hedging strategies with a team of analysts, whose job is to establish a thorough understanding of each convertible's credit quality, expected volatility, and its underlying business's quality of cash flows. In some of the directional hedging, merger arbitrage hedging, and capital structure hedging strategies, it is equally important to value the full capital structure of the company. Because of these necessities, this chapter touches on some of the credit and business valuation methods that will help improve the success of a convertible hedge.

CREDIT EVALUATION

One of the surest ways to wreck a convertible hedge position is to set up the hedge without a clear understanding of the possibility and consequences of credit impairment. The arbitrageur needs to set up a process to monitor the

---

Quotations of Warren E. Buffett throughout this chapter are excerpted with permission from previously published material.

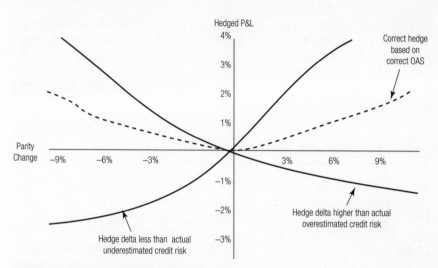

FIGURE 4.1 Profit and Loss Hedge Profile.

risk of the position and identify warning signs that indicate credit deterioration may occur. Indeed, the delta on which the position is hedged is a function of getting the credit assessment and future volatility correct. It is critical to estimate credit risk, including default risk and the expected recovery rate in the event of default. The hedge will not provide proper protection if the credit risk is misunderstood or miscalculated, as the convertible will decline more than expected and the original short position will not be enough to protect against the decline in the convertible's value.

An overly conservative approach to credit risk can cause the opposite problem on the upside of a hedge, too. The profit and loss hedge profile in Figure 4.1 shows how improper credit spread assessment can lead to improper delta estimates and hedge ratios that do not provide the proper risk-reward profile. The dashed line labeled "correct neutral hedge ratio based on correct OAS" (otherwise known as option adjusted spread, a form of credit spread evaluation), shows the risk-reward profile that neutral hedges should achieve. But were the arbitrageur to underestimate the weakness of the credit and therefore set up a hedge with a lower hedge ratio than necessary, the position would suffer a loss as the stock price declines. The line labeled "Hedge delta less than actual" indicates how a hedge, expected to be delta neutral but mistakenly established with a delta less than actual (i.e., actual OAS should have been higher), produces a loss of 2 percent if parity declines by 4 percent.

On the other hand, an overly pessimistic assessment of the credit spread (hedge established with an OAS assumption much wider than actual) can result in a hedged delta that is higher than the actual and the hedge profile breaks down. As the stock price appreciates, the line labeled "hedge delta higher than actual" demonstrates how the expected neutral hedge actually loses 2 percent when the parity level increases by 9 percent. *A miscalculation of the credit quality of the convertible can have significant impact on the success of the hedged convertible.*

CREDIT ANALYSIS AND EQUITY MARKET FEEDBACK

Convertible arbitrageurs almost always monitor the fixed-income markets, credit spreads, and the credit default swap spread market (discussed in Chapter 8). Arbitrageurs also constantly monitor convertible issuers that also have other fixed-income securities trading publicly, as a means to "true up" their spread assumptions used for modeling the convertible. Since the fixed-income (investment) value of a convertible in the low- and mid-grade ranges is in fact a high yield issuer, and high yield paper has a high correlation with the equity markets, some measure of equity feedback is necessary as well. Historically, high-yield debt has demonstrated a 55 percent correlation with their companies' equity price movements on the downside. Clearly, if a company's common stock price has declined significantly, then it is more than likely that its

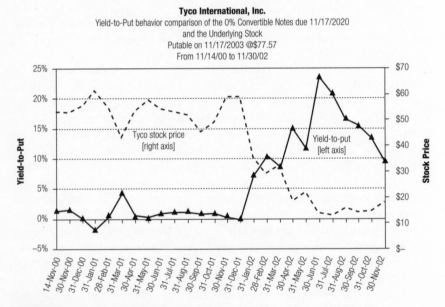

FIGURE 4.2 Relationship between Stock Price of Tyco International and Corresponding Yield to Put.

credit quality is also suspect, especially at very low stock price levels. Figure 4.2 shows the relationship between the stock price of Tyco International and the corresponding yield to put. The credit spread and stock price movements are almost perfect mirror images of one another, demonstrating the link between equity market prices and credit spreads.

The first step is to understand the issue's overall credit rating and standing in terms of both a historical trend and a current relative peer group perspective. Third-party ratings (S&P and Moody's) and their watch lists are helpful, but in my opinion, only insofar as they provide a reference for credit research performed in-house. These ratings lack sufficient gradient; for example, we find substantial differences between two "B" rated issues. For peers in the same rating category and industry, undertaking a typical credit ratio analysis will provide a comparison with regard to liquidity of assets, future earnings and cash flow, capital structure leverage, off balance sheet liabilities, management quality, and industry competitiveness. The bond discount rate incorporates the default probability and expected recovery rate in the event of default as well as the liquidity of the issue. Credit analysis should determine these factors and then provide a relative risk premium to other securities.

$$\text{Estimated bond yield} = \text{average for same credit in market} + \text{individual firm risk characteristics}$$

$$\text{Discount rate} = \text{relative credit spreads} + \text{liquidity} + \text{probability of default} + \text{asset recovery rate}$$

- Pretax interest coverage = pretax income/total interest expense
- Funds-flow interest coverage = cash flow from operations/interest expense
- Quick ratio = current assets − inventories/current liabilities
- Current ratio = current assets/current liabilities
- Equity ratio = common equity/tangible assets − accrued payables
- Total debt service coverage = cash flow from operations after tax + tax adjusted interest + rental expense/interest expense + rent expense + current maturities + sinking fund payments
- Long term debt % capital = long-term debt/(long-term debt + equity + off balance sheet liabilities + short-term-debt)
- Total debt % capital = short-term debt + long-term debt/(long-term debt + short-term debt + equity + off balance sheet liabilities)
- Fund from operations % total debt = working capital from operations/ (long-term debt + short-term debt)
- Operating income as a % sales = operating income/sales

FIGURE 4.3   Credit Analysis—Basic Credit Ratios.

The basic credit ratios in Figure 4.3 are applied in evaluations from a historical trend perspective, relative peer group perspective, and of course a current quality perspective. These credit ratios are just the essentials for beginning to understand a company's balance sheet and cash flow coverage risk. Indeed, weakness discovered in any of these should drive the analysis further and likely raise additional questions concerning both creditworthiness and management.

These credit ratios help provide a relative comparison and will aid in determining the credit spread used to determine the convertible's investment value. But, all of this information is backward looking and available only a few times per year. Using historical ratios and ex-ante credit analysis ignores the valuable information content in market prices. The credit and equity markets are open 250 days per year, and the feedback from these markets is meaningful: Market prices encompass risk measures and uncertainty that need to be evaluated by the arbitrageur in assessing the credit risk.

The discussion of the binomial convertible model in Chapter 2 showed that one of the key benefits of the model was its flexibility to incorporate nonconstant credit spread assumptions. The constant credit spread assumption in convertible valuation will often cause the delta to be mis-specified (usually underestimated), especially as the stock price declines. Chapter 2 does note the mathematical adjustments used to improve the model, but to determine the

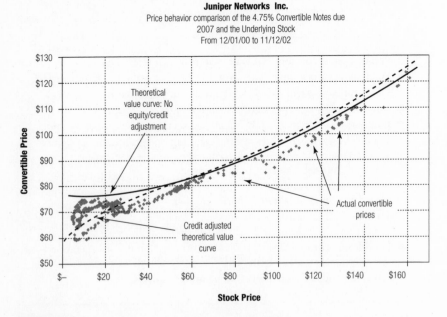

Juniper Networks Inc.
Price behavior comparison of the 4.75% Convertible Notes due
2007 and the Underlying Stock
From 12/01/00 to 11/12/02

FIGURE 4.4   Two Theoretical Convertible Price Tracks.

equity/credit spread link and corresponding discount rate used in the model, market-based credit models are the tool of choice. Figure 4.4 shows two theoretical convertible price tracks; one assumes a constant credit spread, while the other uses the feedback from a market-based credit model (ties in equity value and credit spreads). Clearly, the more robust, credit-adjusted model explains the convertible price track at lower valuations. The constant credit assumption model needs to be continually adjusted for credit changes, but even with such an effort, the original hedge ratio established with a constant-credit spread assumption for all equity prices would have been incorrect. The credit-adjusted model thus provides the highest probability for successful convertible hedging.

ASSET VALUE CREDIT EVALUATION

Arbitrageurs should approach the subject of credit from many angles, including market-based approaches. For example, a stock's value is the present value of future cash flows discounted at a certain rate.

$$Price = Net\ cash\ flow/1 + discount\ rate$$

The discount rate that solves for the current price is helpful in understanding the market's assessment for the equity risk and serves also as a de facto credit discount rate. The credit discount rate should be lower, however, because of debt's preference to claims on assets and its historically higher recovery rate in bankruptcy proceedings. Although this equity-based credit discount rate may be helpful, it is very basic.

Another market-based credit evaluation tool to consider focuses on the fixed dollar coverage that a firm is saddled with and how it relates to both the capital employed in the firm and its equity valuation. In a simple form, a company needs to cover interest on debt, annual lease obligations, working capital, preferred dividends, and some minimal capital expenditures (including R&D in some cases). The combination of the above fixed costs, divided by the number of shares outstanding, converts the dollar coverage into a per share amount. Dividing this number by the discount rate results in an equity price that can be used as another warning price from the equity market. Obviously, this is a single-stage, no-growth discount model, but more extensive models can be developed. Nonetheless, the implication here is that at the implied stock price indicated by this value, the equity markets have determined that the company will just cover fixed operating costs into perpetuity; any price below this level indicates questions as to going concern valuation.

$$P = TFC/1 + r$$

TFC = total fixed costs per share
r = discount rate

On the one hand, the flaw with historical financial ratios is that they ignore market-based risks that are forward looking. On the other hand, the flaw with the equity discount rate basic model is that it does not bring enough of the financial statements into the evaluation process. The current and projected income statement is generally the focus with this model, while it excludes the full capital base of the business, near-term liquidity risks, and other balance sheet risks.

Other, more encompassing market-based credit feedback models have been developed as an extension of the contingent claims valuation for corporate liabilities. In 1971 Black, Scholes and Merton developed an asset value model for valuing a firm's debt and equity on the bases of the firm's asset structure, liabilities and volatility. Merton's work further extended this and developed a method for valuing a business from a contingent claims perspective and quantifying a bond's risk premium as a function of the overall business risk, defined as asset volatility. Merton established that a company's stock and bond values are both derived from the same set of cash flows, and therefore the risks for each type of security are highly dependent and their valuations are closely linked.

$$dV = (\alpha V - C_f)\, dt + \sigma V\, dz$$

V = firm value
α = ROA
σ = standard deviation of firm value
C_f = cash flow

The model also assumes that at maturity the corporate claims are settled in the following way: (Figure 4.5 demonstrates the payoff graphs of each claim)

Debt holders receive at maturity = $F - \text{Max}(F - V,0)$
= Riskless bond – put option while the residual value goes to the equity holders.

Equity payoff = $\text{Max}(V - F,0)$ = Call option with a strike price of F and expiration T.

F = face value of debt
T = mixed maturity date

Merton's formula underscores the links between debt and equity valuations, and of course the links to the business's underlying cash flows and asset volatility. The contingent claims model is directly applicable to the hybrid

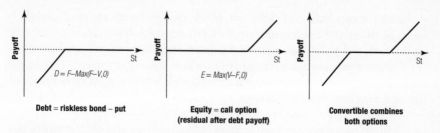

FIGURE 4.5 Convertible Combines Both Options.

convertible, and aids in constructing arbitrage positions. Many credit models exist now that are based on Merton's original work and they are a very useful addition to the arbitrageur's credit toolbox.

Credit spreads have shown a clear link to not only volatility, but also to equity valuations and book value of debt. Figure 4.6 indicates the typical relationship between credit spreads widening and stock prices declining as volatility increases. The market-based models attempt to provide a clear understanding of this relationship and the likely default risk. The increase in equity volatility at lower stock prices reflects both the uncertainty regarding the amount of residual claims on the company's assets that the stockholders would receive in bankruptcy, as well as the market's assessment of the probability of bankruptcy occurring. Meanwhile, the credit spread widening at lower stock prices reflects the debt holders' assessment of the probability of bankruptcy, and of the recovery rate of the debt, based on their prioritized claim on the company's assets.

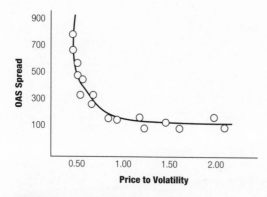

FIGURE 4.6 Relationship between Credit Spreads Widening and Stock Prices Declining as Volatility Increases.

KMV Corp. has expanded on Black, Scholes and Merton's original work to develop a credit risk tool that provides a market-based and financial statement-based evaluation of a given firm's expected default frequency (EDF). Their process estimates a firm's market value and the volatility of assets. They determine the default point as a function of the total liabilities of the firm and calculate the distance to default.

To better understand the KMV model, refer to the Figure 4.7. It is not only helpful for convertible arbitrageurs to incorporate the probability of default into the fixed-income valuation of the convertible, but also to understand the importance of increasing volatility of asset values and the potential default point of a firm. From the default point, we can then estimate the equity value that corresponds to a critical warning based on the debt value per share. The default point indicates the point at which the value of the firm has declined below the total liabilities of the firm. It assumes that as long as the value of the firm is worth more than its total liabilities, the firm will continue to operate. The model also incorporates the default and migration probabilities within the economic cycle. During recessions, default rates increase and access to capital decreases, increasing default migration rates.

Roughly speaking, the default point can be estimated by combining all of the firm's current liabilities and one-half of its long-term liabilities. (This is just a rough estimate that KMV publishes, although in practice they define this level much more precisely.) As the equity approaches this default value, the equity price may be indicating that the credit spread will widen and the

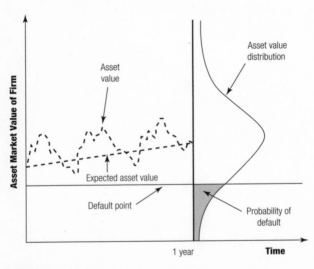

FIGURE 4.7   KMV—Merton Model.

convertible hedge ratio needs to be increased or the position should be closed. It may also be advisable to purchase put options with a strike price close to this value to provide additional protection. The credit default swap market may also have a tighter spread assumption than that indicated by the market-based models, offering an opportunity for a low-cost hedge for the arbitrageur.

The KMV model can be overlaid with the convertible arbitrageur's perspective, shown in Figure 4.8. The convertible price track in the diagram has the asset value distribution overlaid with the credit default point indicated. The vertical line marked "KMV default point" is near the point at which the investment value breaks down as the OAS widens. Around this point, the convertible moves into negative gamma territory and hedging becomes more difficult. The KMV default point is not the exact point at which the credit breaks down, but generally the OAS widens before this point and the investment value has already begun to slide toward the recovery rate.

Using the KMV or similar asset value-based credit models may help target hedges that need additional protection, and may also provide a reasonable estimate regarding a strike price for a protective put purchase. Figure 4.9 shows the convertible payoff at maturity or default with the investment value represented a riskless bond less a put option. The arbitrageur then purchases a long put struck at the level that provides a complete offset to the loss on the short put.

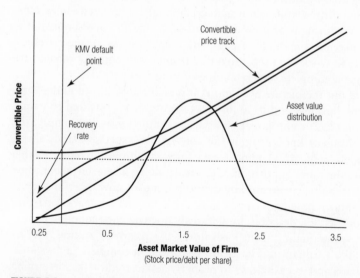

FIGURE 4.8 KMV Model Overlaid with Convertible Arbitrageur's Perspective.

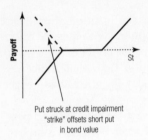

Put struck at credit impairment
"strike" offsets short put
in bond value

FIGURE 4.9   Convertible Payoff at Maturity or Default.

The KMV model can improve the hedging in low-grade convertibles and is another tool to include in the hedging toolbox. *Thorough credit work completed before the hedge is established becomes the foundation for the hedge and also the cornerstone for the theoretical pricing model.*

The market-based models improve the credit process when incorporated into the traditional credit evaluation, because they offset the weakness of ex-ante credit ratio analysis, where the data is stale and new data is only available four times per year. Then again, the weakness of the market-based approach is that, at the extremes, the equity market may overstate the risks or the safety of issues. During the technology bubble of the late 1990s, market-based credit models would have initially signaled a false sense of security for many firms, while traditional credit analysis revealed the extreme risks. Likewise, during recessions the mood of the market overshoots to the downside, and overestimates the default risk of many firms. At the extremes, traditional credit work can keep you out of trouble, but both approaches are valuable to get a complete understanding of a company's risks.

To round out the picture even more, it is also important to understand the underlying business and its ability to generate cash flow, and to gain a perspective on the current valuation and its sustainability. Put simply, the more an arbitrageur knows about the convertible issuer's balance sheet, business model, credit stress points, and equity valuation, the more reliable the hedge and the more opportunities to create alpha. The arbitrageur must exploit market inefficiencies and, by definition, must know more about the convertible and underlying business than does the average market participant. The next section describes how to truly uncover the economic profits of a company, the quality of the cash flows, the return on capital, and finally, the equity's valuation. The arbitrageur needs a complete understanding of a business and its cash flows to properly assign credit risks, determine if the stock price may be subject to large price breaks, takeover risks, or the need to access capital in the future. The following discussion provides a solid framework in which to understand business valuation, a necessary tool for the arbitrageur's toolbox.

CASH FLOW AND VALUING A BUSINESS

Since the value of any security is a function of the underlying business cash flows, the security of the cash flows, and the quality of the cash flows, then it follows that any hedge dependent on credit or equity biases should be backed by a solid understanding of the business and its valuation. Later, it will become even more apparent the extent to which many convertible hedging techniques rely on credit valuation. Moreover, gamma hedges, future volatility estimates, and directional hedges also rely on some equity valuation and opinions on the fundamental strength of the underlying business.

BUSINESS VALUATION MODEL

From the World's Most Successful Investor

Warren Buffett, president of Berkshire Hathaway, is probably the greatest investor of the last 30 years. In this section, I will take an approach toward business valuation that is similar to his. I have included an excerpt from one of Mr. Buffett's annual meetings that discusses his approach toward valuing a company.

> Growth in earnings or sales volume or whatever is a factor which can enhance or diminish—people usually think in terms of enhancing intrinsic value. The value of any purchase made for investment purposes is essentially the discounted [value] of all cash that will ever be received between now and judgment day from that commitment.
>
> And you face (a) determining the cash flows in and out (you have to put money in before you take it out sometimes) and (b) you have to figure out the discount rate. The growth and non-growth or shrinkage of the business is a calculation that goes into determining those items which you're discounting back to the present value.
>
> That's all you're doing as an investor—whether you're buying Coca-Cola or you're buying stock in PS Group or whatever it may

be. We're essentially thinking what's the cash payment capacity of that asset as far as we can see, how sure do we feel about it (the proper discount rate) and how does it compare to alternative choices. That's what's going through our minds.

Growth can be a negative. If you've got to put more money into a business earning sub-par return on capital because it has to grow, then that's a minus. . . . Growth is most positive when it takes no capital at all and produces significant returns.[1]

Mr. Buffett's definition of a business's value serves as our outline for making such determinations. In fact, this business valuation approach is a direct descendent of the approach developed by John Burr William in the 1930s:

The mathematical exercise [of the cash flow approach] is very similar to valuing a bond's value. . . . To determine the value of a business, the analyst estimates the 'coupons' that the business will generate for a period into the future, and then discounts all of those coupons back to the present.[2]

We will use many of Mr. Buffett's writings to provide a framework for estimating these "equity coupons" and determining the intrinsic business value. Equity coupons represent excess cash flow generated by the company and the payment to investors that may take the form of dividends or share repurchases. Unlike bonds, these coupons are variable and there is no principal repayment or maturity date. The analyst must estimate the coupon payments well into the future and discount them at the appropriate rate.

The determination of a company's intrinsic value must be based on sound financial and business analysis; Mr. Buffett provides insight into both aspects. The approach to business valuation must also attempt to put all businesses on a comparable basis. For example, one common denominator among all businesses is employment of capital. This capital can be in a number of different forms, including human, monetary, plant and equipment, natural resources, or any other tangible or intangible asset. But each type of capital is purchased for cash or monetary capital, making business evaluation somewhat easier because it makes all businesses "economic equivalents." It does not matter if the company being analyzed is an energy company or computer manufacturer or any other type of business; a careful assessment of how well the company employs capital becomes the measure against which all

---

[1]Outstanding Investor Digest, Inc. All rights reserved.
[2]Robert G. Hagstrom, Jr., *The Warren Buffett Way*. New York: John Wiley & Sons, Inc., 1994. p. 94.

businesses must ultimately be judged. As a result, the firm that earns the highest return on total invested capital is generally the best business.

In addition to the insights above, we will use additional guidance provided by Mr. Buffett in his annual reports and other published interviews in order to develop a model to determine a company's intrinsic value.

I. CASH INFLOWS: CAPITAL EMPLOYED

Since Mr. Buffett claims that the first step is determining the cash flows into and out of a business, we will also begin there. If a firm has used only equity financing and owns its own plant and equipment, then the capital employed in the business will be largely the retained earnings and equity capital raised.

Unfortunately, most businesses use a mix of financing methods, and there are often accounting discrepancies that obscure the cash flows out of the business. Most people would readily agree that all debt financing, equity financing, minority interests, and retained earnings are considered part of the total capital employed.

The starting points for determining capital inflows or investments (which we will refer to as capital) are very straightforward and easily found on any balance sheet.

Capital = Long-term debt (LTD) plus short-term debt (STD) plus preferred stock (PS) plus common equity (CE) plus minority interests (MI)

But there are some less obvious items that need to be included as part of the capital employed in the business, as follows:

1. Operating Leases

The objective of this model is to determine the on-going value of the business, based on how well management is expected to use the capital entrusted to the business. If one does not adjust for the difference, firms that use operating leases to run their businesses will have an apparent return-on-capital advantage over firms that make outright purchases of assets. The analyst should not assume that an operating lease is not really a necessary portion of capital just because the balance sheet of a firm that decides to use an operating lease does not reflect the lease liability—as it would in an outright asset purchase.

In fact, it may cost a company significantly less capital to make an outright purchase, if the purchase price is inexpensive, compared to the cost of obtaining an operating lease. Adjustments for operating leases become significant in certain industry groups such as retail or restaurants, in which leased space is a significant portion of capital and the company could not operate without that leased space. The analyst must add the value of the operating leases to the capital employed in the business. A simple way to do this is to either capitalize the annual operating lease expense or discount to a present value all future operating lease payments. The book *Security Analyses*, by Warren Buffett's mentors, provides some guidance on this subject: "Practices vary on the matter of operating leases, but we prefer to include them in invested capital."[3] This amount should be added to the capital previously determined to be part of the company's cash outflows. Since the capital equation includes the present value of the operating leases, the net cash flow position must also include the estimated interest component of the lease payment.

This will be discussed further in the cash inflow section. The new capital equation becomes

$$\text{Capital} = \text{LTD} + \text{STD} + \text{PS} + \text{CE} + \text{MI} + \text{present value of all future}$$
$$\text{annual operating leases (OL)}$$

2. Goodwill Amortization

The next adjustment to cash flows into the business concerns the former treatment for goodwill amortization under generally accepted accounting principles (GAAP). Until very recently, GAAP accounting for goodwill was not logical and still today may not reflect accurately the capital invested in the business. Once again, Mr. Buffett provides some insight into the subject:

> We think that the cost of a business is an important factor in determining the success of a business investment. But we do not think that the amortization schedule as provided by GAAP accounting is a particularly representative way of reflecting business results.[4]

Buffett prefers to leave goodwill on the balance sheet and not amortize it because it is important for investors to recognize "just how much the company has paid for goodwill over the years and evaluat[e] the success of the management by whether or not they've made decent returns on it."[5] Keep in

---

[3]Cottle, Sidney, Murray, Roger F., Block, Frank E., *Graham and Dodd's Security Analysis, Fifth Edition, abridged edition for the Institute of Chartered Financial Analysts.* New York: McGraw-Hill, Inc. 1989. p. 351.
[4]Outstanding Investor Digest, Inc. All rights reserved.
[5]Outstanding Investor Digest, Inc. All rights reserved.

mind we want to measure how well a company generates returns on all invested capital (cash flows into the business). The amortization of goodwill shrinks the investment—which has the effect of increasing the returns.

Since we are concerned with the returns generated on the capital, we need to use Mr. Buffett's advice and add back all cumulative goodwill amortization and include this total goodwill as part of the capital employed in the business. The adjusted capital equation is now:

$$\text{Capital} = \text{LTD} + \text{STD} + \text{PS} + \text{CE} + \text{MI} + (\text{OL}) + \text{accumulated}$$
$$\text{goodwill amortization (GA)}$$

3. Investment Write-Down

One of the current trends in corporate America is writing off poor investments. This has the same impact as goodwill amortization, although it occurs more quickly. The effect on book value is an immediate reduction, and the returns on investment seem to increase. However, as an investment advisor, I do not have the luxury of calculating the returns I generate for my clients by writing down their initial investment amount for bad investments. Consider how you would feel if you received this letter from your investment advisor:

Dear Investor,

Your portfolio returned 5% this year, with a $4,500 gain and a closing year-end value of $94,500. Due to poor market conditions in the energy sector, we wrote off an investment we made in Chevron and adjusted your initial investment to $90,000 from $100,000.

Sincerely,

Your Investment Advisor

You would not accept this and neither should we when we determine a company's returns on capital. We add back any losses to capital to ensure that all employed capital is considered. But we must also deduct any gains taken when a company divests or writes off a division to make sure we do not penalize them with an initial investment (capital employed) larger than it actually was. The gains or losses from the initial invested capital will be considered in the business's return on capital and its cash inflows.

We must be careful to assess how well a company employs all capital entrusted to it. Unlike most analysts, we are not forgiving about restructuring charges: These charges will be added back into capital employed. Mr.

Buffett and his partner Charlie Munger have discussed this topic and ridiculed the accounting shenanigan.

> BUFFETT: The whole restructuring charge, incidentally, which has
>   gained enormously in vogue the last few years, presents enormous
>   opportunity for abuse-temptations. People are playing games with
>   restructuring charges—and they'll continue to do so. Most
>   managements are far over-enchanted with the numbers they report
>   rather than the economic reality. And sometimes that gets them
>   into big trouble.
> MUNGER: Think of what you do for earnings by just writing down all
>   of your assets to zero—so that the depreciation charge goes away
>   forever.[6]

The economic reality is that the company had the capital and employed it poorly. As a result, the return on capital was substandard.

The article presented in Figure 4.10 discusses the trend in corporate asset write-downs and the corresponding increase in ROE, although the rate of return on capital would not be affected by these games.

Therefore, the further adjusted capital becomes:

$$\text{Capital} = \text{LTD} + \text{STD} + \text{PS} + \text{CE} + (\text{OL}) + (\text{GA}) + \text{cumulative}$$
$$\text{unusual losses (minus gains) adjusted for taxes (U)}$$

4. Accounting for Acquisitions

Capital outflows into the business might have to be adjusted if one company acquired another and accounted for the acquisition using the pooling method of accounting for acquisitions instead of the purchase method. When one company acquires another using the purchase method of accounting, the balance sheets are combined; any premium paid for assets in excess of their book value is considered goodwill and is initially fully reflected on the balance sheet of the acquiring company. Such acquisitions also require goodwill to be written off as an expense against earnings over a period not to exceed 40 years.

Although the pooling method no longer meets GAAP standards, credit analysts still need to level the playing field for companies that did use the method in the past. Under the pooling method, the acquiring firm uses its stock to purchase the other company. The balance sheets are combined, but any premium paid in excess of the book value of the assets is not reflected

---

[6]Outstanding Investor Digest, Inc. All rights reserved.

INTRINSIC VALUE: THE "20% CLUB" NO LONGER

Once upon a time—say, the year before last—a company making a 20% return on equity was among the elite. A Wal-Mart Stores or a Coca-Cola could obtain the mark, but precious few others.

Now, it seems, the club is open to all. In the first quarter, the average ROE of the Standard & Poor's 500 companies hit 20.12%. This figure (hot off the calculator from Salomon Brothers) represents the highest level of corporate profitability in the postwar era, and probably since the latter stages of the Bronze Age.

If the 20% figure means what it seems, then it is truly historic, akin to the average ballplayer hitting .350. Perhaps it will endure, in which case finance textbooks will be rewritten. More likely, American businesses will revert to the mean, in which case the boom in corporate profits won't last forever and might end tomorrow.

Historically, it has been very hard to maintain an ROE above the low teens for long. At 20%, it would appear that profits are benefiting from an unusually happy alignment of stars, such as a falling dollar, low inflation, continued growth, zero wage pressure and across-the-board cost cutting. As the auto industry is discovering, stars dont' stand still.

ROE, keep in mind, is no inconsequential yardstick. It is the intrinsic measure of profitability: how many cents of after-tax profit on each dollar of shareholder equity.

Until recently, this number varied little. In 1971, a Fortune essayist (investor Warren Buffett) noticed that the ROE of corporate America has been "stuck at 12%" for decades. There was good reason for this. Any company that topped it had to reinvest ever-larger sums at the same rate of profitability or its ROE would fall.

At 20%, a company doubles its profits in four years and sextuples them in 10 years. With capital expanding at such a fearsome rate, few can find attractive places to put it. (Even a Wal-Mart runs out of unstored terrain.) Thus, ROEs return to Earth.

ROEs did rise in the 1980s, when companies leveraged their equity by adding borrowed money to it. The leveraging trend has since flattened; why not the surge in ROEs?

At least a partial answer is that company after company has written off obsolete workers and plants. Corp. just took its second big write-off in as many years.

Corporate bean counters are well aware that such tactics will juice their ROEs. In one convenient stroke, they take a big hit to earnings; then, their books show a lower shareholders' equity, or book value, forever. When the ROE calculation is made, the "equity" in the denominator is smaller. Byron Wien, who is paid to reflect on such matters for Morgan Stanley, says, "There have been tremendous charges taken against book value. So book is tremendously understated. It just doesn't mean anything." If that were so, an ROE of 20% would be no big deal; indeed, it could become the mark of mediocrity. One could then envision corporate boards of the not-too-distant future dismissing slothful CEOs for mustering "only" 15%.

Mr. Wien doesn't quite believe that. To vaporize ("write off") equity overnight is an accounting fiction. Often, the corporate chargetaker is recognizing a deterioration in asset value that actually occurred in the real world over a span of years. The company would have given a truer picture of its business had it depreciated more of the asset all along—which means that, in an economic sense, previous "earnings" were not really as high as reported. Thus, though the current ROE may be juiced, previous ROEs were inflated as well. So in relative terms, the current ROE is still high.

Book values also took a big hit in 1992, when companies changed the way they account for health benefits of future retirees. But since then, ROEs have continued to soar. So it is unlikely that the benefit change fully explains.

According to Jack Ciesielski, who writes the Analyst's Accounting Observer in Baltimore, the ROE signal is "muddy" or inexact—but it has always been muddy. It might not measure true profitability precisely. It does suggest that life in corporate America is about as good as it can get.

ROE at the Top?
Return on corporate equity is at a record

* First quarter
NOTE: Figures for 1978 through the present equal S&P 500 earnings divided by beginning-of-the-year book value. Prior years are S&P Industrial earnings divided by end-of-year book.

FIGURE 4.10 Return on Equity. Source: "Intrinsic Value" by Roger Lowenstein. *The Wall Street Journal*, Central Edition, May 5, 1995. Reprinted by permission of *The Wall Street Journal* via the Copyright Clearance Center.

on the balance sheet, nor is there any charge against earnings. Therefore, if a company acquired another company using pooling instead of purchase accounting, its subsequent earnings will be higher. Of course, many investors are smart enough to understand that earnings do not represent economic value and that GAAP accounting distorts reality.

We are concerned with evaluating how effectively the business employs all capital and therefore we must determine the premium paid in excess of the asset value. If we know the number of shares the company issued in exchange for the acquired company, and multiply the shares exchanged by the market price of the stock on the date of the exchange, we then know the purchase price. Any premium paid for assets in excess of the book value should be added to the acquiring company's balance sheet and be reflected as capital outflows in our model (i.e., goodwill).

Mr. Buffett's insight into this accounting distortion is as follows:

> Most businesses, perhaps, prefer to use the pooling method because they don't like to take the goodwill amortization charge. It actually makes no difference to us what accounting treatment is used. We're interested in the economics of the transaction. . . . We want a standardized way of looking at businesses. And if one company uses the pooling method and another company uses purchase accounting, we're going to recast that in our own minds so that there is comparability.[7]

Mr. Buffett acknowledges the pooling versus purchase problem and addresses it without a complete solution, although I am quite sure our adjustment is the kind of "recasting" necessary to make these transactions comparable. If any pooling acquisitions have occurred, the adjusted capital equation becomes:

$$\text{Capital} = \text{LTD} + \text{STD} + \text{PS} + \text{CE} + \text{MI} + (\text{OL}) + (\text{GA}) + (\text{U}) + \text{price}$$
$$\text{paid in excess of asset value under pooling (P)}$$

5. Deferred Taxes

The deferred-tax reserve is another enigma that results from the difference between GAAP accounting and actual cash payments for taxes. For most firms, including those that are growing or at least maintaining their asset base, this deferred-tax "liability" will never be paid and in fact represents an asset—not a liability. Since it also represents cash that the firm has retained

---

[7]Outstanding Investor Digest, Inc. All rights reserved.

and invested, shareholders clearly expect to earn a return on it regardless of how the cash is accounted for under GAAP. We will add the deferred tax reserve to capital to provide a clearer measure of the capital the company has to work with:

$$\text{Capital} = \text{LTD} + \text{STD} + \text{PS} + \text{CE} + \text{MI} + (\text{OL}) + (\text{GA}) + (\text{U}) + (\text{P}) +$$
$$\text{deferred tax reserves (DT)}$$

6. Inventory Accounting Methods

Businesses have some discretion regarding how to value their inventory. The valuation method chosen will have an impact on reported earnings. The two main methods of inventory valuation used in GAAP accounting are last-in-first-out (LIFO) and first-in-first-out (FIFO). During periods of inflation, LIFO matches the firm's current revenues with current costs much better than FIFO. The LIFO reserve is the amount by which the inventories are understated. Mr. Buffett notes in his 1977 annual report that "During the 1970s there was a pronounced swing by corporations toward LIFO accounting (which has the effect of lowering a company's reported earnings and tax bill)." Earnings, inventory turnover, and valuation are not comparable between those firms using LIFO and those using FIFO. One method of removing this accounting distortion is to add the LIFO reserve (found in the footnotes to a company's financial statements) back into the cash outflows portion, thus eliminating the amount by which the inventories are undervalued. The resulting number represents replacement cost much better and also makes capital comparable across all companies.

Capital is further adjusted to become:

$$\text{Capital} = \text{LTD} + \text{STD} + \text{PS} + \text{CE} + \text{MI} + (\text{OL}) + (\text{GA}) + (\text{U}) + (\text{P}) +$$
$$(\text{DT}) + \text{LIFO reserves (LR)}$$

Annual increases in the LIFO reserve account will also be added into the cash outflows portion of the analysis to adjust for unrealized inventory-holding gains and make the cash flows comparable for all companies.

7. R&D Expense

GAAP accounting calls for research and development investments to be expensed. Although it is difficult to estimate the payoff from R&D investment during the initial stages of a research project, companies undertake these projects with the expectation of some return on capital. We feel that a company's R&D investments should be capitalized and added back to capital.

The analyst should amortize the R&D investment over the expected life of the project. For high technology projects in which rapid change in product technology is the norm, the amortization schedule may be only a few years, but drug companies may have patent protection for many more years. Although I was unable to find any insight specifically on the subject from Warren Buffett, the economic reality is consistent with his other accounting adjustments.

Capitalizing R&D will better match the company's investment-return schedule for a project without unduly penalizing the company in the initial years, although the net capitalized R&D on the balance sheet will ultimately reduce the overall return on capital from the project in the future. In effect, this method allows the R&D investment and its payoff to be matched more smoothly and better reflect the project's economic reality.

The capital employed in the business is adjusted further to become:

$$\text{Capital} = \text{LTD} + \text{STD} + \text{PS} + \text{CE} + \text{MI} + (\text{OL}) + (\text{GA}) + (\text{U}) + (\text{P}) + (\text{DT}) + (\text{LR}) + \text{capitalized R\&D (RD)}$$

So far, we have discussed capital employed in the business from the perspective of the owner's equity and liability side of the balance sheet. Since assets equal liabilities plus owner's equity, investors may prefer to approach capital employed from the operating assets side of the balance sheet. In that case, the investor would need to make the same accounting adjustments discussed above.

Although other additions to capital employed could be made, the significant ones are accounted for here. In an effort to be brief, we will simply state that other such considerations include quasi-equity accounts. Items such as deferred income, deferred gains, bad debt reserves, and other deferred or reserve accounts all represent capital that is employed on behalf of these shareholders, and is thus expected to generate a return to shareholders.

Likewise, many companies have pension liabilities and post-retirement health-care liabilities. These items should be considered debt and added to the capital employed in the business as a cash inflow item. This will reduce the return on capital and shareholder value.

II. CASH OUTFLOWS: ECONOMIC PROFIT

Using Mr. Buffett's model, the next step is to "determine the cash-generating ability of the firm's assets from now until eternity," which means cash outflows. Since reported corporate earnings are not the same as cash profits, we have to make a number of accounting adjustments. Earnings reported by any company will have many assumptions, estimates, expenses, and deferrals that obscure a firm's true cash-generating ability.

1. GAAP Distortions

Generally accepted accounting principles (GAAP) were developed by accountants for accountants and have little relationship to a firm's true economic earnings. We have found that a firm's net income may express an average of 45 percent of cash earnings. Mr. Buffett explains that "The numbers in any accounting report mean nothing per se as to economic value. They're guidelines to tell you something about how to get at economic value."[8] I will attempt to show how adjustments to GAAP on the cash outflows side of the equation can help one value a business's true economic profit. Like Mr. Buffett, we want to ultimately arrive at the true economic value of a firm.

Financial analysts should be concerned with economic earnings—not accounting earnings. Under GAAP, a company can use different depreciation schedules, defer income taxes that will likely never be paid, expense research and development, and use debt financing; furthermore, earnings are subject to other factors that make reported earnings non-comparable. Equally as disconcerting is the fact that a company's income statement reflects only the cost of a firm's debt financing and not the cost of equity capital. In fact, many chief financial officers (CFOs) do not even consider the cost of equity capital when making financing decisions. During a meeting with a CFO from a well-known growth company that has since gone bankrupt. I asked the CFO what he thought his company's cost of equity capital was. He responded, "Zero." I responded that "Clearly, giving away part of your business is costly." Unfortunately, this is the mindset of many investors and corporate managers who evaluate companies only from the perspective of GAAP earnings.

2. Earnings Versus Return on Capital

Many analysts evaluate a company based on the earnings per share that the company generates regardless of the capital employed to generate those earnings. This is similar to an investment manager telling you that he generated $20,000 in profits on average for his clients. If the average client had $100,000 invested, $20,000 profit may be very good. However, if the average client had $1,000,000 invested, the gain is not nearly as exemplary.

In Mr. Buffett's 1977 report to shareholders, he comments on the earnings problem.

---

[8]Outstanding Investor Digest, Inc. All rights reserved.

Most companies define "record" earnings as a new high in earnings per share. Since businesses customarily add from year to year to their equity base, we find nothing particularly noteworthy in a management performance combining, say, a 10% increase in equity capital and a 5% increase in earnings per share.

Profits should be evaluated as a percentage of capital employed to generate those profits.

Less-than-stellar corporate managers and analysts may believe that the objective of a firm is to maximize earnings per share, but truly successful firms—and truly successful analysts—realize that the objective is to maximize shareholder wealth. Accounting earnings do not always achieve this objective, and at times may even run counter to it. Measuring economic-profit return on capital attempts to better reflect reality better.

Buffett recommends looking less at earnings per share than at return on capital, which is what produces the earnings. There are ways of manipulating earnings per share and earnings growth; return on total capital is harder to play with.[9]

Also, the focus on a company's earnings per share also tells you nothing about the total costs of capital employed to earn that "profit." Many companies report positive earnings per share even though the total returns generated are below the firm's total cost of capital. Obviously, a company intends to earn returns above its cost of total capital; otherwise, it would not make economic sense to invest those funds. We are concerned with the firm's economic profits, that is, with profits in excess of all capital costs and adjusted for accounting distortions.

3. EBITDA Analysis: A Starting Point, Not an Ending Point!

Many investors focus on a firm's earnings before interest, taxes, depletion, depreciation, and amortization (EBITDA) as a proxy for the firm's true economic earnings. Many analysts will determine the multiples of EBITDA that a firm should trade for, based on the firm's expected growth rate in EBITDA. EBITDA, however, does not truly represent the going concern value of a business because it ignores depreciation as an expense, other expenses, and many non-cash expense items such as R&D, for example (see below).

---

[9]John Train, *The Money Masters*, New York: Harper & Row, 1980. p. 21.

There is another problem with using EBITDA multiples to determine business value: The firm's total cost of capital is ignored, particularly the cost of equity capital. The multiples used to determine a business value must also be adjusted for the level, growth, and quality of the cash flow and debt; this becomes very subjective. EBITDA analysis also assigns a value to the company's depreciation expense as if the company's tangible assets did not need to be maintained.

Mr. Buffett provides some insight on this subject, although in this instance he refers to EBDIT (earnings before depreciation, interest and taxes) in terms of interest coverage. The point is that depreciation is almost always equal to a company's necessary maintenance expenditure; it represents a return of capital not a return on capital.

> Soon borrowers found even the new, lax standards intolerably binding. To induce lenders to finance even sillier transactions, they introduced an abomination, EBDIT—earnings before depreciation, interest and taxes—as the test of a company's ability to pay interest. Using this sawed-off yardstick, the borrower ignored depreciation as an expense on the theory that it did not require a current cash outlay.
>
> . . . Such an attitude is clearly delusional. At 95% of American businesses, capital expenditures that over time roughly approximate depreciation are a necessity and are every bit as real an expense as labor or utility costs.[10]

Finally, the result does not provide a good measure of economic profits in regards to capital outlays, which is the ultimate goal. The analysis does not determine how much capital was employed in the business to generate the level of EBITDA compared to that of the firm's competitors.

4. R&D Investment

The following adjustments will take the model a few steps beyond EBITDA because some of a firm's operating expenses are not expenses at all. For example, under GAAP accounting, a company must expense R&D costs. Therefore, if you have two firms in the same industry with exactly the same revenue and operating costs, but one firm invests in R&D and the other firm does not, the firm that makes the R&D investment will report lower earnings. However, firms invest in R&D both to remain competitive and because

---

[10]Outstanding Investor Digest, Inc. All rights reserved.

of the potential return R&D represents. R&D expenses are not just an expense, but also an investment and should be recognized as such. One way to reduce the R&D impact is to amortize the expense over an expected payoff time horizon such as three to seven years.

R&D is not the only expense that needs to be recognized as an investment and not just as a cost with no future return; some marketing expenses may also be considered investments. For example, Coca-Cola was spending money advertising in India before it could sell its products there. Coca-Cola invested this money knowing that the dollars spent would help build brand recognition and consumer demand for the time when it had approval to sell in India.

5. An Illustration

To demonstrate some of the problems faced by analysts when trying to compare companies based on earnings per share analysis or EBITDA multiples, I have selected two different accounting scenarios for a sample company I will call GAAP. I will make viable accounting choices to reflect business results. Keep in mind that this is the same company with the same revenue, facilities, and employees. The only difference is how management accounts for business operations and assets. See Table 4.1.

In Scenario A, the company chooses FIFO inventory valuation, an aggressive depreciation period for assets, and does no current R&D, instead choosing to purchase R&D from another company by purchasing the company under the pooling method for acquisitions. The company has used debt in its capital structure and has decided to use operating leases instead of purchasing machinery. The company has taken a write-off for a plant closing.

Under Scenario B, GAAP has chosen LIFO inventory valuation, chosen a conservative depreciation schedule, and invests in research and development. It made an acquisition and accounted for it under the purchase method of accounting for acquisitions. It has no debt in its capital structure and decided to purchase machines instead of using operating leases.

Finally, the company did not take any restructuring charges because it thought that if business picked up in future years, it would need the extra capacity that the closed plant could provide. The income statements and earnings per share for this company look dramatically different under the two scenarios. The return on equity is also misleading. Only the return on capital tells the true profitability story. Both businesses are actually the same. Table 4.1 will demonstrate how to adjust the accounting numbers to make the companies comparable.

TABLE 4.1 GAAP Inc. Income Statement

$ Millions	Scenario A	Scenario B
Sales	1,000.00	1,000.00
COGS (FIFO A, LIFO B)	400.00	440.00
SG&A	150.00	150.00
R&D	—	100.00
Interest expense	50.00	—
Depreciation	75.00	110.00
Pretax income	325.00	200.00
Tax @ 35%	113.75	70.00
Goodwill amortization	—	20.00
Net income	211.25	110.00
Shares	250.00	250.00
EPS	**0.85**	**0.44**
P/E ratio	**11.83**	**22.73**
ROE (%)	**21.13**	**10.00**
Stock price	10.00	10.00
EBITDA multiple	5.56	8.06
Balance sheet		
equity	1,000.00	1,100.00
debt	500.00	—
	Purchase XYZ for $500 in stock 100 @ $50	Purchase XYZ for $500 in cash with $200 goodwill
Acquisition	Pooling	Purchase
R&D investment	No R&D	Yes
Inventory	Fifo investment	Lifo investment
Capital structure	Debt	No debt
Operating leases	Yes	Purchase
Restructuring charge	Equity write-off	None
Depreciation of assets	15 years	10 years

III. CASH-INFLOW MODEL

Evaluating the cash-generating ability of a company begins with a careful analysis of the company's statement of cash flows. The cash outflows that a firm generates can be measured by working through the non-cash charges and adjusting the financial statements for changes that Mr. Buffett suggested when we were determining the cash flows from the business.

1. Cash Basis Accounting

To determine a firm's true economic earnings, the financial statements of all companies need to be revised from accrual basis to cash-on-cash-basis accounting. Accrual accounting has very little to do with true cash flow. We will also at this point remove the firm's financing structure from the picture because the financing decision of a firm has nothing to do with its ability to generate economic profits. We are concerned here not with how the business financed its capital, but rather with the returns that such capital generates for its shareholders. Later, we will consider the financing decision when determining the discount rate used to discount all the firm's expected future economic profits back to the current period.

Since a firm's decision to use debt in the capital structure will affect its tax expense, we will assume for the moment that all firms pay taxes as if they have been financed only with equity capital. Adjusting all firms in this manner puts them on the same basis and helps reveal their true economic profits before the financing decision is considered. Therefore, interest expense on debt is considered non-deductible for tax purposes. Once again, accounting profits are higher if a firm chooses debt capital instead of equity capital to grow its business, but the firm's ability to produce good returns on capital has nothing to do with the decision to finance that capital with debt or equity. An estimate of the interest component of any operating lease must also be included. Including this makes the decision to lease or buy an asset economically equivalent.

The revised statement of cash flows includes interest income and operating interest expense on a fully taxable basis. See Table 4.2. The objective of the adjustments made to the GAAP income statement is to determine the true cash-generating ability of the business. Non-cash charges and other deferred accounting transactions (goodwill amortization, deferred taxes, bad debt reserves, LIFO reserves) are recognized when actual cash is disbursed instead of when GAAP accrual accounting determines. Note that depreciation is added back, but necessary-maintenance capital expenditures are subtracted. It is essential for analysts to determine the on-going maintenance expenditures that a company must make to maintain its operations before

TABLE 4.2 Revised Statement of Cash Flows

Net income available to common stockholders	$294.2
Plus goodwill amortization	57.0
Plus increase in LIFO reserve	18.0
Plus increase in deferred taxes	12.0
Plus increase in bad debt reserves	4.9
Plus increase in net capitalized R&D	30.4
Increase in non-cash adjustments	122.3
Adj. income available to shareholders	416.5
Plus depreciation expense	55.0
Minus necessary-maintenance capital expenditures	50.0
Plus interest expense	20.0
Plus interest expense on operating leases	22.0
Adjusted interest expense	42.0
Minus tax benefit of interest expense (at 35% rate)	(14.7)
Interest expense after taxes	27.3
Net cash operating profit (adjusted for cash taxes)	$448.8

looking at the decision to grow them. We are evaluating the business as a going concern and would not look too kindly upon a company putting off necessary capital expenditures in an effort to preserve cash. If a company's depreciation expense is in excess of necessary capital maintenance expenditures, then the residual is a return on capital. The portion equal to necessary maintenance, however, represents a return of capital.

You will notice that the same accounting adjustments made to determine the cash outflows or capital employed in the business also show up on the cash inflow side of the analysis. The significant difference is that the cash outflow side typically adds back prior write-offs, amortization, or deferred account changes from the past, while the cash inflow analysis deals only with the current period (year) changes in these items.

Some investors will recognize this final operating cash as free cash flow. This is the cash available to investors before management's decision to grow the business. This may be the free cash flow definition that a corporate raider is focused on because he aims to purchase the whole company and alter the company's future growth plans. We are more concerned with the company as a going concern, and therefore would define free cash flow as the cash operating income after tax and necessary capital expenditures (as defined in the table above) but also after the company's growth expenditures. Unlike the corporate raider, we do not have the ability to purchase the firm, change growth plans, and alter the company's life cycle to capture the cash flow before growth expenditures. Free cash flow represents the owner's repayment for taking the risk and employing capital in the business, and is the cash that is available to all investors in the company. The company can pay out this cash in dividends, repurchase stock, pay down debt— or increase reinvestment in the business in order to grow it further and ultimately pay investors a higher dividend in the future.

2. Return on Capital Defined

The net result of the restated operating profits after tax is a cash-on-cash accounting that makes all companies comparable. At this point, we are ready to determine the return on total capital that the firm generates; this is an important component in determining its intrinsic value as outlined by Mr. Buffett.

A company's return on capital can be found by dividing the adjusted operating profit by the adjusted capital as determined by the previous discussions:

(cash operating profit adjusted for tax/adjusted capital invested)
= return on invested capital

Evaluating a business's return on invested monetary capital allows for across-the-board relative comparisons. In each case, a company's return on capital can be compared to its cost of capital to determine the "excess return on investment" or cash value added. Also, note that this analysis considers both the balance sheet and income statement, unlike earnings-per-share analysis, which considers only the income statement. Some companies will have natural capital-cost advantages arising from location, size, governmental subsidies, or a host of other reasons. For example, the Federal National Mortgage Corporation (FNMA) has an implied government backing that results in a debt capital cost that is lower than that of their competitors, which do not have government backing. This gives FNMA a significant cost-of-capital advantage.

The easy part of the model used to estimate a business's intrinsic value is the math and accounting. The difficult part is determining the company's future cash outflows based on a thorough understanding of the business and its competitive advantages, if any. Mr. Buffett explains:

What we refer to as a "moat" is what other people might call competitive advantage. Michael Porter might use that term. . . . There are various types of moats. All economic moats are either widening or narrowing—even though you can't see it. . . . And a good moat should produce good returns on invested capital.[11]

The world's nations and companies all compete for capital. The company that demonstrates its ability to earn high rates of return on the capital employed will also be the company that builds wealth for its investors. Mr. Buffett has a rule that a company must have economic characteristics that allow each dollar of capital employed to eventually be translated into more than a dollar in market value.

This can be accomplished consistently only if the business is generating returns in excess of its capital costs. Mr. Buffett expressed his discontent with big American heavy industries that require continuous massive investment as a "Ponzi scheme because basically the capital raised by the endless new stock and bond issues pays the dividends and interest. The dividends, at least after honest depreciation, are often not being earned."[12] Companies like these often trade at a fraction of capital employed and each dollar in new capital turns into 20 or 30 cents in market value. The companies that successfully employ capital will find that each dollar in new capital employed in the business will generate two or three dollars in market value for its shareholders. Wal-Mart, Coca-Cola, Merck, and many others have been known to generate market value multiples on each dollar of capital employed of better than five to one.

At approximately 11 percent, the return on invested capital for the average American corporation has been remarkably stable during the post-World War II period. Returns are primarily a function of the industry the business operates within and the ability of a company to differentiate its products or services. A very wide range of returns on invested capital exists between industry groups; the list below shows various average industry returns generated on total capital for the past 15 years:

Automotive companies	8%
Food companies	13–15%
Oil companies	8–9%
Consumer products	14–18%
Basic industry	6–10%

To determine a company's economic profit, the return on invested capital needs to be compared to the firm's total cost of capital. If a firm generates returns on capital in excess of the firm's total cost of capital, then an economic profit exists.

---

[11]Outstanding Investor Digest, Inc. All rights reserved.
[12]John Train, *The Money Masters*, New York: Harper & Row, 1980. p. 39.

Cash flow return on total invested capital > Cost of total capital
= economic profit

This economic profit is what actually drives the business value, not the accounting profit that is so widely ballyhooed in the press. If a company earns an accounting profit but does not earn an economic profit, earnings may be in excess of debt costs but do not represent a return in excess of both debt and equity costs. We will discuss this issue at greater length because of its important implications for determining shareholder wealth.

At this point, it is important to determine the company's cost of capital or, to put it another way, the required return on investment the company needs to earn before an economic profit is realized. The firm's after-tax cost of debt is generally easy to determine because in most cases the company has interest-bearing debt on its books. Determining the firm's cost of equity capital is a more confusing issue, though, because GAAP accounting does not provide for this cost. It is essential to remember that the equity cost should represent the opportunity cost of investing. Investors who provide equity capital to a business expect their investment to earn at least a normal return. Equity investments on average have produced an average annual return of 10–12 percent over the past 60 years. Therefore, equity investors will expect at least this return for supplying equity capital to the firm. If the business is unable to generate returns at this level, then investors will not continue to supply capital to the firm or will sell their equity stake. The opportunity cost of capital must be adjusted for the various levels of risk, meaning that a higher discount rate should be used for companies that have a less reliable stream of cash flows.

After completing the above, the firm's capital financing decision comes into play in the analysis. Firms with a considerable amount of debt in their capital structure most likely have a lower credit rating and therefore a higher cost of debt capital. High amounts of leverage may reduce a business's flexibility and impair its ability to take advantage of unforeseen opportunities that may occur in the future. As a result, the equity capital of a highly leveraged firm may need to be discounted at a higher rate, but this is for the analyst to determine.

We can get into some very elaborate formulas when attempting to determine the rate at which to discount the firm's equity capital. One good rule of thumb is to look at average returns available to common stock investors over the years. Large-company stocks have earned annual returns of approximately 10 percent during the last 60 years, while small companies have earned returns of approximately 12 percent in the same period. This is a reasonable starting point for evaluating a firm's cost of capital and will help us arrive ultimately at the discount rate used to determine the business's intrinsic value.

The final step involves multiplying the cost of each portion of the firm's capital by its appropriate weight in the capital structure. For example, if a firm has a cost of debt of 9 percent, a tax rate of 35 percent, a cost of equity of 12 percent, and debt equaling 30 percent of capital, then the firm's weighted cost of capital becomes:

$$WCOC = \{[\text{Debt cost} \times (1 - \text{tax rate})] \times \text{debt \% in capital}\} + (\text{equity cost} \times \text{equity \% in capital})$$

$$WCOC = [9.0 \times (1-0.35) \times .3] + (12.0 \times .7) = 10.16\%$$

Common sense should ensure that you are not discounting the firm at a rate below long-term government bonds plus some premium. Since the company's cash flows are to occur over the life of the firm, it would be inappropriate to assume that companies can finance more cheaply than the government. The U.S. government 30-year bond should represent the risk-free rate of long-term financing. Mr. Buffett provides some guidance on this subject:

> How we determine the discount rates in our discounted cash flow analysis is a very good question. Charlie and I will be affected to some degree by the general long-term rate of interest. But we want a whole lot more than that—whatever it happens to be at the time. We don't calibrate it in any kind of precise way. For example, if [long-term] interest rates were to move from 4% to 8% to 12%, that's significant. But if they go from 8% to 8.5% or 8% to 7.5%, those are meaningless moves to us. We have no precise calculations about them. We look at the capital asset pricing model as . . . a joke.[13]

Buffett will use the long-term rate of interest as a starting point and add a small premium to that rate. The more comfortable he is with a business and the better he understands the firm's present and future ability to generate an economic profit, the lower the discount rate he uses to determine the business's intrinsic value. He then attempts to purchase companies at a significant discount to intrinsic value. He mentions his low opinion of the capital asset pricing model, which other analysts use as the cornerstone for determining a company's cost of equity capital based on its beta. Since beta on an individual stock is usually unreliable and explains very little about a company's quality, capital structure, or any other fundamental business factors, we will also avoid the CAPM approach for our purposes here.

---

[13]Outstanding Investor Digest, Inc. All rights reserved.

It may also be argued that the 30-year Treasury long bond is very sensitive to interest-rate changes and equity evaluation should not incorporate this interest-rate volatility. Therefore, discounting a company's total cost of capital at some premium to the long bond rate is inappropriate. Many investors assume equities are not nearly as interest-rate sensitive as bonds. Mr. Buffett points out that both bonds and equities derive their value from discounting future expected cash flows and both should be considered closely linked to interest rates.

> The value of every business—the value of a farm, an apartment house or any other economic asset—is 100% sensitive to interest rates. That's because all you're doing when you're investing is transferring money to someone now in exchange for a stream of money which you expect to come back in the future. And the higher interest rates are, the less that present value will be. So every business by its nature—whether it's Coca-Cola or Gillette or Wells Fargo—in its intrinsic valuation is 100% sensitive to interest rates.[14]

Remember, Mr. Buffett's approach is to value equities as if they were actually bonds with the coupon not guaranteed but instead to be determined in the future based on the firm's profitability. The analyst must estimate these "coupon payments" and the likelihood of their occurrence.

We do know that during the post-WWII period, American businesses have generated returns on capital of approximately 11 percent. If the company is trading right at its capital value, this is the same as a bond coupon payment of 11 percent. The capital value or capital employed becomes the par value on the equity "bond." If a company generates an 11 percent return on capital but trades for twice the capital value, then the equity yield is only 5.5 percent. This level of return may be attractive if the company has a cost of capital below 11 percent, is improving its returns on capital and growing rapidly or, alternatively, if long-term interest rates are well below 5.5 percent.

IV. INTRINSIC BUSINESS VALUE

> We think in terms of intrinsic business value—which has virtually no connection with book value. It's interesting—back in the mid-20s, Ben Graham wrote an article about why book value is unimportant. He said basically that book value measures what's been put

---

[14]Outstanding Investor Digest, Inc. All rights reserved.

into a business and intrinsic value measures what will be taken out—and that there was often little relationship.[15]

To determine the company's intrinsic value, we can discount the economic profits into the future or we can discount the free cash flow that the company generates into the future. The result will be exactly the same, although using the framework of economic profit, as discussed in this chapter, provides better insight into the business operations.

The simplest way to value a business is to determine the value of a no-growth business. This can be accomplished by using a single-stage model:

$$\text{Cash operating profit after tax/discount rate}$$
$$= \text{No-growth business value}$$

But since most firms are going concerns and growing, or shrinking and shedding non-profitable operations, then the calculation must take into account the growth or non-growth in the business. Since a firm's economic profits are what drive the value of a business, then a firm that can generate an economic profit while growing is worth more than a firm that is growing and not earning an economic profit. In fact, if a firm continues to grow even though it is earning returns below its cost of capital, it is actually reducing the total value of that firm. Remember Mr. Buffett's statement regarding business value and growth:

> Growth can be a negative. If you've got to put more money into a business earning a sub-par return on capital because it has to grow, then that's a minus. . . . Growth is most positive when it takes no capital at all and produces significant returns.

Mr. Buffett thought that the relationship between growth and capital employed was worth considering carefully; this relationship is very instructive when attempting to determine the value of a business.

> We're willing to buy companies that aren't going to grow at all—assuming we get enough for our money when we do it. We're projecting numbers out estimating what kind of cash we're likely to get back over time. . . . But you can certainly have a situation where there's absolutely no growth in a business and it's a much better investment than some company that's going to grow at very substantial

---

[15]Warren Buffett, Outstanding Investor Digest, Inc. All rights reserved.

rates—particularly if they're going to need capital in order to grow. There's a huge difference between the business that grows and requires lots of capital to do so and the business that grows and doesn't require capital. And, generally, financial analysts don't apply adequate weight to the difference between those. In fact, it's amazing how little attention is paid to that. Believe me, if you're investing, you should pay a lot of attention to that. "Capital grows without physical growth in the business."[16]

The growth or variable-growth model will need to take the form of a multiple-stage discounting model. The model should include a life cycle for growth in the company's capital such as a rapid-growth stage, slow-growth stage, and no-growth stage. It should also incorporate multiple stages for the expected life cycle for returns on capital.

In business, as in nature, there is a strong tendency for market returns to revert toward the mean. A company's returns are largely a function of the industry it is in, although by no means does this presume that the industry is the only important component in determining the returns a company can generate. But a business generating high returns will often attract new competitors as well as copy-cats that will put downward pressure on returns. A business generating high returns on capital will also attract capital, and the sheer amount of the capital being re-deployed may force returns toward the industry average. Likewise, a business generating returns well below its industry average may be forced to downsize, replace management, and restructure in an effort to drive returns toward the industry average and—hopefully—above its cost of capital.

The life cycle for growth in a firm's capital or operating assets is very similar to the reversion to the mean explained above. Our model assumes that in time the business returns will revert to the industry average and that the growth rate in the business will also revert to the industry average. The analyst must determine how quickly this will occur, based on an understanding of the industry, the company's competitive advantages, and the quality of the business's investment opportunities.

The final discounting model incorporates many factors and allows for multiple growth, return, and cost-of-capital assumptions.

Value = Capital invested at beginning of forecast + Present value
of forecasted economic profits for the forecast period
+ Present value of forecasted economic profit after forecaster
period (perpetuity)

$$\text{Value} = (EP_{T+1}/WCOC) + (EP_{T+1})(g/ROIC - WCOC)/$$
$$WCOC(WCOC - g)$$

Where:

EP = economic profit
WCOC = weighted average cost of capital
"g" = expected growth rate in EP
ROIC = return on net new capital invested

In the end, understanding the importance of economic profits and the distortion of GAAP accounting will improve the analyst's ability to determine a business's value. But the truth is that each person has his or her own set of economic realities that will alter the results obtained from this model. This is true because the model determines value by estimating future cash flows and, as a wise old man once said, the success of a meal is determined more by the cook than the recipe.

Hopefully, this introduction to the credit analysis and business valuation tools that are essential to the arbitrageur's full understanding of the securities risks and opportunities lays the final stone in the foundation for the reader's understanding for convertible arbitrage. Up to this point, the book has attempted to provide a basic understanding of convertibles, the history of convertible arbitrage, and its role in a hedge portfolio. I have also provided an overview of typical valuation models that are used by the convertible community and the various risk measures (the "greeks") that describe the security. The first four chapters should provide the tools necessary to apply to the hedging techniques discussed in the remainder of this book.

CHAPTER 5

Convertible Arbitrage Techniques—Delta Hedging

onvertible hedge funds employ delta hedges, gamma hedges, leverage, and many other techniques to alter the risk profiles of the position. This chapter will discuss the delta neutral hedge, considered the bread-and-butter hedge for the convertible arbitrage funds. Delta neutral hedging is one of the lower-risk hedge techniques because of its ability to significantly reduce the equity sensitivity while taking advantage of the equity volatility. Since the hedge can control risks well, the use of leverage is nearly always associated with the delta neutral hedge.

The next few chapters will discuss many techniques employed by convertible arbitrageurs. To better understand some of the basic applications of the various hedges, referring to Figure 5.1 may help. As prices change and time passes, the risks and hedge opportunities change, too. The convertible price track in Figure 5.1 outlines the typical investment grade convertible hedge techniques employed at the different bands of the convertible price track spectrum, along with the commensurate risk levels that accompany each band of the price track. The full price track offers different hedging opportunities with greeks that can be exposed or hedged to complement other positions in the portfolio. It is imperative that the convertible arbitrageur utilize the full spectrum of opportunities in the marketplace not only because of the need to manage risk exposure, but also because the market does not always offer the plain vanilla delta neutral hedge opportunity in significant quantity or with high enough return potential. The arbitrageur needs to understand his or her own level of competency regarding the various hedge techniques and exploit the ones that he or she has an advantage in, while avoiding or minimizing the portfolio's exposure to the other hedge types.

Utilizing the full range of the opportunity set can help balance the portfolio and also keep it invested throughout the market cycle. Deep-in-the-money convertibles are exposed to a low degree of omicron, rho, or gamma

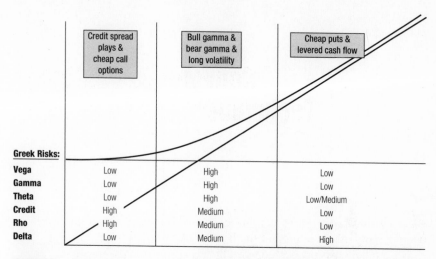

Greek Risks:			
Vega	Low	High	Low
Gamma	Low	High	Low
Theta	Low	High	Low/Medium
Credit	High	Medium	Low
Rho	High	Medium	Low
Delta	Low	Medium	High

FIGURE 5.1   Greek Exposure at Various Points along the Convertible Price Track.

but may offer the opportunity to capture a highly predictable, levered cash flow or free put options. Alternatively, the busted convertible is exposed to a high degree of omicron and rho but offers the opportunity to capture free or cheap call options for issues that are significantly undervalued from a credit perspective.

The greeks' risk levels stated in the distressed or low-grade range of the curve assumes that the credit quality holds: It is especially relevant for synthetic convertibles, structured convertible notes, and exchangeable convertibles.

The hedge opportunity set and the risk levels can dramatically change in the distressed zone of the price track, because the investment floor protection is elusive due to the now-high correlation between the convertible's underlying stock and its credit quality. Figure 5.2 indicates the changes in risk for low-grade issues. The negative gamma, along with a reversal in delta, causes many hedge positions to disintegrate. Careful credit assessment and an appreciation for the more subjective nature of hedging in this risky credit zone will help the arbitrageur to properly adjust the hedge and avoid disaster.

Arbitrageurs with a strong credit background or supporting analyst staff can exploit the significant price discrepancies that are prevalent in the low-grade convertible marketplace. The credit default swap market and other behaviorally correlated hedges can be established to reduce risk and gain profits in distressed convertibles.

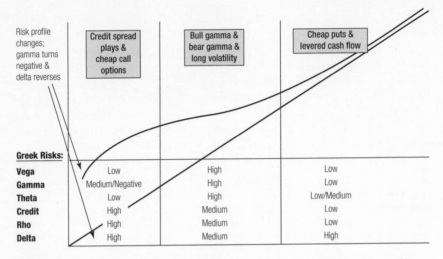

Greek Risks:	Credit spread plays & cheap call options	Bull gamma & bear gamma & long volatility	Cheap puts & levered cash flow
Vega	Low	High	Low
Gamma	Medium/Negative	High	Low
Theta	Low	High	Low/Medium
Credit	High	Medium	Low
Rho	High	Medium	Low
Delta	High	Medium	High

FIGURE 5.2   Greek Exposure at Various Points along the Low-Grade Convertible Price Track.

DELTA NEUTRAL HEDGE (LONG VOLATILITY)

The popular neutral hedge often found in convertible hedge funds and the one most commonly discussed in the press involves the delta neutral hedge setup. As we've noted, the idea of the delta neutral hedge is to purchase a long convertible and short the underlying stock at the current delta. The position is set up so that no profit or loss is generated from very small movements in the common stock price, but the cash flow is captured from both the convertible's yield and the short's interest rebate. The hedge neutralizes the convertible's equity risk (or delta, as the name implies) but is exposed to interest rate risk (rho) and long volatility risk (vega). Because of the vega risk, this hedge is also called a long volatility hedge. In effect, the major portion of the non-income return must come from the long vega exposure. This of course means that the implied volatility of the convertible must increase from the initial setup's implied volatility. The arbitrageur seeks undervalued convertibles based on the low current implied volatility level relative to the implied volatility level he or she expects in the near future. As the implied volatility level increases, so does the theoretical value of the long convertible, adding to the return on the hedge. Should the implied volatility level decrease, the hedge may show a loss until income flows from the coupon interest and short interest rebate offset the loss over time. Should the implied volatility level remain the same, the position will only earn the income flow. As you can see, the more volatile the implied volatility of the position, the more trading opportunities. The hedge is rebalanced as the stock price and/or convertible price move. Rebalancing may result in adding to or reducing the long or short position.

One note on delta and volatility: Convertibles with very little or no call protection remaining can be subject to a perverse effect of increased volatility. *As volatility increases, it has the effect of reversing the time value of an option and as volatility decreases, it has the effect of increasing the time value of an option.* The arbitrageur should evaluate the impact of volatility shifts on the callable convertible to understand the impact on the delta and theta and how the hedge is going to actually react. (See Appendix 5.1.)

The first opportunity scan an arbitrageur conducts is generally one that attempts to identify delta neutral hedge opportunities using the criteria set out below.

Convertible Characteristics Used to Identify the Opportunity

- Theoretically undervalued convertible (implied volatility or credit misspricing).
- Yield advantage that is higher than LIBOR rate.
- Expectation that implied volatility will increase for low cash flow positions or increase or stay the same for high cash-flow positions.
- Stable or improving credit opinion.
- Minimal liquidity risk.
- Ample stock-borrow available.
- Vega higher than omicron.

Risks to Consider

- Implied volatility decreases.
- Credit spread widens.
- Surprise call from issuer.
- Yield curve shift up at short end.
- Theta consumes vega gains.

Consider this example: A convertible trading at 105 percent of par with 19.65 percent conversion premium that converts into 22.50 shares of stock and trades with a delta of .594. The arbitrageur purchases 1,000 bonds for a long investment of $1,050,000 and shorts the underlying stock an equivalent dollar hedge based on the .594 delta. With the stock trading at $39 per share, shorting 16,000 shares sets up the neutral hedge. The stock price then moves up 1 percent to $39.39 and the convertible moves up to 105.624 percent of par. The gain of $6,240 from the long convertible position is matched with an equivalent loss on the short stock position, netting the arbitrageur no gain or loss on the position:

Initial hedge—delta neutral hedge ratio of .594

	Quantity	Price	Value	Profit/(Loss)
Convertible long	1,000	1,050.00	$ 1,050,000	
Short stock	16,000	39.00	$ (624,000)	
Stock price moves 1%				
Convertible long	1,000	1,056.24	$ 1,056,240	$ 6,240
Short stock	16,000	39.39	$ (630,240)	$(6,240)

Net Profit/(Loss) $ 0

In theory, each time the stock price moves up a few percentage points, the arbitrageur adds to the short position because the delta has increased on the position and the neutral hedge needs to be maintained. Likewise, as the stock price declines, the arbitrageur buys back some of the short position to reflect the decreasing delta.

In our example above, after the stock price has moved up 1 percent to $39.39, the new delta for the convertible is .605. To maintain the proper hedge ratio, an additional 223 shares of stock should be shorted. If not, the position's original hedge ratio would realize a gain or loss on the next move up or down in the stock. As shown below, if no adjustment to the hedge ratio occurs and the stock price moves up another 1 percent, the long convertible position gains $6,390 while the short stock position loses $(6,304) for a net gain of $86. The arbitrageur must constantly measure the position hedge ratio and compare it to the convertible's current theoretical delta. Of course, the trading costs and liquidity of the short position must be considered before the hedge is adjusted.

Original hedge after 1% stock move (delta increases to .605)

	Quantity	Price	Value	Profit/(Loss)
Convertible long	1,000	1,056.24	$ 1,056,240	
Short stock	16,000	39.39	$ (630,240)	
Stock price moves another 1%				
Convertible long	1,000	1,062.63	$ 1,062,630	$ 6,390
Short stock	16,000	39.78	$ (636,544)	$(6,304)

Net Profit/(Loss) $ 86

While the objective of the delta neutral hedge is to capture the cash flow from the convertible and the interest on the short credit balance while eliminating the equity market risk, the delta neutral position can also capture gains from mispricing in the convertible market.

The best example of the optimal delta neutral hedge strategy is one in which the arbitrageur purchases a theoretically undervalued convertible. For example, in Figure 5.3, this long volatility hedge described above may be theoretically undervalued if it is purchased with an implied volatility of 35 percent, yet the arbitrageur expects the volatility to increase to 40 percent. The convertible with a current implied volatility of 35 percent and stock price at $39.00 is purchased for 105 percent of par. But if theoretically priced with 40 percent volatility, the convertible is worth 106.5 percent of par. The position is long vega and expected to pick up five volatility points. The position is set up with a delta neutral hedge to eliminate equity risk and capture the valuation discrepancy. Since the price discrepancy may exist for an extended period of time, the yield on the convertible and interest from the short position should be sufficient to carry the position. With the hedge in place, the arbitrageur does not care if the stock price moves up or down, but that volatility reverts back to the 40 percent level. The convertible should realize a vega of .28 for each point move in volatility.

In this example, let's assume that the stock price declines 1 percent to $38.61, and the convertible actually increases in value because it once again trades at the 40 percent volatility level that the arbitrageur expected. Even

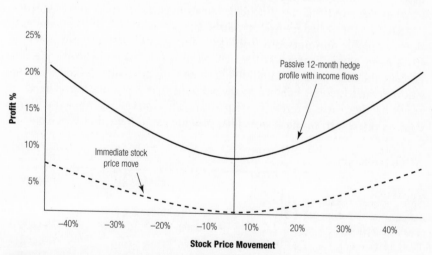

FIGURE 5.3 Passive Hedge—Delta Neutral Risk-Reward Profile.

though the stock price declines, the increase in the implied volatility more than offsets the stock price decline's impact on the convertible valuation. The theoretical convertible value increases $5 per bond to $1,055. In effect, the vega impact offset the delta impact of the stock price decline. Both the short position and the long side of the trade return a profit.

Initial hedge implied volatility 35%—expected volatility 40%

Hedge ratio = .594
Convertible market price 105 % of par
Convertible theoretical price 106.5% of par

	Quantity	Price	Value	Profit/(Loss)
Convertible long	1,000	1,050.00	$ 1,050,000	
Short stock	16,000	39.00	$ (624,000)	
Stock price moves down 1% and volatility rises to 40%				
Convertible long	1,000	1,055.00	$ 1,055,000	$ 5,000
Short stock	16,000	38.61	$ (617,760)	$ 6,240

Net Profit/(Loss) $11,240

In practice, a correction of a theoretical valuation may take days or weeks to manifest itself in the marketplace. In the meantime, the arbitrageur maintains the neutral hedge by adjusting the hedge to match the changing delta in the position. Should the convertible trade at the expected implied volatility of 40 percent or higher, the hedge position is closed for a low risk profit.

Delta neutral hedges are established as a means of capturing the cash flows available on some convertible positions as well as the profit potential from being long cheap volatility. The convertible example above yields 6 percent annually, while the underlying stock pays no dividend. The short position creates a credit balance in the account that earns interest. The short credit balance earns interest at 5.5 percent. This interest, combined with the coupon interest from the convertible, provides a total yield of 9 percent.

Annual cash flows

Convertible coupon	$60 per bond	1,000 bonds	= $60,000
Short interest rebate	$39	16,000 shares @ 5.5%	= $34,320
Stock dividend due	$0	16,000 shares	= $0
Total cash flow			**$94,320**
Long investment	$1,050,000		
Return on investment	$94,320/$1,050,000	= 9 % AROI	

Purchasing the convertible issue when it is undervalued and closing out the hedge when the convertible trades at a premium to fair value can further enhance the 9 percent annual cash flow return. Astute traders could effectively add 2 percent to 3 percent to the total return to this position for an annual return in the range of 11 percent to 12 percent.

DELTA ESTIMATES VERSUS THEORETICAL DELTAS

In practice, the theoretical delta is nothing more than a starting point to begin the hedge analysis. The theoretical continuous time delta only becomes relevant when the other greeks and the arbitrageur's expectations are brought into the analysis. The correct hedge ratio depends upon the expected change in implied volatility of the convertible and the resulting changes in gamma and delta. The arbitrageur also considers the magnitude of the underlying stock price moves upward and downward over what he perceives to be a relevant time period for the hedge to be held or rebalanced. The modified delta, explained in Chapter 3, is the relevant hedge ratio to use when establishing a position. This is true because all of the greeks can then be filtered into the analysis for a better representation of the market neutral hedge and the various risks.

DYNAMIC REBALANCING OF THE DELTA NEUTRAL HEDGE

Dynamic hedging in theory implies determining a minimum or maximum greek exposure and rebalancing continuously to maintain the neutrality of the convertible hedge or the desired greek exposures. Determining the appropriate time to rebalance the delta neutral hedge is a function of the amount of volatility that is acceptable in the return and the degree of returns sought after from the change in gamma, vega, rho, or theta. Of course, trading costs must also be considered in the rebalancing equation. The less frequently the rebalancing occurs, the larger the bleed in returns from equity correlation. Since convertibles represent non-linear derivatives, they are time dependent in their price and also may be subject to considerable instability in valuation. For this reason, dynamic hedging is necessary. Other non-linear derivatives such as swaps and forwards require none or very little dynamic hedging. Static hedging or at least infrequent rebalancing may be desirable in an un-levered portfolio when trading costs are high or the total income flow is low. Of course, some types of directional hedging call for a more passive rebalancing of the hedge. Rebalancing of a hedge position must occur more frequently when the position has a high gamma. The high gamma results in the delta hedge moving quickly out of neutrality with stock price moves.

Frequent rebalancing offers the arbitrageur the opportunity to lock in gains and build trading profits that may otherwise be forsaken in a strategy with less frequent rebalancing. For example, in the graph in Figure 5.4, the stock price fluctuates in a wide range, offering rebalancing opportunities as

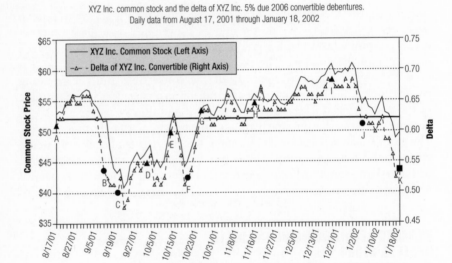

XYZ Inc. common stock and the delta of XYZ Inc. 5% due 2006 convertible debentures.
Daily data from August 17, 2001 through January 18, 2002

Active Hedging "Points" Labeled on the Chart Above:							
	Date	Action	# of shares	Delta	Hedge Ratio	Stock Price	Bond Price
Point A	8/17/2001	Long/Short	300 /−2850	0.61	0.67	52.75	100.00
Point B	9/7/2001	Cover	−200	0.54	0.62	51.50	99.50
Point C	9/19/2001	Cover	−400	0.50	0.53	43.14	91.25
Point D	10/2/2001	Short	200	0.55	0.57	46.86	95.75
Point E	10/11/2001	Short	125	0.60	0.61	50.79	99.25
Point F	10/18/2001	Cover	−200	0.52	0.56	45.01	95.00
Point G	10/24/2001	Short	250	0.63	0.62	53.21	102.88
Point H	11/15/2001	Short	300	0.65	0.69	56.01	106.25
Point I	12/19/2001	Short	200	0.68	0.74	60.80	110.25
Point J	1/3/2002	Cover	−300	0.61	0.69	54.28	104.88
Point K	1/18/2002	Closed	−300 / 2825	0.54	0.64	49.60	100.43

FIGURE 5.4   Adjusting Your Convertible Hedge More Often . . .

indicated. The move from point A to point K results in many trading opportunities. The initial position was established at point A with the stock at $52.75 and the convertible at 100 percent of par. The delta was .61 and shorting 2,850 shares against 300 bonds long established the hedge. The hedge ratio was slightly higher than the delta because of the downside gamma in the security. The table in Figure 5.4 indicates that the rebalancing points in the active hedge occurred at roughly five delta point changes from the previous rebalancing point. Figure 5.5 demonstrates the return improvement from the active hedge as compared to the more passive hedge.

In a passive hedge position, the potential gains at points B through J are not realized. In this scenario, more frequent hedging also serves to lower volatility because less equity sensitivity bleeds into the return.

Each convertible hedge position needs to be closely monitored according to the individual pre-determined hedge strategy. Delta neutral hedges should be established with an expected game plan regarding the approach to rebalancing the delta drift. For example, given the current delta and gamma of the position, the hedge will be rebalanced for every 5-point move in delta between the delta range of .6 and .75. The convertible's gamma and stock

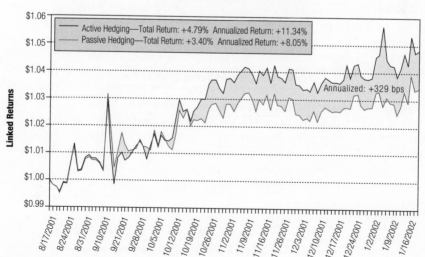

Linked returns of an active versus passive convertible hedge of XYZ Inc. common stock and the
5% due 2006 convertible debenture
From August 17, 2001 through January 18, 2002

FIGURE 5.5 ... Leads to Greater Returns!

liquidity determine the frequency of the rebalancing of the position. As the delta rises or falls and the gamma falls the rebalancing becomes less frequent in relation to stock price movements.

The only situation in which active hedging produces lower returns than a passive strategy is one in which the stock price moves in only one direction. In practice, this is rare, but when it occurs, trading costs eliminate the benefits of active hedging and the only return potential must come from income and a convergence to theoretical value.

In a market-neutral hedge program, the hedge rebalancing should occur more frequently than in a diversified convertible hedge strategy, because the volatility of the hedge is largely determined by how much delta changes between rebalancing. Positions with a high gamma need to be rebalanced more frequently than positions with low gamma, all other things being equal. More-volatile stocks also necessitate more frequent rebalancing of the hedge.

DELTA NEUTRAL HEDGE ON LEVERAGE

The most common delta neutral hedge setup involves borrowing money to establish the position. The convertible hedge position allows for significantly more leverage than would be allowed by Regulation T (the Federal Reserve Bank's regulation that governs the amount of credit that brokerages may extend to customers). Most hedge funds lever the portfolio or convertible arbitrage positions from 4 to 1 to as much as 9 to 1. The prime broker that custody's the hedge account will establish how much leverage can be utilized as well as assess risk-based capital charges over and above regulatory capital charge requirements, based on various hedge positions. For example, the risk-based capital charges are lower for investment grade issues as compared to non-investment grade issues to compensate for the credit risk difference. In-the-money convertible hedges require less capital than out-of-the-money issues because of the lower equity risk and credit risk. Bonds require less capital than preferred issues to compensate for the latter's lower recovery rates and status in the event of default. Long-term bonds require more capital than short-term bonds because of the higher duration. Private placements and 144A issues require more capital than registered issues because of the liquidity differences. Unhedged bonds above par require more capital than unhedged bonds below par. Just as the type of security changes capital requirements, so too does the type of hedge also alter capital requirements. Under the Net Capital Requirements for Brokers or Dealers, the capital requirement for a hedge position under Convertible Debt Securities reads as follows:

G. In the case of a debt security not in default which has a fixed rate of interest and a fixed maturity date and which is convertible into an equity security, the deductions shall be as follows: If the market value is 100 percent or more of the principal amount, the deduction shall be determined as specified in subdivision (J) below; if the market value is less than the principal amount, the deduction shall be determined as specified in sub division (F) above; if such securities are rated as required by subdivision (F) above.

J. In the case of all securities or evidences of indebtedness, except those described in Appendix A, Rule 15c3-1a, which are not included in any of the percentage categories enumerated in paragraphs (c)(2)(vi)(A) through (H) of this section, the deduction shall be 15 percent of the market value of the greater of the long or short positions and to the extent the market value of the greater of the long or short exceeds 25 percent of the market value of the greater of the long or short positions, the percentage deduction on such excess shall be 15 percent of the market value of such excess.

The capital requirements above recognize the effects of leverage on the hedging of investment grade issues and assigns capital charges to minimize leverage where risks are highest. This does not ensure that leverage will not magnify mistakes and even ruin your portfolio, it only provides a layer of protection against such an outcome for a well-diversified global broker or dealer with a trading book of fixed income, convertible, equity, and other securities.

The economics of the levered delta neutral hedge is shown below. Consider the same delta neutral position setup in the example above. The $1,050,000 position is established by borrowing 85 percent of the investment at a cost of 6 percent. The established position now generates the following series of cash flows in and out:

Annual cash-flows:
Convertible coupon $60 × 1,000 bonds	= $60,000
Short interest rebate $39 × 16,000 @ 5.5%	= $34,320
Stock dividend due	= 0
Total cash flow	= $94,320

Long investment $1,050,000

Capital required for hedge:
a) 15% of the unhedged long market value (LMV) plus the lesser of; b) 15% of the hedged long market value or c) the total dollar premium of the hedged portion of the position. Mathematically this can be expressed as

a) $.15 \times ((1 - delta) \times LMV) = .15 \times ((1 - .60) \times \$1,050,000) = \$63,000$
Plus the lesser of;
b) $.15 \times (delta \times LMV) = .15 \times (.60 \times \$1,050,000) = \$94,500$

Or

c) $((LMV - parity) \times delta) = (($1,050,000 - $875,000) \times .60) = $105,000$

Total capital required = $63,000 + $94,500 = $157,500

Carrying cost of position @ 6%:
(Long market value − capital required) × interest rate
    = ($1,050,000 − $157,500) × .06 = $53,550

Position cash flow in $ 94,320
Position cash flow out $ 53,550
Net cash flows $ 40,770

Total leveraged ROI = $40,770/$157,500 = 25.9%

The leverage returns provided by borrowing money to establish convertible hedges that are correctly set up and rebalanced can be exceptional. In some situations, the only way to generate double-digit returns on a hedge profile is to borrow capital. In other situations, the hedge may become too unstable with the capital borrowed. The use of borrowed capital magnifies the returns but also magnifies the risks. Unfortunately, the risks are magnified slightly more than the returns because the returns are reduced by the cost of the borrowed capital. Because the risks are magnified, the arbitrageur must rebalance the hedge more often when it is levered and also run tighter controls on the greek drifts. The long vega and negative rho exposure that is acceptable for a cash-only position may be unacceptable for a position using borrowed capital. The need to hedge the other greek exposures using various hedge techniques increases as the use of borrowed capital increases. But, the use of leverage should be considered as a possibility in each of the hedge examples discussed in this book.

The degree of leverage (after considering prime broker capital restrictions) for each hedge is a function of the ability to control the unwanted risk exposure and the degree of confidence the arbitrageur has in the hedge itself. For simplicity, many of the hedge examples in this book do not include the use of leverage; however, the reader can quickly estimate the impact of leverage on the returns and risks.

DELTA HEDGE—CURRENCY HEDGE OVERLAY

The global convertible securities and warrant market is extensive, and will continue to expand as democracy, capitalism, and privatization encompass the world. Many of the arbitrage opportunities found outside of the U.S. market will be exposed to currency risks.

Currency hedging attempts to lock in the exchange rate of the two currencies involved in the hedge and allow only the greeks desired to remain. Most hedging is accomplished by entering into a forward contract that guarantees the exchange rate at a date in the future. The forward contracts range in time but are generally from 3 to 6 months.

A brief introduction to currency exposure and currency hedging may be useful. A convertible investor purchases 1,000 Euro denominated bonds at 100 with the Euro/USD exchange rate at 1.10 Euro for each dollar. The investor purchases 1,000,000 Euros for $909,091 USD (1.10/1.0) and then purchases the bonds. Three months later, the bonds are at the same price in Euros but the Euro has decreased in value relative to the dollar, falling to 1.15 per 1 USD. The investor is a dollar investor and now has a currency loss, because if he sells the bonds, he would receive 1,000,000 Euros, but when they were exchanged for dollars, he would receive 1,000,000/1.15= $869,565, for a loss of -$39,526 ($869,565 - $909,091). The investor could have hedged the position by entering into a forward contract to sell 1,000,000 Euros in 3 months at 1.10 per 1 USD. Three months later, with the Euro at 1.15 to 1.0 USD, the forward contract could be closed, locking in a gain of $39,526 [(1,000,000/1.15) - (1,000,000/1.10)], offsetting the loss on the long bond.

The convertible arbitrageur must monitor each position's currency exposure and aggregate the portfolio exposure to determine the amount of forward contracts to enter into. The hedged convertible portfolio's currency exposure changes with movements in the underlying stocks, in interest rates, and of course in currency rates, so the process of actively monitoring each position is essential to maintaining the proper currency hedge.

Consider the delta neutral hedge at the beginning of this chapter, but with various combinations of currency exposure. I will demonstrate a few brief examples of the currency risk (chi) in the various convertibles that needs to be hedged and also how the delta neutral stock hedge changes the chi exposure.

Example 1—Dollar Denominated Bond Convertible into Foreign Stock

In the first example, the convertible bond is a US dollar pay issue convertible into a foreign stock. The long bond is exposed to currency movements via the change in parity. But, since arbitrageurs short stock against the long parity value of the convertible, the arbitrageur does not need to hedge the currency. As seen in Table 5.1, when the Euro declines 2 percent from 1.0 to 0.98 against the dollar, the bond's USD value does not change, but the underlying stock's USD value declines from $39 to $38.22; the short position, however, completely offsets the currency impact.

TABLE 5.1 Long Dollar Convertible

EXAMPLE 1 Long dollar convertible—Foreign underlying stock—Neutral stock hedge

Euro/$	1.00 Quantity	Price	Value $	Parity $	Change in Long	Change in Parity	Change in Short	Net P&L
Long bond	1,000	$ 1,050	$1,050,000	$624,000				
Short stock	(16,000)	Eur 39	($624,000)					
Euro/$	0.98							
Long bond	1,000	$ 1,050	$1,050,000	$611,520	$0	($12,480)		($12,480)
Short stock	(16,000)	Eur 39	($611,520)				$12,480	$12,480
								$0

No change in bond value—parity and short offset

No currency hedge needed—short stock offsets long parity

Example 2—Foreign Currency Bond Convertible into Foreign Stock

In this example, the convertible is a foreign currency denominated issue convertible into a foreign stock. The full value of the long position is exposed to currency if unhedged, but with a delta neutral stock hedge only the premium above parity is exposed to currency. As in the first example, the short stock position eliminates the currency impact on parity. See Table 5.2.

Example 3—Foreign Currency Bond Convertible into USD Stock

In this example the convertible is a foreign pay issue convertible into a USD stock. The short stock position and parity is not exposed to currency risk because they are USD based. The bond is exposed to currency because all interest payments and par value pay in foreign currency. The convertible's fixed income (investment value) represents the present value of the remaining interest payments and par value payment at maturity and therefore this value needs to be hedged. See Table 5.3.

The international convertible market includes issues with fixed exchange rates built into the security, convertibles with multiple currency exposure (Yen bond convertible into Euro stock), and even a third currency exposure, due to convertibles that convert into more than one underlying stock. The arbitrageur addresses multiple currency positions by hedging back to one currency and then back to the arbitrageur's domestic currency.

In any hedge example discussed in the next few chapters, foreign currency exposure may be involved. The arbitrageur needs to evaluate the bond exposure, the embedded warrant exposure, and the currency risk in each. Then he must evaluate the hedge vehicle's impact on the currency risk of each. The final foreign currency hedge that is applied is easy to evaluate, but difficult to monitor unless each position is earmarked with an ongoing currency hedge risk type, as described in the above three examples.

TABLE 5.2 Long Foreign Currency Convertible

EXAMPLE 2 Long foreign currency convertible—Foreign underlying stock—Neutral stock hedge

Euro/$	1.00 Quantity	Price	Value $	Parity $	Change in Long	Change in Parity	Change in Short	Net P&L
Long bond	1,000	Eur 1,050	$1,050,000	$624,000				
Short stock	(16,000)	Eur 39	($624,000)					
Euro/$	0.98							
Long bond	1,000	Eur 1,050	$1,029,000	$611,520	($21,000)	($12,480)		($33,480)
Short stock	(16,000)	Eur 39	($611,520)				$12,480	$12,480
								($21,000)

Change in parity and stock offset—
premium above parity exposed to currency

Need to hedge difference
between bond price and parity

TABLE 5.3 Long Foreign Currency Convertible

EXAMPLE 3 Long foreign currency convertible—USD dollar underlying stock—Neutral hedge

Euro/$	1.00 Quantity	Price	Value $	Parity $	Change in Long	Change in Parity	Change in Short	Net P&L
Long bond	1,000	Eur 1,050	$1,050,000	$624,000				
Short stock	(16,000)	$39	($624,000)					
Euro/$	0.98							
Long bond	1,000	Eur 1,050	$1,029,000	$624,000	($21,000)			($21,000)
Short stock	(16,000)	$39	($624,000)			$0	$0	$0
								($21,000)

No change in parity and short

Need to hedge fixed income value of convertible

APPENDIX 5.1

Delta, volatility, and time effects: As mentioned earlier in the chapter, convertibles with very little or no call protection remaining can be subject to a perverse effect of increased volatility. *As volatility increases, it has the effect of reversing the time value of an option and as volatility decreases, it has the effect of increasing the time value of an option.* The arbitrageur should evaluate the impact of volatility shifts on the callable convertible to understand the impact on the delta and theta and how the hedge is going to actually react. A significant increase in volatility may result in the theta changing enough to offset the vega, in turn causing the delta and gamma to change and possibly even miss a dividend or interest payment because of an earlier-than-expected call.

To demonstrate how the volatility price distribution changes with time refer to Figure 5.6.

One way to think about a callable convertible is to consider when and why it would be called. Convertibles may be called to refinance at a lower interest rate or they may be called because they are deep enough in the money to force conversion to stock. Since most companies calling a convertible to force conversion to stock have call notices of 30 days, they must allow the parity level to move up in the money enough to ensure that under reasonable circumstances (volatility assumptions), parity will not fall below

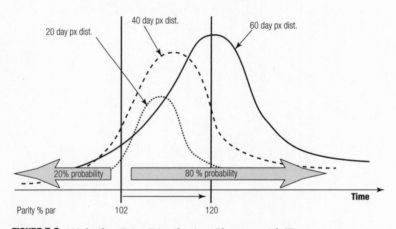

FIGURE 5.6 Volatility Price Distribution Changes with Time.

the call price. But since the amount of time it takes for the convertible's parity level to reach the trigger level is a function of volatility, then as volatility levels change, so does the expected life of the convertible and its value.

If parity does fall below the call price, the company will be forced to pay cash instead of stock to the holders. Although the optimal call price for a convertible is when parity reaches the call price, a cushion is necessary to protect the issuer. Convertibles that are convertible into cash at the company's option should be evaluated as if the issue will be called at the optimal call price with little or no cushion. If it is determined that the convertible will not be called to refinance, but will be called as it moves up into the money to force conversion, the option volatility time effect can be clearly understood. The equation below demonstrates the volatility and time link. (The NORMSINV in the denominator is an Excel function that calculates the Z-value or inverse of the standard normal cumulative distribution for a given probability with a mean of zero and standard deviation of one.)

$$\text{Time} = \left(\frac{\text{Log(est. trigger level)} - \text{Log (parity level)}}{\sigma \times \text{NORMSINV(probability)}} \right)^2 \times \text{(number of trading days in year)}$$

If the convertible has no call protection remaining and will only be called to force conversion, then the arbitrageur can estimate how much above the call price the parity level (trigger) should move before it may be called with a given probability and expected volatility. If it is determined that the parity level must be, for example, 120 percent of the call price for the company to safely call the issue, then the arbitrageur can use the following formula to estimate the amount of time premium that should be built into the convertible's embedded option. For example, how much time will it take with an 80 percent probability for the trigger level to be reached for a convertible with a parity level of 102 and trigger level of 120 and a 3-month annualized volatility of 40 percent. The answer can be found by using the following equation:

$$\text{Log}(120) - \text{Log}(102)/(0.40 \times 0.84162)^2 = (0.1625/0.3366)^2$$
$$= 23.30 \% \text{ of the trading days in a year}$$

With 255 trading days in the year, the time value should be roughly 59 trading days. But if volatility increased to 60 percent, then the time premium would shrink and the delta and theta would have been incorrect. At a 60 percent implied volatility level, the time would shrink to

$$(0.1625/0.5050)^2 = 10.35 \% \text{ of the 255 trading days or 26.4 days.}$$

By rearranging the formula to determine time, the arbitrageur may also use this equation to estimate what the trigger level might be for a given time period and probability level.

Call trigger = call price parity $\times$ (1 + ($\sigma\sqrt{dt}$ $\times$ NORMSINV(probability)))

An example of an application of this equation would be a callable convertible with a 30-day notice with the same parity level of 102 that is equal to the call price parity. The convertible has a 3-month annualized implied volatility of 60 percent and the arbitrageur wants an 80 percent probability on the trigger:

$$\text{Trigger} = 102 \times (1 + (.60\sqrt{30 / 255} \times .84162)) = 102(1 + (.2058 \times .84))$$
$$= 102 \times 1.1732 = 119.666$$

In some situations, such as covered call writing and income capture hedges, estimating time premium is helpful. The arbitrageur may want to match a covered call write expiration with the convertible's expected life or if the interest or dividend payment date is factored into the expected return, but it is not certain, depending on when the issue is called. Of course, calculating the correct delta and a "shadow" delta based on changes in volatility and its impact on the convertible is also subject to the effects discussed above.

It may also be useful to estimate the parity trigger level for a fixed time period. Once again, a covered call write at the trigger level may be preferred. The conversion premium at the parity trigger level should be zero, making the forecast delta and gamma easy at that point on the curve. The arbitrageur should understand the effects of changes in volatility on the time premium of a callable convertible and also how a trigger level can be estimated for a given time interval. These formulas should be included as part of the arbitrageur's toolbox.

APPENDIX 5.2 General Rules and Regulations Promulgated under the Securities Exchange Act of 1934 Rule 15c3-1—Net Capital Requirements for Brokers or Dealers

Definitions

c. For the purpose of this section: . . .

Net Capital

2. The term "net capital" shall be deemed to mean the net worth of a broker or dealer, adjusted by: . . .

Securities Haircuts

vi. Deducting the percentages specified in paragraphs (c)(2)(vi)(A) through (M) of this section (or the deductions prescribed for securities positions set forth in Appendix A) of the market value of all securities, money market instruments or options in the proprietary or other accounts of the broker or dealer. . . .

Nonconvertible Debt Securities

F.

1. In the case of nonconvertible debt securities having a fixed interest rate and a fixed maturity date and which are not traded flat or in default as to principal or interest and which are rated in one of the four highest rating categories by at least two of the nationally recognized statistical rating organizations, the applicable percentages of the market value of the greater of the long or short position in each of the categories specified below are:

   i.   Less than 1 year to maturity-2%
   ii.   1 year but less than 2 years to maturity-3%
   iii. 2 years but less than 3 years to maturity-5%
   iv.   3 years but less than 5 years to maturity-6%
   v.   5 years but less than 10 years to maturity-7%
   vi.   10 years but less than 15 years to maturity-7\1/2\%
   vii. 15 years but less than 20 years to maturity-8%
   viii. 20 years but less than 25 years to maturity-8\1/2\%
   ix.   25 years or more to maturity-9%

2. A broker or dealer may elect to exclude from the above categories long or short positions that are hedged with short or long positions

in securities issued by the United States or any agency thereof or non-convertible debt securities having a fixed interest rate and a fixed maturity date and which are not traded flat or in default as to principal or interest and which are rated in one of the four highest rating categories by at least two of the nationally recognized statistical rating organizations if such securities have maturity dates:

i.   Less than five years and within 6 months of each other;
ii. Between 5 years and 10 years and within 9 months of each other;
iii. Between 10 years and 15 years and within 2 years of each other; or
iv. 15 years or more and within 10 years of each other.

    The broker-dealer shall deduct the amounts specified in *subparagraphs (3)* and *(4)* below.

3. With respect to those positions described in *subparagraph(2)* that include a long or short position in securities issued by the United States or any agency thereof, the broker or dealer shall exclude the hedging short or long United States or agency securities position from the applicable haircut category under *paragraph (c)(2)(vi)(A)*. The broker or dealer shall deduct the percentage of the market value of the hedged long or short position in nonconvertible debt securities as specified in each of the categories below:

   i.   Less than 5 years to maturity-1\1/2\%
   ii. 5 years but less than 10 years to maturity-2\1/2\%
   iii. 10 years but less than 15 years to maturity- 2\3/4\%
   iv. 15 years or more to maturity-3%

4. With respect to those positions described in *paragraph (2)* above that include offsetting long and short positions in nonconvertible debt securities, the broker or dealer shall deduct a percentage of the market value of the hedged long or short position in nonconvertible debt securities as specified in each of the categories below:

   i.   Less than 5 years to maturity-1\3/4\%
   ii. 5 years but less than 10 years to maturity-3%
   iii. 10 years but less than 15 years to maturity-3\1/4\%
   iv. 15 years or more to maturity-3\1/2\%

5. In computing deductions under *paragraph (c)(2)(vi)(F)(3)* of this section, a broker or dealer may include in the categories specified in *paragraph (c)(2)(vi)(F)(3)* of this section, long or short positions in securities issued by the United States or any agency thereof that are deliverable against long or short positions in futures contracts relating to Government securities, traded on a recognized contract market approved by the Commodity Futures Trading Commission, which are held in the

proprietary or other accounts of the broker or dealer. The value of the long or short positions included in the categories shall be determined by the contract value of the futures contract held in the account.

The provisions of *Appendix B* to Rule 15c3-1 will in any event apply to the positions in futures contracts.

Convertible Debt Securities

G. In the case of a debt security not in default which has a fixed rate of interest and a fixed maturity date and which is convertible into an equity security, the deductions shall be as follows: If the market value is 100 percent or more of the principal amount, the deduction shall be determined as specified in *subdivision (J)* below; if the market value is less than the principal amount, the deduction shall be determined as specified in *subdivision (F)* above; if such securities are rated as required by *subdivision (F)* above; . . .

All Other Securities

J. In the case of all securities or evidences of indebtedness, except those described in *Appendix A*, Rule 15c3-1a, which are not included in any of the percentage categories enumerated in *paragraphs (c)(2)(vi)(A)* through *(H)* of this section or *paragraph (c)(2)(vi)(K)(ii)* of this section, the deduction shall be 15 percent of the market value of the greater of the long or short positions and to the extent the market value of the lesser of the long or short positions exceeds 25 percent of the market value of the greater of the long or short positions, the percentage deduction on such excess shall be 15 percent of the market value of such excess. No deduction need be made in the case of:
  1. A security that is convertible into or exchangeable for another security within a period of 90 days, subject to no conditions other than the payment of money, and the other securities into which such security is convertible or for which it is exchangeable, are short in the accounts of such broker or dealer; or
  2. A security that has been called for redemption and that is redeemable within 90 days.

CHAPTER 6

Gamma Capture Hedging

The convexity in the convertible price track offers convertible arbitrageurs the ability to capture this gamma with minimal risk. Gamma hedging can be established with a risk profile very close to that of delta neutral but allowing for less frequent rebalancing and some equity market alpha bleed. Gamma hedging can also take the form of a slight directional bias hedge offering significant payoff if the directional bias pays off.

CAPTURING THE GAMMA IN A CONVERTIBLE HEDGE

A static hedge ratio combined with a changing delta provides the opportunity for gamma capture and is both a significant contributor to the total return of the position and a major reason convertible hedging is effective. As discussed in detail in Chapter 3, gamma measures the change in the convertible's delta with respect to changes in the underlying stock price. A convertible's gamma offers arbitrageurs an opportunity to take advantage of the security's unique risk-reward profile, particularly when higher gamma positions can be hedged to capture this risk-reward trade-off. When establishing gamma hedges, it is useful to calculate the "shadow gamma" by determining how the delta changes based on the expected change in implied volatility and its impact on the hedge return. The position is again re-evaluated using the new implied volatility parameters and the shadow gamma. The shadow gamma is the expected gamma if the targeted implied volatility is reached.

The delta neutral gamma hedge can benefit from capturing gamma regardless of the direction of the stock price move. In fact, every delta neutral hedge is established to capture some gamma because even with a very small stock price move, gamma capture will occur before the hedge is rebalanced. Figure 6.1 depicts the "bow-tie" return profile of the gamma capture with a

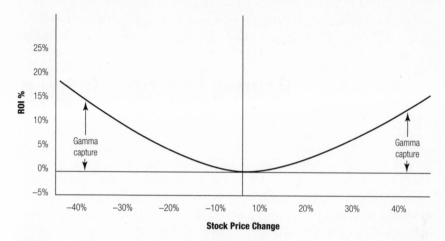

FIGURE 6.1 Delta Neutral Hedge—Gamma Capture Bow-Tie Return Profile.

passive hedge, showing how returns mount as price changes get more extreme. Of course, with such large stock price movements, this passive hedge would over time be subject to a large amount of equity market volatility and correlation. Instead, the position is typically dynamically hedged as delta changes, allowing for a measurable degree of gamma capture before the hedge is rebalanced back to neutral. Frequent rebalancing can capture incremental gamma, but it is worth noting that the smaller the gamma capture, the lower the volatility: Total return may not be significant unless the position is leveraged. Less frequent rebalancing, say, at every 10-point change in delta, can increase the gamma capture but also slightly increase the equity correlation and volatility of the hedge return. The neutral gamma hedge position works best for convertibles with a high degree of gamma and also a highly volatile underlying stock price. The volatile underlying stock offers small amounts of gamma capture that can be captured weekly. A stock price that exhibits jumps in price can be especially rewarding since the mismatch in the hedge is over a greater share price movement and occurs quickly. The arbitrageur may be the beneficiary of a 3 or 4 percent move up in the stock price before the delta neutral position is re-established. This means the position was exposed to a higher degree of equity risk and return before re-hedging occurred.

Since a high gamma convertible will result in a relatively large change in the delta as the stock price changes, the convertible may offer good equity upside with low equity exposure on the downside. Unlike the delta neutral hedge, a gamma hedge will generally force the arbitrageur to make a slight price direction bet on the underlying security to maximize returns with an unlevered hedge. The hedge portfolio should have both bullish-tilt gamma hedges and bearish-tilt gamma hedges to reduce overall equity market exposure in the portfolio. These positions also typically have a longer expected holding period due to the larger stock price moves desired before a hedge adjustment is made. The gamma hedge will also subject the portfolio to slightly more volatility in returns because of the slightly higher equity exposure.

The tilt of a gamma hedge can be measured by comparing its hedge ratio to what would be required for a delta neutral stance: Bullish tilted issues are hedged less than the ratios called for by the convertible's delta, and bearish tilted ones are hedged more. Both bullish and bearish tilted positions may be set up with their respective hedge ratio's allowing for a break-even return or a return matching the risk-free rate over a 3-month period should the position move against the desired direction of the initial setup. But, if the positions indeed move in the direction of the desired tilt, then substantial capital gains can be added to the cash flow returns. See Figure 6.2.

Bull Gamma Hedge

The bull gamma hedge captures upside gamma with a semi-directional tilt on the hedge. The hedge ratio for a bull gamma tilt hedge is established slightly below the true delta neutral position. The degree of the gap between the true delta neutral hedge ratio and the bull gamma is a function of the downside risk tolerance for the position and the conviction regarding the short-term upward trend in the underlying stock.

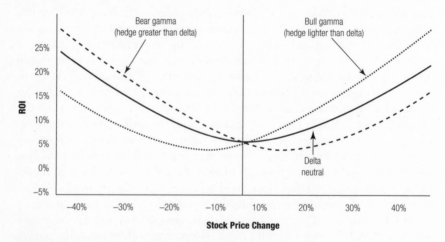

FIGURE 6.2 Tilt Hedges Can Add Substantial Capital Gains.

Characteristics to Identify the Opportunity

- Theoretically undervalued or fairly valued convertible.
- Convertible with a high gamma—preferably high upside gamma and low downside gamma.
- Convertible with stable or improving credit opinion.
- Yield advantage above the common stock. Amount depends on gamma upside/downside opportunity.
- Volatile common stock—offers many trade readjustment opportunities.
- Underlying stock with improving technical opinion. Improving relative strength index (RSI), positive EPS estimate revisions, acceleration in earnings trend.
- Fundamental opinion justifies higher stock price levels.

Risks to Consider

- Significant stock price decline.
- Implied volatility declines. (vega risk)
- Yield curve shifts. (rho risk)
- Time to capture gamma. (theta risk).
- Credit deterioration.
- Surprise call from issuer.
- Liquidity swings in convertible.
- Takeover of company below current convertible price with no put protection.

Bullish hedges in effect sacrifice some slight cash flow in return for hopefully larger capital gains. The cash flow sacrificed is that portion of the short interest credit missed due to the lighter hedge relative to the delta. The bad-case scenario achieves a break-even or risk-free rate of return, while the good-case scenario typically provides a return on investment in the mid-teens, without leverage. The bullish tilt positions work best when the upside gamma is smaller than the downside gamma in the position. This convexity allows for a better bullish tilt profile, offering capital gains potential without undue downside equity risk.

The arbitrageur needs to depend on fundamental or technical research to determine the position tilt. As the stock price increases, the gamma starts to decline while the delta increases, requiring close monitoring of the position and adding to the hedge so that the hedge ratio closes in on the delta neutral ratio as the gamma approaches zero or the stock price objective is reached. Should the stock price appreciate to the potential upside objective, the lower hedge will create capital gains. See Figure 6.3.

The bullish tilt position should be set up using a delta based on the potential lower stock price instead of the current stock price, demonstrated in

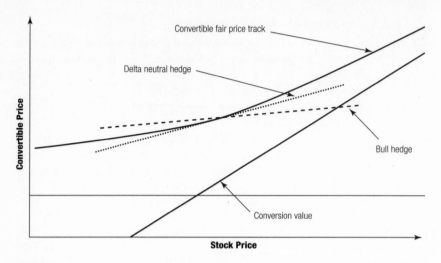

FIGURE 6.3   Delta Neutral Hedge versus Bull Hedge.

Table 6.1 and Figure 6.4. For example, set up a hedge with a stock price of $53; the convertible price is $950 with a delta of .54 and an upside gamma of .85 and a downside gamma of .76. Consider a 12-month holding period for this position, where the stock price is expected to move −33 percent to the downside with a one standard deviation move based on the 12-month expected volatility. The stock downside target is now $35.50 and the convertible's delta with the stock at $35 twelve months from today is calculated at .30. The bullish position is set up at a mid-point delta below the current .54 but above the expected level of .30 with the expectation to generate a return commensurate with the risk-free rate of return should this occur. In this example, when the stock trades down to $35, the convertible is valued at $830 and the hedge generates a total return of +6.2 percent over twelve months. The amount of income flow from the position over the holding period is determined in order to adjust the hedge ratio up or down to achieve the fine-tuning necessary for a risk-free rate of return on the downside. As with this and all other hedge examples, in reality the holding period is typically not a year and the opportunity to re-hedge and reverse hedge direction occurs often. Nonetheless, the hedges, if even held a few days, can offer annual returns that are at least as good as the more static hedges demonstrated in this chapter.

The light hedge relative to the current delta offers excellent upside gains should the stock price appreciate from the establishment of the original hedge. The high gamma makes this type of position a fruitful one: The con-

TABLE 6.1 Bullish Tilt Profit and Loss

	Downside Target Price		Current Price		Upside Target Price
Stock price	35.50		53.00		79.05
Convertible price	830.00		950.00		1,192.50
Delta	0.30		0.54		0.75
Long bonds	100	bonds at	950.00	Total investment	95,000.00
Borrow	0				95,000.00
Short stock	−700	shares at	53.00	Net investment	−37,100.00
P/L convertible	−12,000.00		0.00		24,250.00
P/L stock	12,250.00		0.00		−18,235.00
Convertible income	4,250.00		4,250.00		4,250.00
Stock dividends	0.00		0.00		0.00
Short credit interest	1,394.00		1,669.50		2,080.00
Total P/L	5,894.00		5,919.50		12,346.00
12 month ROI	6.20%		6.23%		12.99%

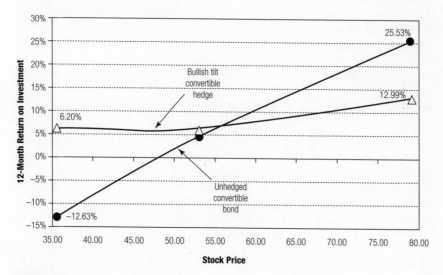

FIGURE 6.4 Bullish Tilt Position.

vertible will participate in an increasing amount of the stock's upside as the stock price and the delta both rise. If the upside stock target of $79.05 is reached, the convertible will trade for $1,192.50. Gains with income over the twelve-month period will approximate +12.99 percent. In practice, some slight additions to the short position on the way up will lock in some gains and avoid a hedge ratio that is extremely low relative to the delta.

Bullish Tilt Gamma Hedge on Leverage

A leveraged bullish tilt position can produce extraordinary returns, but not without subjecting the position to additional risk. The hedge ratio on a leveraged bullish tilt position should generally be slightly more than the hedge ratio on the un-leveraged bullish tilt position to reduce some of the added volatility in the return. As the Table 6.2 shows, adding significant leverage to the prior example changes the return profile dramatically.

The upside total annual return to the bullish gamma hedge on leverage is now an outstanding 46.90 percent if the upside stock price objective is reached. See Figure 6.5. The downside return is also much lower, returning only 1.66 percent if the downside stock price objective was achieved. Should the stock price end up at the same price it was at the setup, the return over one year would be only 1.87 percent. Increasing the hedge would lower the return on the upside and increase the downside protection. Although this is an extremely bullish tilt example, it does demonstrate the heavy directional tilt that can be achieved, and by increasing the hedge ratio, the tilt can change considerably.

TABLE 6.2 Bullish Tilt Gamma Hedge on Leverage

	Downside Target Price		Current Price		Upside Target Price
Stock price	35.50		53.00		79.05
Convertible price	830.00		950.00		1,192.50
Delta	0.30		0.54		0.75
Long bonds	100	bonds at	950.00	Total investment	95,000.00
Borrow	85% LMV at 7% cost			Net investment	14,250.00
Short stock	−700	shares at	53.00		−37,100.00
P/L convertible	−12,000.00		0.00		24,253.00
P/L stock	12,250.00		0.00		−18,247.00
Convertible income	4,250.00		4,250.00		4,250.00
Stock dividends	0.00		0.00		0.00
Short credit interest	1,394.00		1,669.50		2,080.00
Margin interest	−5,652.50		−5,652.50		−5,652.50
Total P/L	241.50		267.00		6,683.50
12 month ROI	1.69%		1.87%		46.90%

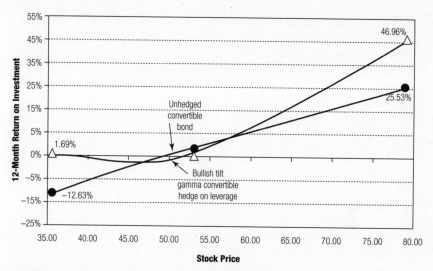

FIGURE 6.5 Bullish Tilt Gamma Convertible Hedge.

BEARISH TILT GAMMA CONVERTIBLE HEDGE

The bearish tilt hedge position is similar in design to the bullish hedge with a tilt designed to make money should the underlying stock price decline. Once again, the potential gains from this tilt position can be very large if the stock price moves in line with the hedge's expectation. Should the stock price move up, the loss should again be limited to a return that approximates the risk-free rate. As with a bull tilt, the arbitrageur should once again have a fundamental or technical opinion on why the stock price should decline over the expected holding period, but here she or he needs to also be confident that the stock price decline is not indicative of significant credit deterioration. Should the convertible issuer's credit deteriorate, the gamma in the position may not be realized and the hedge will not achieve the expected returns.

Characteristics to Identify the Opportunity

- Theoretically undervalued or fairly valued convertible trading relatively close to its investment value.
- Convertible with a high gamma–preferably high downside gamma and low upside gamma.
- Convertible with stable or improving credit opinion.

- Yield advantage above the common stock. Amount depends on gamma upside/downside opportunity.
- Volatile common stock–offers many trade readjustment opportunities.
- Underlying stock with deteriorating technical opinion. Declining RSI, negative EPS estimate revisions, declining in earnings trend or negative earnings surprise.
- Fundamental opinion justifies much lower stock price levels.

Risks to Consider

- Significant stock price appreciation.
- Implied volatility declines. (vega risk)
- Yield curve shifts. (rho risk)
- Time to capture gamma. (theta risk)
- Credit deterioration–very important.
- Surprise call from issuer.
- Liquidity swings in convertible.
- Takeover of company below current convertible price with no put protection.

The arbitrageur needs to depend on fundamental or technical research to accomplish the objective of this hedge. The more conviction in the directional alpha bet, the lower the hedge ratio in the opposite side of the hedge as Figure 6.6 demonstrates for a bearish hedge relative to a neutral hedge delta line.

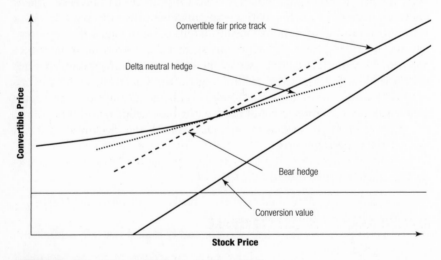

FIGURE 6.6 Delta Neutral Hedge versus Bear Hedge.

TABLE 6.3   Example of Bearish Hedge

	Downside Target Price		Current Price		Upside Target Price
Stock price	35.50		53.00		79.05
Convertible price	830.00		950.00		1,192.50
Delta	0.30		0.54		0.75
Long bonds	100	bonds at	$950.00	Total investment	$95,000.00
Borrow	0			Net investment	$95,000.00
Short stock	-900	shares at	$53.00		-$47,700.00
P/L convertible	-12,000.00		0.00		24,250.00
P/L stock	15,750.00		0.00		-23,445.00
Convertible income	4,250.00		4,250.00		4,250.00
Stock dividends	0.00		0.00		0.00
Short credit interest	1,793.00		2,147.00		2,674.00
Margin interest	0.00		0.00		0.00
Total P/L	9,793.00		6,397.00		7,729.00
12 month ROI	10.31%		6.73%		8.14%

To demonstrate the bearish tilt gamma hedge, the same high gamma issue that was used for the bull tilt position can now be assumed regarding a bearish one, and re-hedged at a ratio in excess of the delta neutral hedge ratio. Since the current delta is .54 and we are expecting a stock price decline, the hedge ratio should be established with the issue's high gamma in mind, expecting an upside return competitive with the risk-free rate and a downside return in the double digits. As Table 6.3 and Figure 6.7 show, the selected hedge calls for 900 shares short against the convertible to provide a 66.5 percent hedge ratio compared to the delta neutral 54 percent hedge. If the stock price declines to the desired target price of $35.50, the bear hedge returns 10.3 percent over the 12-month period. Should the stock price actually increase and move against the hedge, the bear hedge will still provide a relatively respectable 8.1 percent for the period. If the stock price remains the same, the hedge returns 6.73 percent. (Again, the 12-month time frame serves only as an example, and we would expect more frequent activity by the typical arbitrageur.)

BEARISH GAMMA HEDGE ON LEVERAGE

Employing leverage, the downside returns on the hedge are excellent and the upside returns are still very good. Table 6.4 and Figure 6.8 show how the

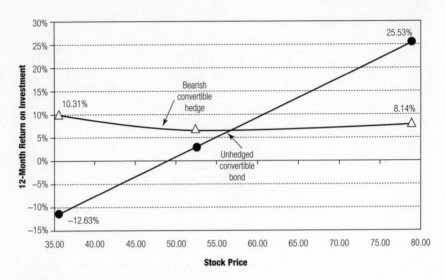

FIGURE 6.7   Bearish Convertible Hedge.

TABLE 6.4   Use of Heavy Leverage Improves Downside Returns

	Downside Target Price		Current Price		Upside Target Price
Stock price	35.50		53.00		79.05
Convertible price	830.00		950.00		1,192.50
Delta	0.30		0.54		0.75
Long bonds	100	bonds at	950.00	Total investment	95,000.00
Borrow	85% LMV at			Net investment	14,250.00
	7% cost				
Short stock	−900	shares at	53.00		−47,700.00
P/L convertible	−12,000.00		0.00		24,250.00
P/L stock	15,750.00		0.00		−23,445.00
Convertible income	4,250.00		4,250.00		4,250.00
Stock dividends	0.00		0.00		0.00
Short credit interest	1,793.00		2,147.00		2,674.00
Margin interest	−5,652.50		−5,652.50		−5,652.50
Total P/L	4,140.50		744.00		2,076.50
12 month ROI	29.06%		5.22%		14.57%

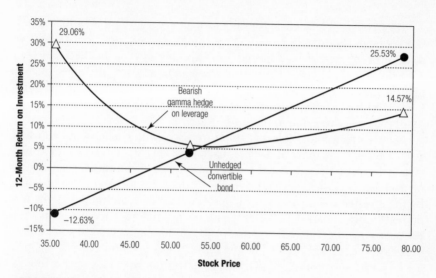

FIGURE 6.8 Bearish Gamma Hedge on Leverage.

use of heavy leverage can dramatically improve the downside returns of the bear gamma hedge, returning 29 percent as compared to only 10.3 percent without the use of leverage. The upside returns on the hedge are also better at 14.57 percent as compared to 8.14 percent. The hedge ratio could be increased even more if the arbitrageur has a stronger conviction that the stock price will decline. While the upside return potential declines as the hedge ratio increases, the downside returns increase at a higher rate as a result of the downside gamma being higher than the upside gamma.

THE GAMMA TILT HEDGE'S ROLE IN A MARKET NEUTRAL PORTFOLIO

Many hedge fund consultants would consider anything more than a very mild directional tilt inappropriate for a convertible arbitrage portfolio. While it is true that the heavy directional bull tilt convertible hedges are subject to significant equity volatility and delta exposure, it is also true that slight tilts do allow the convertible arbitrage shops with a strong equity analyst staff to help add alpha to the portfolio through some delta exposure. Also, the hedges are more passive, thereby reducing the trading costs and time to monitor the positions and these savings can be funneled into further equity research and more active hedge opportunities.

The convertible arbitrageur should make every attempt to maintain a market neutral portfolio by setting up complementary positions to achieve a sector or industry delta-adjusted beta exposure of zero. In effect, the high cash flow of the convertible position is combined with an equity market neutral strategy to enhance the portfolio's alpha. The success and the number of positions in the portfolio with gamma tilts are dependent on the quality of the equity research in the shop.

The worksheet in Table 6.5 demonstrates how to reach a delta-adjusted zero beta for the gamma tilt hedges. Each position's dollar exposure to delta is calculated by netting out the difference between the theoretical market neutral delta and the hedge ratio implied delta. This difference is multiplied by the invested dollars in the long position, and then multiplied by the underlying stock's market beta. The result is the delta-adjusted beta exposure for each position. The bull gamma hedges in this example have a net dollar beta exposure of $31,850, while the bear gamma positions have a negative net dollar beta exposure of –$31,960. At a net of only –$110, the portfolio's bull gamma and bear gamma delta-adjusted beta exposure is effectively zero. In the example in Table 6.5, the six hedges were all in the same industry to also further increase the probability of market neutrality. The arbitrageur should at least offset the bull and bear gamma positions in the broader economic sector if industry specific opportunities are too small.

TABLE 6.5 Delta-Adjusted Beta Worksheet—Semiconductor Industry

Bull Gamma

Position	Position Size	Beta	Theo. Delta	Hedge Delta	Delta $ Exposure	Delta Adj. Beta
ABC	$100,000	1.10	0.65	0.55	$10,000	$11,000
DEF	$100,000	1.35	0.57	0.50	$ 7,000	$ 9,450
GHI	$100,000	0.95	0.75	0.63	$12,000	$11,400
					Net beta exposure =	**$31,850**

Bear Gamma

Position	Position Size	Beta	Theo. Delta	Hedge Delta	Delta $ Exposure	Delta Adj. Beta
XYZ	$100,000	1.45	0.65	0.75	($10,000)	($14,500)
UVW	$100,000	1.24	0.57	0.66	($ 9,000)	($11,160)
RST	$100,000	0.90	0.75	0.82	($ 7,000)	($ 6,300)
					Net beta exposure =	**($31,960)**
Portfolio's net bull and bear gamma beta exposure →						($110)

Gamma hedging convertibles from mild bull or bear tilts to extreme bull/bear tilts takes advantage of the convertible's unique non-linear relationship with the underlying stock and the high cash flows thrown off by the hedge. But, gamma hedging also allows convertible arbitrageurs an additional means to add alpha to the portfolio while controlling the delta exposure. Arbitrageurs with a strong equity analyst support team should look to add gamma tilt hedges to the diversified convertible hedge portfolio.

CHAPTER 7

Convertible Option
Hedge Techniques

Since the various types of convertible securities include embedded call options (both long and short) as well as embedded or contractual put options, many arbitrage opportunities occur between a convertible issuer's listed option and the convertibles embedded options. Selling the expensive option and purchasing the cheaper option is the main objective, although convertible hedging with options also can augment a stock hedge position or completely change the risk-reward profile. *In most convertible option hedge techniques, the arbitrageur takes advantage of the volatility time skews that present themselves in the market.* Typically, the longer-term embedded convertible option's implied volatility is much lower than that of the shorter-term call option implied volatility at or close to the same strike price. Setting up a monitor that compares the differences in the implied volatility of the convertible to the implied volatility of a targeted option will aid the arbitrageur in identifying some opportunities. The monitor in Figure 7.1 compares the implied volatilities and when the difference widens, such as the opportunity on 1/20/01 in which the difference spiked from 4 to 5 volatility points to 25 volatility points, indicating that a call write opportunity might exist.

The convertible arbitrageur can also utilize the listed and OTC options markets to create some interesting hedge profiles that are not available with the traditional long convertible and short stock hedge. Many of the publicly traded convertibles have listed options available: Since a convertible can be converted into the underlying stock, a call or put option can be purchased or sold against the convertible security. Typically, the arbitrageur will be selling a call option on a covered or partially covered basis and/or purchasing a put option to provide additional protection. The arbitrageur may also utilize the options market as a temporary hedge profile if the short stock position is called in or if the stock borrow is difficult to obtain. Or stock hedges with high-dividend-paying stocks can be covered before the stock dividend

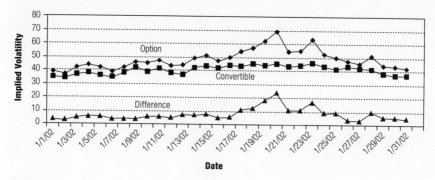

FIGURE 7.1   Implied Volatility Differences.

record-date and an option hedge temporarily established to protect the position until the dividend is paid. This tactic avoids the negative cash flow from the dividend due as a result of the short stock. Once the stock pays the dividend, it can be shorted again without the negative cash flow impacting the hedge.

Selling call options against a long convertible is considered a covered hedge as long as the number of shares the options can be exchanged for does not exceed the number of shares of stock that the convertible can be exchanged for. Selling call options provides additional income that is immediately available to the arbitrageur and reduces the total cost of the hedge. The option premium represents the maximum gain available from the option but the loss theoretically is unlimited. But, since the long convertible is in effect part long call option, the gain on the embedded call option from the convertible will offset or reduce the loss on the call short should the stock price move above the option strike price plus the call option premium. Determining the correct hedge ratio to avoid upside loss is a function of the convertible's delta, gamma, and theta. It is important for arbitrageurs to use a good convertible graphics package that will create a graph of the call option hedge overlay return profile to demonstrate how the hedge will pay off at the extremes.

Figure 7.2 shows how a covered out-of-the money call write with a $30 exercise price performs for a wide range of stock prices. The hedge was established with the stock trading at $25, and the return profile looks good until the stock price moves above $32 ($30 strike plus the $2 in option premium received). At stock prices above $32, the convertible's gains do not offset the loss on the call option, and at prices above $35, the hedge drops into negative return territory. A consideration of each option hedge should include the expected price range graph along with a wide range of prices to understand the effects at the extremes.

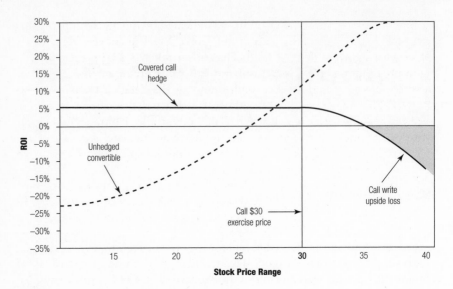

FIGURE 7.2   Covered Call Write—Upside Risk.

In each scenario, a break-even or minimum return point should be established because the option hedge profile offers some surprises, particularly because the short call puts a cap on the upside, but does not protect against large stock price declines. Covered call write hedges for stocks that have recently experienced a price collapse present an excellent hedge opportunity because they typically offer high implied volatility (generally, volatility is inversely related to stock price moves), and such stocks are not likely to gain significant ground. In these cases, the upside risk of the option hedge is mitigated and the implied volatility is high on the option. Due to the unfavorable prospects of the underlying equity, the outright convertible community may also be net sellers of the convertible, pushing the convertible's implied volatility lower.

For purposes of simplicity and brevity, in the next two option hedge examples, the long convertible will include the same issue with the following characteristics: The long convertible bond has a 4.5 percent coupon rate and the bond matures 11/15/2006. Each bond converts into 54.253 shares of stock, and the underlying stock pays no dividend. The expected implied volatility for the convertible is 50 percent and the current implied volatility is 40 percent, indicating that the convertible is 2.4 percent undervalued at the current price of $1,000 (or par value). The convertible's upside gamma is higher than the downside gamma, as indicated by the much higher upside capture than the downside capture in Table 7.1. The convertible's vega is 0.41 with a current delta of 0.68. The convertible has 22.9 percent conversion premium and 31.3 percent investment value premium. The XYZ convertible example is helpful in understanding the hedging techniques, but convertibles with considerably different characteristics can be utilized in option hedging situations as well. The convertible arbitrageur identifies mispriced options both long and short, and then calculates worksheets and adjusts the hedge ratio, option strikes, and option expiration periods to obtain the risk return profile objective.

Each example here includes a worksheet that describes the long position, option positions, and the stock short if included. The worksheets also show the profit and loss for various stock price ranges for the time period indicated. The time period or holding period for the hedge is determined by the expiration of the option nearest to expiration. The stock price range is based on a one standard deviation move in the stock price based on the holding period and the stock's expected volatility. The percentage change in the stock's price moves is also based on a log normal distribution. At each stock price, the theoretical convertible price is calculated based on the expected implied volatility and assumes constant interest rates over the holding period. The options at each price point are one day before expiration. Many of the hedge examples do not employ borrowed money, but in each case the use of leverage can dramatically increase the returns. The annualized return calculations assume that the same type of hedge can be found and re-established for the remainder of the year. The current example cannot actually produce the AROI because a portion of the return profile is a result of capturing under-valuation in the long convertible, which obviously cannot be recaptured again. The worksheets in the examples immediately following also assume passive hedging, although active hedging is preferred and will most likely improve the return profile.

COVERED OR PARTIALLY COVERED CONVERTIBLE CALL OPTION HEDGE

The traditional call option convertible hedge provides enhanced income to the hedge profile for generally sideways or declining stock price moves. To pursue this hedge, the arbitrageur's expectation for the stock price movement would be a price that, at the call's maturity, is below the call strike price plus the call premium. Because the call hedge profile is capped on the upside, a bullish tilt is not possible in most cases. The risk-reward profile favors a narrow stock price range for an enhanced return.

Characteristics to Identify the Opportunity

■ Convertible that is undervalued—implied volatility < expected volatility.
■ Convertible with higher upside gamma than downside gamma.
■ Call option implied volatility > expected volatility > convertible's implied volatility.
■ Call option 3 to 4 months until expiration with enough premium income to justify capping the return profile.
■ Convertible income plus call option premium meets minimum return expectations.
■ Underlying stock currently demonstrating weak or marginal technical support.
■ Underlying stock price fundamentally overvalued.
■ No catalyst for upside stock move present.

Risks to Consider

■ Take-over of convertible issuer.
■ Stock price moves significantly above call option strike.
■ Volatility time skew widens: Longer-term convertible embedded option volatility drops while shorter- term call option short volatility increases.

Sample Worksheet and Profile—Covered Call as a Stock Hedge Alternative with I-T-M Call Write

The worksheet in Table 7.1 shows a position long 100M of the XYZ convertible bond and short in-the-money call options. The short in-the-money call option has a strike price of $10, with the current stock price at $15. In effect, the short call options act as a synthetic stock hedge for prices at and above $10 for the stock. The hedge ratio is close to the delta neutral hedge ratio used with a stock hedge. Using the characteristics we have presumed in this example, 37 call option contracts are sold against 5,425 shares underlying the 100M convertible bonds to establish the neutral hedge (3,700 options shares/5,425 convertible share = .68 percent). This in-the-money call option hedge is preferred if a stock borrow cannot be obtained, or if the underlying stock pays a high dividend that the arbitrageur wants to avoid. Like a stock hedge, the risk-reward profile can be established to meet a neutral profile but should the stock price decline significantly below the option strike price the option will not protect the hedge as would a short stock position. Therefore, a true risk-neutral profile has not been established. Nonetheless, the call write in this example will provide an attractive risk-reward profile for a wide range of stock prices. The highest probability of stock price ranges over the 4-month holding period offers a range of returns

TABLE 7.1 Long Convertible/Sell Calls—XYZ Company

Convertible	*Common Stock*						
		Symbol	XYZ				
		Price $	15.00		Dividend $	—	
		Volatility %	50		Yield		0.000%
	Convertible	Floor Yield	12.00		Quantity	100	
		Symbol	XYZ-X		Maturity	11/15/06	
		Price $	100.000		Conv. Prem.	22.88 %	
		Yield	4.50%		Coupon	4.50 %	
		Adj Strike $	14.093		Conversion Ratio	54.2530	
Short Call	*Short Call*				Quantity	37	
		Symbol	BQXYZ		Expiration	2/16/03	
		Strike $	10.00		Time to Expiration	0.325 years	
		Price $	5.40		Implied Volatility %	50	

Hedge ratio: 68%	Holding period: *3.9 Months*				
% Change 1 Std. Deviation	−24.9%	−18.3%	Current	22.4%	30.0%
Assumed Stock Px	11.27	12.25	15.00	18.35	19.50
Est Convertible Px	88.01	91.75	102.38	114.91	120.87
Convertible Px % Moves	−12.0%	−8.2%	2.4%	14.9%	20.9%
Est Short Call Px	1.27	2.45	5.15	8.38	9.50
Call Px % Moves	−75.3%	−52.4%	0.0%	62.7%	84.5%
Profit/Loss Convertible	−11,990	−8,250	2,386	14,910	20,870
Income/Dividend	1,463	731	1,463	731	1,463
Profit/Loss Short Call	15,281	10,915	925	−11,026	−15,170
Total Profit/Loss	4,754	3,396	4,778	4,615	7,163
ROI	5.94%	4.24%	5.97%	5.77%	8.95%
AROI	18.28%	13.05%	18.37%	17.75%	27.54%

(*Profit & Loss Information*)

at expiration between approximately 5 and 9 percent or 15 to 27 percent annually. Figure 7.3 shows the return profile of the hedge position and compares it to the long convertible to demonstrate how effective the hedge is at altering the risk-return profile.

Covered call writing against convertibles can also be established with at-the-money and out-of-the-money option strikes. The out-of-the-money strike option hedge offers better upside participation, but generally less downside protection. The at-the-money hedge offers the highest return

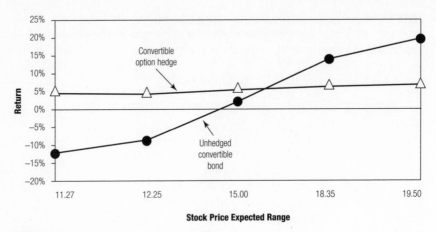

FIGURE 7.3   Convertible Covered Call Write.

profile for small stock price trading ranges around the strike price. Although the stock hedge offers more protection should the stock price decline significantly, covered call writing with convertibles that are trading relatively close to their fixed income values may in fact offer a much *better neutral return profile than stock hedging.* That is because the premium income from the call write often offers a much higher income flow than the short credit from the short stock position. But, it is important to understand the limits of the option in regards to protecting the position against significant stock price drops and the upside cap that will limit upside returns.

LONG CONVERTIBLE STOCK HEDGE WITH CALL WRITE OVERLAY

Option hedging can enhance the traditional convertible stock hedge, too. The call write can be used to change a bullish gamma hedge to a more neutral profile or a neutral hedge to a higher-yielding profile. As we will see, establishing a stock hedge with a delta neutral profile and then overlaying a partial call write position can significantly enhance the total return of the position without compromising the neutrality. If the arbitrageur believes the stock price will not trade up through the current resistance level, then a call write overlay will enhance an otherwise mediocre hedge return profile, adding as much as 2–3 percent in a quarter. This hedge takes advantage of the lower long-term implied volatility by establishing a delta neutral hedge with stock locking in the long-volatility and selling the higher short-term volatility with a covered call write overlay. Changes in the volatility skew will result in gains on both sides of the position.

Characteristics to Identify the Opportunity

- Current stock hedge position offers mediocre total return in a sideways market.
- Call option implied volatility above near-term expected implied volatility.
- Stock price expected to trade within a narrow range over holding period of option.
- Additional stock borrow may be difficult.
- Call option premium income significantly higher than stock's short interest rebate over holding period.
- Call options with strike at near-term resistance level offers enough premium income to sell.
- Call option implied volatility > than convertible's implied volatility.

Risks to Consider

- Take-over of convertible issuer at stock price above option strike.
- Combined stock and option hedge ratio below 100 percent to avoid upside losses.
- Implied volatility calendar skew widens.

In the worksheet in Table 7.2, the arbitrageur establishes a convertible stock hedge by shorting 3,750 shares against the 100M long convertibles with a delta neutral hedge ratio of 68 percent. Since the arbitrageur's technical and fundamental analysis indicates that the stock has limited upside in the near term, while the downside risks also seem marginal, the most likely scenario for the stock is range bound trading. Surveying the listed options market, the arbitrageur sees that the issuer's call options expiring in 4 months are trading at an implied volatility level of 70 percent, as compared to the convertible's implied volatility of 40 percent. The arbitrageur sells 10 call options with a strike price of $20 to further enhance the sideways total return on this position. This option hedge adds about 1 percent (3 percent annually) to the 4-month total return for any stock price at or below $20 at expiration. Further, an at-the-money call write would have increased the premium an additional 1 percent, or a total of 6 percent annually. As the worksheet indicates, the call write does come at a cost should the stock price move above $21.

However, as Figure 7.4 shows, with the stock price moving up to $25, the call option hedge reduces the total return of the position to near zero.

TABLE 7.2   Long Convertible/Sell Calls/Short Stock—XYZ Company

Convertible	**Common Stock**				
		Symbol	XYZ		
		Price $	15.00	Dividend $	—
		Volatility %	50	Yield	0.000%
Short Call	**Convertible**	Floor Yield	12.00	Quantity	100
		Symbol	XYZ-X	Maturity	11/15/06
		Price $	100.000	Conv. Prem.	22.88 %
		Yield	4.50%	Coupon	4.50 %
		Adj Strike $	14.093	Conversion Ratio	54.2530
	Short Call			Quantity	10
		Symbol	BQXYZ	Expiration	2/16/03
		Strike $	20.00	Time to Expiration	0.325 years
		Price $	1.00	Implied Volatility %	70
Short Stock	**Short Stock**				
		Symbol	XYZ	Quantity	3,750
		Price $	15.00	Fed Fund Rate	1.80%

Hedge ratio: 68%   Holding period: 3.9 Months

% Change 1 Std. Deviation	−24.8%	−18.3%	Current	22.4%	33.1%	66.7%
Assumed Stock Px	11.27	12.25	15.00	18.35	19.95	25.00
Est Convertible Px	88.01	91.75	102.38	114.91	120.87	139.70
Convertible Px % Moves	−12.0%	−8.2%	2.4%	14.9%	20.9%	39.7%
Est *Short* Call Px	0.01	0.01	0.01	0.01	0.01	5.00
Call Px % Moves	−100.0%	−100.0%	−100.0%	−100.0%	−100.0%	400.0%
Est *Short* Stock Px	11.27	12.25	15.00	18.35	19.95	25.00
Short Px % Moves	24.9%	18.3%	0.0%	−22.3%	−33.0%	−66.7%
Profit/Loss Convertible	−11,990	−8,250	2,380	14,910	20,870	39,700
Income/Dividend/ Short Interest	2,107	1,478	2,286	1,646	2,513	2,695
Profit/Loss *Short* Call	1,000	1,000	1,000	1,000	1,000	−4,000
Profit/Loss *Short* Stock	13,988	10,313	0	−12,563	−18,563	−37,500
Total Profit/Loss	5,105	4,541	5,666	4,993	5,820	895
ROI	5.16%	4.59%	5.72%	5.04%	5.88%	0.90%
AROI	15.87%	14.11%	17.61%	15.52%	18.09%	2.78%

The left margin labels (rotated): Convertible / Short Call / Short Stock / Profit & Loss Information

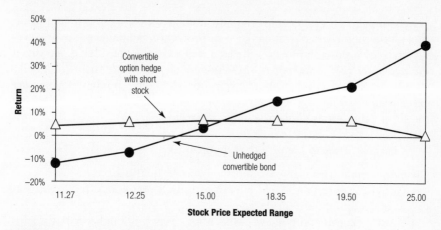

FIGURE 7.4   Convertible Covered Call Write/Short Stock.

Thus, it is important to monitor and close such an option position should a large enough upside move look possible. Figure 7.4 shows how the call write cuts into the upside return profile and is no longer neutral above the $21 stock price level. The arbitrageur may cover the call hedge or reduce the stock hedge to avoid further upside losses above this level.

SYNTHETIC BOND—LONG BUSTED CONVERTIBLE WITH CALL WRITE AND LONG OUT-OF-THE-MONEY CALL FOR PROTECTION

The next call option hedge example, while untraditional, does offer attractive total returns. This hedge can be considered a synthetic bond because its sole purpose is to add income to an already high-yielding busted convertible. Because both its delta and gamma are near zero, the busted convertible is unsuitable for a stock hedge. The major risks for this type of hedge are omicron, upsilon, and rho, which are all related to credit and interest rate risks. The arbitrageur must therefore identify a busted convertible with a strong balance sheet to mitigate the credit spread risk and recovery rate risks, while the overall interest rate risks can be hedged or monitored at the portfolio level. The final major risk relates to the potential for a take-over. Should the convertible issuer be acquired at a stock price significantly above the current stock price and option exercise price, the short calls will produce a large loss that may not be offset by the embedded convertible option and income. The risk is higher for convertibles that do not have take-over protection, although the vagueness of some take-over protection language in the prospectus presents a false comfort level that should also be considered. To offset the take-over risk, a far out-of-the-money long call option near the break-even point with the same term to expiration should be purchased. The long call amount should also match the short call amount to completely negate the short call options above the long call strike price.

Characteristics to Identify the Opportunity

- Convertible with stable or improving credit quality.
- Current convertible's yield plus short option premium offers returns at or above minimum hurdle rate.
- Short call option implied volatility above expected implied volatility (to minimize interim months' loss).
- Long call option implied volatility is low enough to keep costs in line with total return objectives.
- Convertible issuer's industry is not in the midst of consolidation through M&A activity.
- Stock price not demonstrating exceptional technical strength.
- Convertible trading at, through or very near investment value—avoid embedded call option premium collapse.

Risks to Consider

- Credit event or credit spread widens.
- Take-over with no change of control put and near long call strike price.
- Take-over by a company with a weaker credit rating causing bond value to decline.
- Interest rates move up.
- Further stock price declines will evaporate any premium above fixed-income value.
- Traditional high-yield buyers supporting the busted convertible market move into net selling position, removing price support for issue and pushing bonds below current levels.

Worksheet Example, Table 7.3 and Figure 7.5— Busted Hedge—Covered Call with Long Call for Protection

The busted hedge example in Table 7.3 and Figure 7.5 is long 100M XYZ convertible bonds with a 5 percent coupon, maturing 2/1/2007, trading at 78 percent of par with a current yield of 6.41 percent. The current stock

TABLE 7.3 Busted Covered Call with Protective Out-of-the-Money Long Call—XYZ Company

Convertible	*Common Stock*				
		Symbol	XYZ		
		Price $	6.00	Dividend $	—
		Volatility %	60	Yield	0.000%
	Convertible	Floor Yield	13.00	Quantity	100
		Symbol	XYZ-X	Maturity	2/1/07
		Price $	78.000	Conv. Prem.	364.85 %
		Yield	6.41%	Coupon	5.00 %
		Adj Strike $	27.762	Conversion Ratio	27.9660
Short Call	*Short Call*			Quantity	22
		Symbol	BQXYZ	Expiration	2/22/03
		Strike $	7.50	Time to Expiration	0.3534 years
		Price $	1.00	Implied Volatility %	104
Long Call	*Long Call*			Quantity	25
		Symbol	BQXYZ2	Expiration	2/22/03
		Strike $	12.50	Time to Expiration	0.3534 years
		Price $	0.25	Implied Volatility %	98

Profit & Loss Information	Hedge ratio: 79%	Holding period: 3.9 Months					M&A Scenario
	% Change 1 Std. Deviation	–29.0%	–21.5%	Current	27.4%	40.9%	235.0%
	Assumed Stock Px	4.26	4.71	6.00	7.65	8.45	20.10
	Est Convertible Px	79.69	79.69	78.00	79.69	79.69	84.07
	Convertible Px % Moves	2.2%	2.2%	0.0%	2.2%	2.2%	7.8%
	Est *Short* Call Px	0.01	0.01	0.01	0.16	0.95	12.60
	Call Px % Moves	–100.0%	–100.0%	–100.0%	–84.0%	–5.0%	1160%
	Est *Long* Call Px	0.01	0.01	0.01	0.01	0.01	7.61
	Call Px % Moves	–100.0%	–100.0%	–100.0%	–100.0%	–100.0%	4973%
	Profit/Loss Convertible	1,690	1,690	0	1,690	1,690	6,070
	Income/Dividend	1,625	813	1,625	813	1,625	1,625
	Profit/Loss *Short* Call	2,200	2,200	2,200	1,848	110	–25,520
	Profit/Loss *Long* Call	–625	–625	–625	–625	–625	19,025
	Total Profit/Loss	**4,890**	**4,078**	**3,200**	**3,726**	**2,800**	**1,200**
	ROI	**6.40%**	**5.34%**	**4.20%**	**4.88%**	**3.66%**	**1.57%**
	AROI	**18.11%**	**15.11%**	**12.88%**	**13.81%**	**10.36%**	**4.44%**

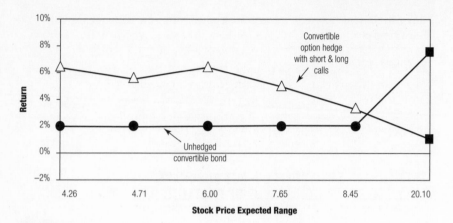

FIGURE 7.5   Busted Hedge—Covered Call with Long Call Protection.

price is $6.00 and yields nothing. The convertible is exchangeable for 27.966 shares of stock per bond and the current conversion premium is a very high 364.85 percent, typical for a busted convertible. The convertible is very close to its fixed-income value and has an investment premium of only 3 percent. The short call premium enhances the 4-month yield by 2.82 percent or almost 8 percent annually. The long out-of-the-money call option is considered catastrophic insurance and costs about 0.8 percent or 2.26 percent annually. The net option income is 2 percent over the 4-month period or 5.7 percent annual income enhancement.

The coupon income from the convertible, plus both the net option income and the bond accretion toward par value as a result of time decay, results in an excellent sideways return of 6.4 percent or 18.1 percent annually. The worksheet in Table 7.3 and Figure 7.5 also demonstrates the point that is very close to break-even for the hedge. If the stock price should move up 235 percent to $20 per share in the 4-month period, the position will only earn about 1 percent. Figure 7.5 shows the sharp decline in the return on investment as the stock approaches $20 per share. The long out-of-the money call protects the position against this unlikely but possible scenario. Without the long call option overlay as insurance, the hedge would have lost –$17,825, for a 4-month loss of –23.5 percent. The long call insurance policy is well worth the cost.

In establishing this type of hedge, the arbitrageur may also believe that the credit spreads in general will contract 50 basis points over the next 4 months for the convertible's credit grade. In this example, since the issue has an omicron of 0.37, a 50 basis point contraction in credit spreads would add another 1.85 percent of return to the 6.4 percent return, for a 4-month return of 8.25 percent and an annualized return of 23.3 percent. Once again, this hedging technique is not the traditional market neutral convertible hedge but actually is much closer to an enhanced fixed-income position. Nonetheless, positions with this type of risk-reward profile do work their way into a diversified convertible arbitrage portfolio if the arbitrageur has confidence in the credit quality of the issue.

CONVERTIBLE STOCK HEDGE—PUT PURCHASE PROVIDES ADDITIONAL DOWNSIDE PROTECTION

The options market also can be used to improve stock hedge positions when the convertible's downside risk is high or the investment floor proves to be elusive. As noted in Chapter 1, the fixed-income value of a convertible acts as a put option and can also be modeled as one when determining the theoretical value of a convertible. The purchase of put options on the underlying stock can improve the risk-reward of a hedge. Options purchased at-the-money or close-to-the-money can provide the downside protection that is necessary for a more neutral return profile when the convertible's investment value premium is too large to protect the hedge properly.

Put options can also be used as a *means to hedge the credit risk* for issues that do not have a well-defined investment value. Many low-grade convertible preferreds and bonds have investment values that are moving targets because of the high correlation between declining stock prices and their companies' corresponding credit spreads (negative gamma results). The arbitrageur may choose to carry this type of position with a stock hedge that is much higher than the theoretical delta implies (bearish hedge), but this profile may cause significant upside losses if the stock price moves up sharply.

Since the strike price of the embedded convertible is a function of the fixed-income value, puts can be purchased with a strike price near the expected fixed-income value's determined strike. The puts are very effective because they are perfectly correlated with the common stock but lack all credit risk. The embedded put option or investment value in a convertible does have credit risk, with credit deterioration resulting in a declining fixed-income value and downside protection. With put options in place, a hedge can be established that does not have significant upside risks and also active rebalancing of the hedge on the downside can occur without undue delta exposure. This ability to rebalance is important because many low-grade hedges are difficult to rebalance on the downside because the delta does not change and the gamma is very low or becomes negative. In such cases, instead of covering some of the short positions and locking in gains, the position will not realize a gain and may trade only dollars at best. The purchase of put options, however, establishes a floor and allows active rebalancing, enabling short stock gains on the downside to be booked.

Put options can also be purchased as *catastrophic insurance* or instead of credit default swaps. Arbitrageurs may set up a stock hedge position and then purchase deep out-of-the-money put options that will provide the protection in the event of a sharp stock price decline and perceived credit event. Figure 7.6 shows the return profile for a stock hedge that experiences a credit event on the downside (negative gamma) with no put options. The position provides the neutral profile until the stock price declines through $15, at which point the returns decay and even move into the negative territory because the convertible's delta begins to rise and the stock hedge is insufficient to offset the negative gamma. The graph also shows the same hedge with the purchase of out-of-the-money put options with a strike price at $15. Because the puts were originally purchased when the stock hedge was established with the stock price at $25, the puts were 40 percent out-of-the-money and therefore very inexpensive. As seen in the graph, the cost of the puts results in a slightly lower return profile for all stock prices above $15,

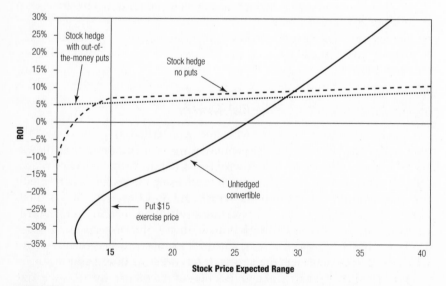

FIGURE 7.6 Stock Hedge with Catastrophic Put Protection.

but once the stock price drops below $15, the puts provide excellent protection and preserve the hedge's neutral profile.

Typically, these deep-out-of-the money puts can be purchased for a very minimal cost. The strike price on the put option should be struck at the stock price level at which the arbitrageur feels negative gamma may occur in the convertible.

Characteristics to Identify the Opportunity

- Convertible demonstrates low downside gamma but offers high volatility, good yield carry, and high liquidity.
- Put option's implied volatility is reasonably low and the total cost of protection does not compromise the total net income of the position.
- Convertible not trading in the distressed zone but is of low credit quality. Purchasing a deep-out-of-the money put will protect the hedge against severe credit and equity price breaks.
- Convertible not demonstrating downside gamma as expected and investment value not well defined.
- Credit default swap protection costly or not available.

Risks to Consider

- Put strike price below the level needed to prevent downside loss and negative gamma in position.
- Under-hedging of short stock position and incorrect designation of negative gamma point.
- Put costs are a negative cash flow item reducing overall return for stock prices above put strike.

Worksheet Example, Table 7.4 and Figure 7.7— Long Put to Augment Stock Hedge Risk-Reward Profile

In this example, the neutral hedge profile desired is difficult to achieve when hedged at the current delta. The downside risks of the hedge can be reduced by adding to the short stock position and increasing the hedge ratio from 68 percent to 75 percent but the upside returns are then lowered and unattractive. Purchasing put options one strike out-of-the-money at $0.60 each on a partial hedge basis provides enough protection over the expected stock price range to make the hedge achieve the neutral profile. It is necessary to purchase only 11 put contracts, even though 54 contracts would be needed to cover the total convertible position. Because of the 68 percent stock hedge, the puts provide a minor adjustment to the overall hedge by tweaking the

TABLE 7.4 Long Convertible/Long Put/Short Stock—XYZ Company

Convertible	*Common Stock*					
		Symbol	XYZ			
		Price $	15.00	Dividend $	—	
		Volatility %	50	Yield	0.000%	
	Convertible	Floor Yield	12.00	Quantity	100	
		Symbol	XYZ-X	Maturity	11/15/06	
		Price $	100.000	Conv. Prem.	22.88 %	
		Yield	4.50%	Coupon	4.50 %	
		Adj Strike $	14.093	Conversion Ratio	54.2530	
Long Put	*Long Put*			Quantity	11	
		Symbol	BQXYZ	Expiration	2/16/03	
		Strike $	12.50	Time to Expiration	0.325 years	
		Price $	0.60	Implied Volatility %	50	
Short Stock	*Short Stock*					
		Symbol	XYZ	Quantity	3,700	
		Price $	15.00	Fed Fund Rate	1.80%	

Hedge ratio: 89%   Holding period: *3.9* Months

% Change 1 Std. Deviation	−24.8%	−18.3%	Current	22.4%	33.1%
Assumed Stock Px	11.27	12.25	15.00	18.35	19.95
Est Convertible Px	88.01	91.75	102.38	114.91	120.87
Convertible Px % Moves	−12.0%	−8.2%	2.4%	14.9%	20.9%
Est *Long Put* Px	1.25	0.26	0.01	0.01	0.01
Put Px % Moves	108.3%	−56.7%	0.0%	0.0%	0.0%
Est *Short* Stock Px	11.27	12.25	15.00	18.35	19.95
Short Px % Moves	24.8%	18.3%	0.0%	−22.4%	−33.1%
Profit/Loss Convertible	−11,990	−8,250	2,380	14,910	20,870
Income/Dividend/Short Interest	2,099	1,469	2,286	1,634	2,499
Profit/Loss *Long Put*	715	−374	−660	−660	−660
Profit/Loss *Short Stock*	13,801	10,175	0	−12,395	−18,315
Total Profit/Loss	4,625	3,020	4,006	3,489	4,394
ROI	4.59%	3.00%	3.98%	3.47%	4.36%
AROI	14.14%	9.23%	12.25%	10.26%	13.43%
Leverage ROI	8.20%	5.01%	6.97%	5.94%	7.74%
Leverage AROI	25.22%	15.40%	21.43%	18.27%	23.80%

(Profit & Loss Information)

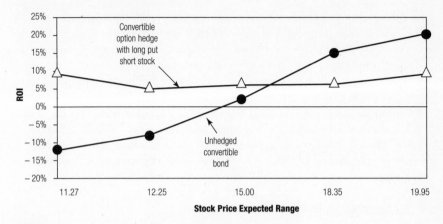

FIGURE 7.7 Convertible Covered Long Put/Short Stock.

risk-reward ratio and shifting it into line with the arbitrageur's objectives. The hedge has an expected 4-month holding period and an expected stock price range over this period between $11.27 and $19.95. The hedge worksheet shows a passive return profile of around 4 percent for the expected stock price range, which works out to a 12 percent annualized return. The puts support the downside range and help maintain this return profile. Figure 7.7 shows the hedge profile compared to the unhedged convertible return. The bottom of the worksheet also shows the returns for a low-levered hedge with only 50 percent margin. The levered hedge works out to about a 20 percent annualized return even before including any active trading profits that can be captured.

CONVERTIBLE HEDGE CALL WRITE WITH PROTECTIVE LONG PUT

Protective put options can also be used with a covered call write overlay hedge. This hedge is similar to the stock hedge with deep-out-of-the-money puts purchased to provide insurance or the at-the-money puts to raise the investment value of the convertible. The convertible's downside gamma and income determine what type of hedge may be established, but in all cases the call option premium must also be high enough to justify the hedge. A convertible trading with high downside gamma may need put options purchased with an exercise price that is close to or at-the-money to protect the downside risk of the position. This hedge opportunity is less prevalent because the cost of the put option protection often will offset the call option premium, making the stock short alternative more attractive than purchasing put options or significantly reducing the number of puts needed.

Put options can be purchased deep OTM for issues that appear to have high downside gamma, but because of the potential for credit impairment, an additional layer of protection is purchased. In either hedge scenario, the cost of the put options must be significantly less than the call option premium received. Put options can enhance a covered call write or provide insurance to the hedge, but either way, they are a negative cash flow item to the hedge.

Characteristics to Identify the Opportunity

- Stock expected to be range bound until the call options expire. No catalyst and technically not attractive.
- Call option's implied volatility > convertible implied volatility and > expected volatility.
- Convertible has low theta risk and low call probability.
- Convertible income plus call option premium less put costs meets minimum return targets.
- Stock short may be difficult or the amount of short interest rebate over holding period is significantly less than call option premium.

Risks to Consider

- Take-over of convertible issuer causes upside loss or premium collapse.
- Interim volatility shifts, causing loss on hedge for a portion of the holding period.
- The convertible becomes significantly under-priced, impairing the hedge.
- Stock price at expiration is above call strike price.

Worksheet Example, Table 7.5 and Figure 7.8— Convertible Hedge Call Write with Protective Long Put

The worksheet in Table 7.5 is an example of a covered call write that offers 2.77 percent premium over 4 months should the stock remain below the $25 strike price. Since the arbitrageur expects the stock—currently at $20—to remain range bound over the next 4 months, a covered call write offers a better sideways return than a stock hedge. By purchasing 100M convertibles that are undervalued or even fairly valued and selling over-priced call

TABLE 7.5 Long Convertible/Long Put/Short Call—XYZ Company

Common Stock							
	Symbol	**XYZ**					
	Price $	20.00		Dividend $		0.32	
	Volatility	35%		Yield		1.60%	

Convertible

		Quantity	100
Symbol	**XYZ-X**	Spread over Treasuries	312 bps
Price $	98.50	Maturity	4/15/08
Coupon	4.50%	Conversion Premium	37.90%
Yield to Maturity	4.80%	Investment Premium	3.32%
Conversion Ratio	35.714	Delta	0.21
Adj Strike $	26.692	Vega	0.30

Short Call

		Quantity	35
Symbol	**BQXYZ**	Expiration	2/16/03
Strike $	25.00	Time to Expiration	0.325 years
Price $	0.78	Implied Volatility	50%

Long Put

		Quantity	30
Symbol	**BQXYZ**	Expiration	2/16/03
Strike $	15.00	Time to Expiration	0.325 years
Price $	0.12	Implied Volatility	35%

Dollar Protection: 2.77%   **Holding period:** *3.9 Months*

% Change 1 Std. Deviation	−40.0%	−17.9%	−13.0%	Current	15.0%	21.8%	40.0%
Assumed Stock Px	12.00	16.41	17.39	20.00	22.99	24.36	28.00
Est Convertible Px	87.65	95.25	96.51	98.50	101.50	103.00	109.00
Convertible Px % Moves	−11.0%	−3.3%	−2.0%	0.0%	3.1%	4.6%	10.7%
Est *Short* Call Px	0.01	0.01	0.01	0.01	0.01	0.01	3.00
Call Px % Moves	−100.0%	−100.0%	−100.0%	−100.0%	−100.0%	−100.0%	285.0%
Est *Long Put* Px	3.00	0.01	0.01	0.01	0.01	0.01	0.01
Put Px % Moves	2400.0%	−99.9%	−99.9%	−99.9%	−99.9%	−99.9%	−99.9%
Profit/Loss Convertible	−10,850	−3,250	−2,000	0	3,000	5,307	10,500
Income/Dividend/ Short Interest	1,463	1,463	732	1,463	732	1,463	1,463
Profit/Loss *Short* Call	2,730	2,730	2,730	2,730	2,730	2,730	−7,770
Profit/Loss *Long Put*	9,000	−360	−360	−360	−360	−360	−360
Total Profit/Loss	2,343	583	1,102	3,833	6,102	9,140	3,833
ROI	2.44%	0.61%	1.15%	3.99%	6.35%	9.51%	3.99%
AROI	7.39%	1.84%	3.47%	12.28%	19.54%	29.26%	12.28%

options, the return over the next few months is in excess of 1 percent per month without leverage, with the use of leverage significantly improving the return. But, because the arbitrageur is concerned that this low-grade convertible issuer needs some catastrophic insurance, 30 out-of-the-money put option contracts are purchased with a strike price of $15. The hedge has 35 calls written against the convertibles, representing 35 long calls or a 100 percent hedge. If the stock price closes above $25 at expiration, it results in a lower return profile. The worksheet and graph show the P&L for a $28 stock price at expiration, which clearly reduces the return on the hedge and at even higher stock prices the return continues to decay and move into negative territory.

The 30 put options provide enough protection to help the hedge in the event of negative gamma occurring. The worksheet in Table 7.5 shows the P&L should the stock price decline severely and why the put options are necessary. If the stock price closes at $12 on expiration, the hedge is protected. The position without put options would have realized a loss at this point of −6.8 percent or −20.8 percent annually. The small costs of the puts helped shift the P&L into positive territory and avoid a disaster. The convertible was moving on a .18 downside delta originally, but as the stock price declined through $15 the delta increased to .30, putting stress on the hedge return profile and demonstrating the need for put protection. The exact put option amount is dependent on the arbitrageur's credit analysis and estimate of impairment, as well as the delta that the convertible may be expected to trade with if the credit event occurred. Figure 7.8 shows the return on the hedge as compared to the unhedged convertible over the ex-

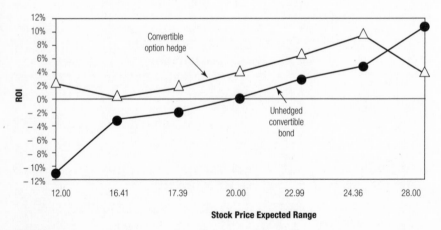

FIGURE 7.8 Convertible Covered Call Write/Long Put.

pected 4-month trading range. It also demonstrates that the covered call write causes upside loss potential at one extreme and the put provides protection at the other extreme.

MANDATORY CONVERTIBLE PREFERRED— STOCK HEDGE WITH CALL WRITE OVERLAY

Option hedging can also improve the return profile of a mandatory convertible issue. Mandatory issues such as DECS and Prides have embedded short and long call options that can be offset by the reverse hedge if the listed call options demonstrate a significantly higher implied volatility level than the embedded options. Return profiles for stock hedging with mandatory issues can also be enhanced with covered call write overlays. The typically high-yielding mandatory issue, with a stock hedge and call write overlay, produces an excellent high-yield hedge. But, the high-yield capture does come with some additional risks. *Mandatory issues have delta, gamma, and vega risks that transition quickly and can be subject to reversals with sharp stock price moves, making the hedging of these issues a very high maintenance and difficult prospect, at times.*

Characteristics to Identify the Opportunity

- Call option implied volatility > mandatory convertible's implied volatility at upper strike.
- Stand still yield not subject to high theta risk.
- Stock price with no catalyst for major price breaks.
- Clearly defined delta and gamma price track.

Risks to Consider

- Net negative vega exposure moves against hedge.
- Volatility of stock becomes high and subject to jumps in price.
- Active monitoring of theta, vega, gamma, and delta to avoid return collapse is time intensive.
- Take-over and other event risks are substantial.
- Liquidity of mandatory issues presents some significant price risks over short periods of time.

Example Worksheet, Table 7.6 and Figure 7.9— Mandatory Stock Hedge with Call Write Overlay

The worksheet in Table 7.6 is an example of a stock hedge with a mandatory convertible issue in which the 10-point trading range on the stock offers excellent sideways returns. Keep in mind that a graph showing the hedge

TABLE 7.6 Long Mandatory/Sell Calls/Short Stock—XYZ Company

Convertible	*Common Stock*					
		Symbol	XYZ			
		Price $	21.40	Dividend $		0.2500
		Volatility %	41	Yield		4.673%
	Convertible	Floor Yield	11.00	Quantity		10,000
		Symbol	XYZPRC	Maturity		11/15/05
		Price $	25.000	Stand Still Yield		8.87%
		Yield	8.87%	Qtrly Div		0.55
		Lower Strike $	21.400	Upper Strike		25.680
		Lower Price $	4.600	Upper Price $		3.600
		Lower Conv Ratio	1.1682	Upper Conv Ratio		0.9735
Short Call	*Short Call*			Quantity		37
		Symbol	BQXYZ	Expiration		1/17/03
		Strike $	25.00	Time to Expiration		0.25 years
		Price $	2.68	Implied Volatility %		95
Short Stock	*Short Stock*					
		Symbol	XYZ	Quantity		7,200
		Price $	21.40	Fed Fund Rate		1.90%

	Hedge ratio: 93%	Holding period: *3* Months				

	% Change 1 Std. Deviation	−18.5%	−13.5%	Current	15.6%	22.8%
Profit & Loss Information	Assumed Stock Px	17.44	18.51	21.40	24.74	26.28
	Est Convertible Px	22.11	23.1	25.00	27.70	29.12
	Convertible Px % Moves	−11.5%	−6.6%	0.0%	12.6%	18.8%
	Profit/Loss Convertible	−28,900	−19,000	0	27,000	41,200
	Income/Dividend/Short Interest	3,661	625	3,767	625	3,899
	Profit/Loss Short Call	9,916	9,916	9,916	9,916	4,736
	Profit/Loss Short Stock	28,512	20,808	0	−24,048	−35,136
	Total Profit/Loss	13,189	12,349	13,683	13,493	14,699
	ROI	5.49%	5.14%	5.70%	5.62%	6.12%
	AROI	21.97%	20.57%	22.80%	22.48%	24.49%

with a wider range of stock prices is a necessary check against return collapse. The convertible in this example already offers a high 8.87 percent annual yield and the stock hedge should provide some additional protection and a slight yield. The call option hedge overlay adds another 4 percent to the hedge and takes the total hedge ratio up to 66 percent. The position is

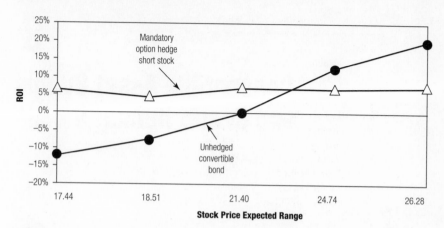

FIGURE 7.9   Mandatory Covered Call Write/Short Stock.

long 10,000 shares of the mandatory issue and short 7,200 shares of stock with an additional 37 call options written against the hedge. The call options have a strike price of $25 so they are OTM with the current stock price at $21.4. The call options have an exceptionally high volatility of 95 percent, while the convertible's lower and upper strikes have implied volatility levels much lower, at around 40 percent.

The hedging of mandatory issues offers less attractive trading profits if the stock moves consistently in one direction because of the need to add to the stock hedge on the downside and reduce it on the upside (the opposite of the desired). This can be accomplished by selling the mandatory as the stock price appreciates and buying more as it declines, in order to lock in some trading profits. But, adjusting the long position often also necessitates adjusting the call write, which increases trading costs.

The hedge example offers a return profile that ranges from 5 to 6 percent over the 3-month holding period should the stock price remain in the 10-point range. The annualized returns are from 22 to 25 percent, as indicated at the bottom of the worksheet.

Many variations of option hedges can be employed by the arbitrageur, who is limited only by his creativity and the markets' opportunity sets. Numerous other hedges are too extensive to include in this chapter, but I hope that the variety of examples that have been presented here convey the range of possibilities. The arbitrageur should include option hedge techniques in his toolbox along with a good option calculator and graphics package to improve his understanding of the hedge profiles and price risks.

CHAPTER 8

Convertible Asset Swaps and Credit Default Swaps

CONVERTIBLE ASSET SWAPS—EXTRACTING CHEAP OPTIONS FROM INVESTMENT-GRADE CONVERTIBLES

The convertible arbitrageur identifies an undervalued investment-grade convertible as a result of a non-priced or very low priced embedded equity option. An asset swap provides a means of extracting the mispriced option from the security. The convertible asset swap provides a pure play on the embedded option for the arbitrageur while minimizing the capital outlay and credit risk. The credit default swap (CDS) market provides a means of extracting mispriced options embedded in low-grade convertibles or to protect the hedge against credit spread expansion. Since the theoretical value can be more easily attainable by utilizing an asset swap, the convertible market efficiency will improve.

The convertible arbitrageur may be able to utilize the swap market to extract cheap equity options from mispriced investment-grade convertibles because of the potential demand for investment-grade corporate credit by the fixed-income community. The swap convertible market is especially active in Europe due to the less-developed corporate bond market and the relatively higher proportion of investment-grade convertible debt. In Japan, the active convertible swap market results from the large number of "busted" convertible issues and the opportunity to capture cheap equity options embedded in these securities. The U.S. swap market, however, is somewhat less active, thanks to this country's more developed corporate bond market and the overall lower quality of the convertible credits available. During 1999 and 2000, the U.S. swap market exhibited a wave of activity after issuance slowed in the commercial paper market: In response, high-premium, zero-coupon, short-dated puttable convertibles were issued and swapped via the commercial paper market spreads. High quality and large issue size helped boost demand for this paper in the commercial paper markets, as did the lower durations that resulted from the frequent, short-dated puts available on these zero-coupon convertibles.

The swap market offers the convertible arbitrageur an opportunity to sell the fixed-income portion of the convertible and retain the cheap equity option. The equity option component is then hedged with stock, providing an attractive neutral hedge opportunity. In fact, the short interest rebate reduces and may even completely cover the total dollar investment in the equity option stub! To initiate the asset swap, a fixed-income buyer willing to take on the credit risk of the issue in the form of an asset swap must be found. It is for this reason that investment grade paper is usually used in asset swaps. The credit buyer may find the convertible asset swap attractive because it may be the only means to invest in the issuer's credit or with the term to maturity desired. The swap yield spread is also wider than is available in the corporate market, but this is somewhat offset by the lower degree of liquidity in the swap structure.

THE MECHANICS OF CONVERTIBLE ASSET SWAPPING

A basic convertible asset swap entails synthetically separating the convertible's fixed-income component from its embedded equity option component as illustrated by Figure 8.1. Examples are provided in Table 8.1. Figure 8.2 demonstrates the mechanics of a typical convertible asset swap. The arbitrageur identifies a convertible that is inexpensive and purchases the issue, and then sells the convertible to an investment broker and receives an option to repurchase the convertible. The arbitrageur's loss exposure is limited to the capital invested in the equity option component. The investment broker finds the bond investor who is interested in the credit and structure of the issue. The arbitrageur's option provides the equity exposure, while the bond buyer holds the fixed-income component. Most often, the bond buyer is interested in a floating-rate income stream, so the swap is structured to provide this. The bond buyer purchases the fixed-income component or credit value for a price determined by discounting the security by a predetermined spread over LIBOR. The spread allows the bond buyer to receive a floating rate, while the investment broker retains the fixed rate. The asset swap credit value is protected against an early call or conversion with a recall spread that determines the price at which the credit seller must repurchase the convertible. This penalty spread provides the credit buyer a minimum return, while a lockout provision provides a minimum holding period for the security.

TABLE 8.1 Partial Listing of Convertible Asset Swaps as of December 10, 2002.

Issuer	Coupon	Maturity	Swap Date	Credit Rating*	Swap Spread	Convertible Bid	Offer
Allergan, Inc.	0%	01 Nov 20	02 Nov 03	BBB+	LIBOR + 160/140	64.50	64.88
Alza/Johnson & Johnson	0%	28 Jul 20	28 Jul 03	BBB–	LIBOR + 50/40	80.13	80.63
American International Group	0%	09 Nov 31	09 Nov 06	AAA	LIBOR + 70/60	63.44	63.93
Amgen Inc.	0%	01 Mar 32	01 Mar 05	A	LIBOR + 135/125	72.88	73.13
Anadarko Petroleum Corp.	0%	07 Mar 20	07 Mar 03	BBB+	LIBOR + 85/75	61.38	61.88
Avon Products	0%	12 Jul 20	12 Jul 03	A	LIBOR + 60/60	54.38	54.75
Baxter International Inc	1.25%	01 Jun 21	01 Jun 06	A–	LIBOR + 120/105	99.13	99.38
BJ Services Co	0.40%	24 Apr 22	24 Apr 05	BBB	LIBOR + 170/150	81.13	81.63
Chiron Corp	0%	12 Jun 31	12 Jun 04	BBB+	LIBOR + 110/100	57.94	58.44
Cooper Cameron	1.75%	17 May 21	18 May 06	BBB+	LIBOR + 150/130	99.00	100.00
Costco Companies	0%	19 Aug 17	19 Aug 07	A–	LIBOR + 85/70	71.44	71.81
Countrywide Credit	0%	08 Feb 31	08 Feb 04	A–	LIBOR + 150/140	78.69	79.19
CSX Corporation	0%	30 Oct 21	30 Oct 03	BBB	LIBOR + 160/140	83.63	84.13
Danaher Corporation	0%	22 Jan 21	22 Jan 04	A	LIBOR + 120/110	66.44	66.69
Devon Energy	0%	27 Jun 20	27 Jun 05	BBB	LIBOR + 150/140	52.19	52.69
Diamond Offshore	1.50%	15 Apr 31	15 Apr 08	A–	LIBOR + 110/100	90.69	91.19
First Data Corporation	2.00%	01 Mar 08	01 Sep 04	A	LIBOR + 120/100	111.19	112.19
Franklin Resources	0%	11 May 31	11 May 03	A	LIBOR + 130/120	58.69	59.06
General Mills	0%	28 Oct 22	28 Oct 05	BBB	LIBOR + 150/140	69.44	69.69
Global Marine, Inc.	0%	23 Jun 20	23 Jun 05	BBB	LIBOR + 140/120	54.00	54.50
Health Management Associates	0.25%	16 Aug 20	16 Aug 03	BBB–	LIBOR + 225/200	67.06	67.56
International Paper Co.	0%	20 Jun 21	20 Jun 04	BBB	LIBOR + 160/150	52.81	53.06
Jones Apparel Group	0%	01 Feb 21	01 Feb 04	BBB–	LIBOR + 180/160	54.94	55.31
Kohl's Corporation	0%	12 Jun 20	12 Jun 03	BBB	LIBOR + 225/200	63.13	63.50
Lowe's Companies.	0%	16 Feb 21	16 Apr 04	BBB+	LIBOR + 100/90	76.06	76.44
Medtronic Inc	1.25%	15 Sep 21	15 Sep 04	A+	LIBOR + 160/140	104.69	104.94
Merrill Lynch	0%	13 Mar 32	13 Mar 05	AA–	LIBOR + 160/140	97.69	98.06
Nabors Industries, Inc.	0%	05 Feb 21	05 Feb 06	A–	LIBOR + 110/100	62.13	62.50
Omnicom Group Inc	0%	31 Jul 32	31 Jul 03	A–	LIBOR + 225/200	99.88	100.25
PMI Group	2.50%	15 Jul 21	15 Jul 04	A+	LIBOR + 200/175	106.19	106.35
Radian Group, Inc	2.25%	01 Jan 22	01 Jan 05	A	LIBOR + 235/215	101.63	102.63
Reebok International	4.25%	01 Mar 21	19 Jan 04	BBB–	LIBOR + 175/150	108.19	108.94
Teva Pharmaceuticals	0.75%	15 Aug 21	20 Aug 04	BBB–	LIBOR + 275/250	107.06	107.81
TJX Companies Inc.	0%	13 Feb 21	13 Feb 04	BBB+	LIBOR + 130/115	80.75	81.13
Transocean Sedco Forex	1.50%	15 May 21	15 May 04	BBB	LIBOR + 175/160	91.44	92.44
Verizon	0%	15 May 21	15 May 04	A+	LIBOR + 200/175	57.31	57.56
XL Capital Ltd	0%	23 May 21	23 May 04	A+	LIBOR + 200/180	64.19	64.44

Source: Credit Suisse First Boston, LLC. Used with permission.

*Source: Moody's Investor Service, Inc., and/or its affiliates. Reprinted with permission.

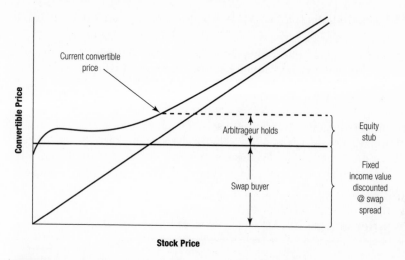

FIGURE 8.1   Asset Swap Components of a Convertible Bond.

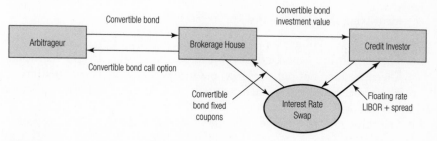

FIGURE 8.2   Typical Convertible Asset Swap.

The credit buyer often receives a spread wider than that of other corporate bonds available, due to the lower liquidity of the issue. The credit buyer is assuming the credit risk until maturity of the contract or until the contract is called. While the equity stub holder is protected against credit spreads widening, he can benefit if credit spreads narrow by recalling the asset swap and then re-selling it at the current credit spread.

Traditionally, convertibles in the U.S. market have been valued on a spread to government debt basis, but with the growth of the asset swap market, many high-grade issues are valued on the basis of the appropriate swap curve (LIBOR, Euribor, etc.). To determine valuation, the convertible arbitrageur must assess the viability of the paper as an asset swap or against the appropriate government curve if a swap is unlikely. The equity stub option, considered long rho, has a variable strike price that also protects the option from increasing interest rates. As seen in the formula below, the strike on the option is equal to the bond value, determined by discounting par value and the convertible coupons by LIBOR plus the credit spread:

$$\text{Investment Value} = \Sigma \, PV \, (\text{coupons}) - \Sigma \, PV \, (\text{LIBOR} + \text{Spread})$$

Importantly, the equity stub option has significant credit spread protection and some interest rate protection. That is because an increase in interest rates or credit spreads will lower the bond value and also the strike price of the option, making the option more valuable (assuming all other factors are constant).

SWAP HEDGE SETUP

The equity stub remaining from the bond asset swap can be hedged to provide a low-capital-outlay, levered position while reducing many of the risks that concern an arbitrageur.

Identifying the Opportunity

- Convertible bond has an investment-grade credit rating.
- The convertible, from a LIBOR spread discount perspective, looks cheap.
- The embedded option is volatile and priced below expected volatility.
- The embedded option, when isolated and leveraged, offers exceptional return potential.
- The terms and/or structure of the convertible are attractive to fixed-income buyers.
- The convertible issue is large enough to offer a swap large enough to entice fixed-income buyers.
- The underlying stock can be easily borrowed.
- The convertible call/put terms are long enough in duration to establish a swap.
- Desire to reduce credit exposure and capital employed in hedge.

Risks to Consider

- Liquidity of position reduced considerably—position can only be closed with party initially entering into agreement.
- Counter-party risk increases.
- Convertible issuer calls bonds for early redemption.
- Position is long rho, vega, and theta: need to watch for decay or shifts.
- Documentation and deliverable risk.

To begin, the arbitrageur will set up a neutral stock hedge against the equity option component of the asset swap. The position now requires much less capital and provides a leveraged play on the underlying stock. The delta neutral hedge position on the option component has lowered many of the greek risks and further lowered the capital required. The credit risk has been eliminated, while the equity risk is neutralized. The interest rate or rho risk has also been significantly reduced. The rho is lower as a result of swapping the credit and removing much of the negative rho that exists in the original convertible structure. Also, it is important to note that the option strike price is a function of the credit value of the swap, so that if interest rates rise, the strike price of the option goes lower. The neutral stock hedge against the option does retain long volatility risk or vega as well as theta risk. But often options embedded in some convertibles are assigned little or no value and as a result the greek risks are minimal. Table 8.2 shows the greek risks and trade offs, comparing a convertible hedge to an equity stub swap hedge. Also, the Bloomberg asset swap calculator offers investors a quick means to assess swap values.

Let's examine an example of a swap opportunity, using a hypothetical XYZ convertible that carries a very high credit rating and is theoretically undervalued. The convertible is currently priced at 103, and the arbitrageur purchases $10 million face value of this bond for a purchase price of $10.30 million. This security is a candidate for an asset swap if a fixed-income buyer can be enticed to purchase the bond value of this security. The bond value is determined by discounting the present value of the fixed-income payments and par value at the current swap rate; in this case the spread is 50 basis points over LIBOR. The bond value of 93.1 becomes the value at which the arbitrageur sells the convertible back to the investment bank and in return receives the call option to purchase the convertible at a cost derived

TABLE 8.2   Greek Risks and Trade Offs

Greek Measures	Convertible Hedge	Swap Equity Stub Hedge	Trade Off
Delta	+	+	
Gamma	+	+	
Vega	+	+	
Rho	+	−	Reduce interest rate risk
Theta	+	+	
Credit-default	+	0	Eliminate credit risk
Liquidity	+	−	Lose liquidity
Credit spread	+	0	Eliminate spread risk

from the price difference between 103 and 93.1. The credit or fixed-income investor then purchases the convertible asset swap fixed-income portion for par value (100) and receives floating rates with a spread above LIBOR. The arbitrageur establishes a market neutral hedge position with the option component and then dynamically hedges the option with short stock each time the position delta changes enough to warrant a rebalance. This occurs until the option gets fully priced (trades with an implied volatility that is higher than it was at the hedge's original setup) or until maturity. At maturity, the option investor or arbitrageur will exercise the call option if the convertible's parity level is above the redemption value. If parity is below the redemption value, then the option expires worthless and the asset swap expires. If the swap contract is exercised early, the arbitrageur (option holder) must pay the fixed-income buyer the bond value at the time based on the remaining cash-flows and some pre-determined penalty spread.

The hedged equity swap stub offers an improved risk-reward trade off: Leverage amplifies the gains attainable, while the position also reduces credit spread, bankruptcy, and interest rate risks. Table 8.3 compares the returns

TABLE 8.3 Comparison of Returns

Stock price	$14	$20	$30
Convertible price	90	103	137
Conversion premium	42.9%	14.4%	1.5%
Stock price % change	−30%	0%	+50%
Convertible % change	−12.6%	0%	+33%
Equity stub value	0.5	10	44
Equity stub % change	−95%	0%	+340%
Convertible hedge			
Stock short P&L	+$180	0	−$300
Convertible P&L	−$130	0	+$340
Convertible interest	+$60	+$60	+$60
Short credit rebate	+$20	+$20	+$20
Total P&L	+$130	$80	+$120
AROI %	+12.6%	+8.0%	+11.65%
Equity portion of swap hedge			
Stock P&L	+$180	0	-$300
Equity option stub	−$95	0	+$440
Short interest rebate	+$20	+$20	+$20
Total P&L	+$105	+$20	+$160
AROI %	+ 5%	+ 20%	+ 60%

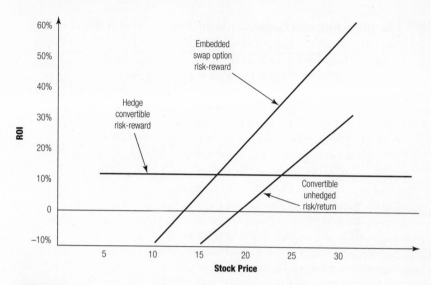

FIGURE 8.3   Asset Swap Hedged Equity Stub Risk-Reward.

attainable from a passive delta neutral hedge that offers approximately 12 percent in return for up- or downside moves in the underlying stock with those of an equity stub hedge. As indicated below, the latter offers a substantially higher return profile—except on the downside. The hedge ratio has been kept consistent for both hedges in the table to allow an easy comparison to be made, although in practice the equity stub hedge ratio should be slightly higher to provide a more balanced return profile. The equity stub risk-reward comparison graphs in Figure 8.3 show the striking difference in return profiles and the levered effect of equity swap stub hedging.

Moreover, the equity swap stub could also be established with borrowed capital to further lever the return profile. See Figure 8.4. The stub hedge is similar to a warrant or leap hedge (long-term option).

CONVERTIBLE BOND CREDIT DEFAULT SWAP— TRANSFER CREDIT RISK IN A HEDGE

Since much of the global convertible issuance comes from companies carrying credit ratings below what is typically asset swapped (single A or better credit rating), the credit default swap (CDS) market is another useful tool that can be used by the convertible arbitrageur to expand his methods for managing credit risk. Examples are provided in Table 8.4. The increased de-

TABLE 8.4 Partial Listing of Convertible Credit Default Swaps (CDS) as of April 25, 2003

Issuer	Ticker	Moodys Rating	S&P Rating	Basis Points per Annum	
				Bid	Ask
American International Group, Inc	AIG	Aaa	AAA	35	41
Amgen Inc	AMGN	A2	A+	29	37
AOL Time Warner Inc	AOL	Baa1	BBB+	150	170
Arrow Electronics, Inc	ARW	Baa3	BBB–	284	316
Baxter International Inc	BAX	A3	A	38	46
Carnival Corporation	CCL	A3	A	84	94
Cendant Corporation	CD	Baa1	BBB	142	162
Chiron Corporation	CHIR	Baa1	A–	29	37
Clear Channel Communications, Inc	CCU	Baa3	BBB–	117	137
Computer Associates International, Inc	CA	Baa2	BBB+	173	203
Countrywide Home Loans, Inc	CFC	A3	A	42	62
Cox Communications, Inc	COX	Baa2	BBB	86	106
Cummins Inc	CUM	Ba2	BB+	403	453
Devon Energy Corporation	DVN	Baa2	BBB	50	60
Electronic Data Systems Corporation	EDS	Baa2	A–	160	186
Ford Motor Credit Company	F	A3	BBB	344	350
Gap, Inc (The)	GPS	Ba3	BB+	230	250
General Mills	GIS	Baa2	BBB+	45	55
General Motors Acceptance Corporation	GMAC	A2	BBB	234	240
Hewlett-Packard Company	HPQ	A3	A–	45	53
International Paper Company	IP	Baa2	BBB	69	79
Kerr-McGee Corporation	KMG	Baa2	BBB	73	93
Liberty Media Corporation	L	Baa3	BBB–	190	210
Lowe's Companies	LOW	A3	A	29	39
Medtronic Inc	MDT	A1	AA–	22	30
Merrill Lynch	MER	Aa3	A+	34	44
Motorola, Inc	MOT	Baa2	BBB	145	161
Northrop Grumman Corporation	NOC	Baa3	BBB–	40	50
Prudential Financial, Inc	PRU	A3	A–	42	56
Raytheon Company	RTN	Baa3	BBB–	94	104
Toys R Us, Inc	TOY	Baa3	BBB–	290	320
Tyco International Ltd	TYC	Ba2	BBB–	309	325
Viacom Inc	VIA	A3	A–	41	51
Walt Disney Company (The)	DIS	Baa1	BBB+	85	95
Washington Mutual, Inc	WM	A3	BBB+	36	46
Weatherford International, Inc	WFT	Baa1	BBB+	40	50
XL Capital Ltd	XL	A1	A+	65	81

Source: Goldman Sachs. Used with permission.

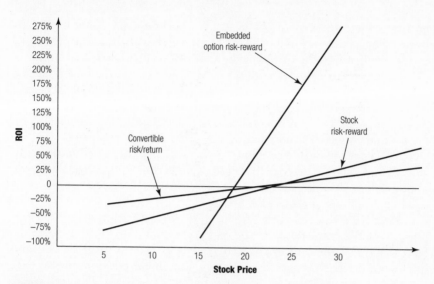

FIGURE 8.4   Equity Stub Risk-Reward Comparison with Leverage.

mand for credit protection in the late 1990s and early 2000s spurred the growth of the CDS market. The CDS market improves credit pricing and liquidity and allows the transfer of risk from one market participant to another. The growth of the CDS market in the late 1990s and early 2000s has also had an influence on how convertibles are valued. An issue's CDS spread has become the de facto discount-rate spread used to value that convertible's fixed-income component. Although a CDS is not available for every convertible issue, the existence of the market has helped improve the transparency in the low-grade debt and convertible market.

The CDS provides the convertible arbitrageur with a means of transferring the credit risk of an issuer to the swap seller for a specified time period and at a fixed spread over LIBOR. The spread of course takes into consideration the duration of the position and the issue-specific credit risks, including default probability and recovery rate estimates. Although the credit risk is transferred, the ownership of the convertible is not. Instead, the CDS is like an insurance policy purchased against the specific issue.

Credit Spread Movements

The convertible hedge with CDS protection will not gain from credit spread tightening from the CDS, but the convertible itself should gain in value, capturing some of the benefits of the spread contraction. As credit spreads widen, though, the price of credit spread protection increases and the CDS profits as the convertible drops in value. Thus, the CDS does not directly benefit from credit spread narrowing but it will directly benefit from spread expansion. In effect, the CDS acts like a put option because of its payoff profile and the fact that the buyer of the CDS has the right to sell the protected bond back to the CDS seller for par value if a credit event occurs. The cost of purchasing puts to cover the difference between par value of the bonds and the recovery rate can be compared to the present value of the CDS premiums to determine if equity put options offer a better opportunity to protect the hedge. Because the equity price is highly correlated with credit spreads and volatility, especially as the credit becomes impaired, equity put options offer a viable alternative to CDS. Chapter 7 discussed the use of equity put options to protect the hedge.

When the credit risk is sold to the CDS seller, the arbitrageur has effectively created a synthetic short sale on the credit portion of the convertible. Since this is a synthetic short position, there is no optionality in the CDS and the CDS seller has purchased a synthetic long bond position, providing a fixed return for the terms of the swap contract. The CDS seller may in fact purchase the synthetic bond at a price that is superior to what is available in the bond market for the same or similar paper. The CDS seller may also short the actual convertible bond in the marketplace as a hedge against the swap sold. If the CDS seller shorts the bond first in an illiquid market, the bond price may decline and the swap spread widen, causing the credit to appear riskier only because a swap was established.

The swap seller is only obligated to make payments when a credit event occurs (see Figure 8.5). The convertible CDS does have some additional risk if a company on the brink of technical default is able to restructure its obligations but still leave the credit in a questionable or tenuous position. The CDS buyer may in fact be left holding a bond with only minor protection. The International Swaps and Derivatives Association, Inc. (ISDA) credit derivative definitions in 1999 defined a credit event and full protection for investors in the event of bankruptcy, obligation default of acceleration, failure to pay, repudiation/moratorium, and restructuring events.

Since the credit portion of the convertible can be hedged via the CDS market, the arbitrageur can focus on the inexpensive option in the convertible and the delta hedge. The value added in this type of hedge can be twofold: First, the dynamic delta hedge can be managed without concern regarding the default risk, and second, the busted issue with negative gamma does in fact have a floor with this hedge. The CDS market is a tradable market, and should the buyer want to break the swap before the contract expiration, the credit would have to be repurchased in the marketplace at the then-prevailing spread over LIBOR. The CDS does not hedge the interest rate exposure in the position—only the credit risks. Overlaying an inter-

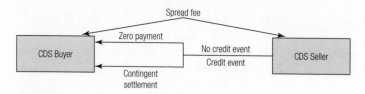

FIGURE 8.5 CDS Credit Event.

est rate hedge with the CDS leaves the convertible arbitrageur the long equity call option. The long equity call option can then be delta hedged to capture the undervalued opportunity and dynamic hedge opportunities. Of course, the cost of both hedges can weigh heavily on the potential return of the position.

The CDS does not provide leverage on the position as would the convertible asset swap, but the arbitrageur may be more willing to establish a position with borrowed money on certain issues if the credit risk could be reduced or eliminated. On the other hand, the CDS increases the cost of the hedge, thus reducing the amount of leverage used. Table 8.5 provides a comparison between the convertible asset swap features and a credit default swap. Either tool is useful, depending on the situation and the overall convertible arbitrage portfolio risks.

Characteristics to Identify the Opportunity

- CDS available and liquid.
- Convertible's embedded equity option is undervalued.
- Stock borrow is ample.
- Concerns about the company's creditworthiness are revealed during analysis.
- Counter-party risk is low.
- The arbitrage return potential is high enough to comfortably cover CDS premium and fees.

Risks to Consider

- Credit spreads are narrow.
- Bid/ask spread on CDS too wide for short-term arbitrage opportunity.
- Counter-party credit deteriorates.
- Embedded option loses premium.
- Documentation risks and deliverable risks.
- CDS was overpriced and eats into the return of the position as it moves back to fair value.

TABLE 8.5 Comparison of Convertible Asset Swap and Credit Default Swap

Convertible Asset Swap	Credit Default Swap
Eliminate credit risk	Eliminate credit risk
Eliminate credit spread risk	Eliminate credit spread risk
Reduces interest rate risk	No interest rate risk reduction
More expensive than CDS	Less expensive than asset swap
Callable	Not callable
Less liquidity	Better liquidity
Provides leverage	No leverage
Non standard contracts	Standard contracts

Convertible Credit Default Swap (CDS) Example

Imagine a scenario where the convertible arbitrageur identifies an attractive hedge candidate in a telecom equipment manufacturer, but his portfolio is currently already fully exposed to low-grade credits in the telecom equipment sector. The arbitrageur enters into a credit default swap with a broker/dealer who sells credit protection on XYZ telecom to the arbitrageur to protect the $5 million investment with a term of three years. The arbitrageur pays a spread over LIBOR for the protection that is 1.75 percent per year, paid quarterly for the three-year period. Should a credit event occur, the broker dealer pays the arbitrageur $5 million and receives as physical settlement the XYZ telecom convertible bonds from the arbitrageur to terminate the contract. The CDS produces a negative cash flow, so additional trading opportunities from the hedge must be available or the convertible pricing discrepancy must offer an excellent opportunity to cover the cost of the CDS.

The proliferation of multiple convertible issues from the same company enhances the value of entering into a CDS for an extended time horizon. A CDS purchased against a multiple convertible issuer can remain on the books because the arbitrageur has multiple issues to choose from and maintain a hedge with the most attractive issue at any point in time for the duration of the CDS contract.

Hedging Credit Risk—Basket Approach

Another means of providing credit protection is to structure a swap on a basket of credits. This is desirable if the individual position size is small relative to the CDS average size, or if the arbitrageur wants to simplify the paperwork. The downside, of course, is that even when individual positions leave the portfolio, the hedge is still in the portfolio via the basket swap. Alternatively, arbitrage funds can get around this problem and still hedge credit risk by shorting a high-yield index product. The index hedge, however, is difficult to match with the portfolio because of significant position variation and convexity risks. (A convertible portfolio will demonstrate different convexity as a result of the long option embedded in the vehicle.) Matching credit risk with duration will still leave a relatively large and difficult level of convexity risk in the portfolio. Because of the difficulty of matching the hedge perfectly, the basket hedge should be conservatively positioned and re-evaluated once portfolio drift falls outside of tolerance guidelines.

APPENDIX 8.1   ASSET SWAP AND CREDIT DEFAULT SWAP TERM SHEETS

Each swap entered into must be accompanied by a swap term sheet and agreement. The following is an example of an asset swap followed by a credit default swap term sheet. The arbitrageur will be expected to provide a credit letter as a counter party that determines to some extent the final terms and pricing of the swap agreements.

Sample Documentation: Asset Swap Term Sheet

APPENDIX I ASSET SWAP TERM SHEET

This is a DRAFT Confirmation for discussion purposes only. This does not constitute a contract between [Party] and [Counterparty].

Dear Sirs:

The purpose of this letter agreement (this "Confirmation") is to confirm the terms and conditions of the Bond Option Transaction, including the Hypothetical Swap Transaction (the "Swap Transaction"), each as defined below and together the "Transaction" entered into between you and us on the Trade Date specified below. This Confirmation constitutes a "Confirmation" as referred to in the Agreement specified below.

The definitions and provisions contained in the 2000 ISDA Definitions (the "Swap Definitions") and in the 1997 ISDA Government Bond Option Definitions (the "Bond Definitions" and, together with the Swap Definitions, the "Definitions") (each as published by the International Swaps and Derivatives Association, Inc.) are incorporated into this Confirmation. In the event of any inconsistency between the Definitions and this Confirmation, this Confirmation will govern. References herein to a "Bond Option Transaction" shall be deemed to be references to a "Government Bond Option Transaction" for the purposes of the Bond Definitions.

The Bond Definitions apply in relation to the Bond Option Transaction (paragraphs 1 to 9 (inclusive) below) and the Swap Definitions apply in relation to the Swap Transaction (Appendix A below). Notwithstanding the above, the 1999 ISDA Credit Derivatives Definitions (as published by the International Swaps and Derivatives Association, Inc.) apply to the definition of "Default Date" in paragraph 2 below.

This Confirmation supplements, forms part of, and is subject to, the 1992 ISDA Master Agreement dated as of [] as amended and supplemented from time to time (the "Agreement"), between you and us. All provisions contained in the Agreement govern this Confirmation except as expressly modified below. If such Agreement does not currently incorporate provisions relating to Physical Delivery of Bonds, you and we agree to use our best efforts promptly to negotiate an amendment to the Agreement incorporating such provisions as we may in good faith agree are necessary.

Party A and Party B each represents to the other that it has entered into this Transaction in reliance upon such tax, accounting, regulatory, legal, and financial advice as it deems necessary and not upon any view expressed by the other.

In this Confirmation (including the attached Appendix A), "Party A" means [Party] and "Party B" means [Counterparty].

The terms of the particular Bond Option Transaction to which this Confirmation relates are as follows:

1. General Terms:

Trade Date:	[]
Effective Date:	[Trade Date + 3 Business Days]
Termination Date:	DD/MM/YYYY
Option Style:	American
Option Type:	Call
Seller:	Party A
Buyer:	Party B
Bonds:	USD 10,000,000 stated principal amount of x.xx% exchangeable bonds issued by XYZ Corp (the "Issuer") due DD/MM/YYYY (ISIN No.)
Number of Options:	1
Option Entitlement:	USD 10,000,000
Multiple Exercise:	Inapplicable
Exercise Price:	An amount equal to the sum of (a) the product of (i) 100% (ii) the Option Entitlement and (iii) the number of Options exercised or deemed to be exercised on the relevant Exercise Date, and (b) the Additional Amount in paragraph 4. below.
Seller Business Day:	London
Calculation Agent:	Party A, whose determinations and calculations will be binding in the absence of manifest error. The Calculation Agent will have no responsibility for good faith errors or omissions in making any determination as provided herein.

2.   Procedure for Exercise:

Exercise Period: Until the Expiration Time on all Seller Business Days in the period from and including the Effective Date to and including the Expiration Date.

Expiration Date: The first to occur of:

   (a)   the date that is five Clearance System Business Days prior to the Termination Date

   (b)   two Seller Business Days following the Default Date

"Default Date" means any day upon which Party A gives notice to Party B that any of the following has occurred:

   (i)   Bankruptcy;

   (ii)   Failure to Pay;

   (iii)   Obligation Default;

   (iv)   Repudiation/Moratorium; or

   (v)   Restructuring

where:

"Obligations" means Bond or Loan; and

"Reference Entity" means the Issuer.

Expiration Time: 3.00 p.m. in the time zone of the Seller Business Day.

Exercise Date: The day during the Exercise Period on which the Buyer exercises the Option.

3.   Settlement Terms:

Settlement: Physical

Bond Payment: The Exercise Price

Settlement Date: Five Clearance System Business Days after the relevant Exercise Date.

Clearance System: The principal clearance system customarily used for settling trades in the Bonds, or any successor to or transferee of such clearance system. If the Clearance System ceases to clear the Bonds, the parties will negotiate in good faith to agree on another manner for delivery.

Clearance System Business Day: Any day on which the Clearance System is (or, but for the occurrence of a Settlement Disruption Event, would have been) open for the acceptance and execution of settlement instructions.

4.   Additional Amounts:

(a) Swap Cash Settlement Amount:

The Calculation Agent shall determine the Swap Cash Settlement Amount as provided below. If the Swap Cash Settlement Amount is payable by Party A it is a positive amount. If the Swap Cash Settlement Amount is payable by Party B it is a negative amount.

"Swap Cash Settlement Amount" means either

(i) an amount agreed between the parties as the amount payable in respect of the early termination of the Swap Transaction on the applicable Settlement Date; or

(ii) if the parties are unable to agree on the Swap Cash Settlement Amount by the Expiration Time on the applicable Settlement Date, an amount calculated by the Calculation Agent in accordance with Section 6(e)(ii)(1) of the 1992 ISDA Master Agreement, the necessary changes being made, as though (i) the Swap Transaction were the sole Terminated Transaction, (ii) the applicable Settlement Date were an Early Termination Date, (iii) Party B were the sole Affected Party and (iv) Market Quotation applies.

In both cases, the Swap Cash Settlement Amount shall be calculated on the basis that the Notional Amount equalled the Notional Reduction Amount.

(b) Early Call Premium:

If the Option is exercised on any Seller Business Day from and including the Effective Date to and including the day which is five Clearance System Business Days prior to [Effective date + [] Months], then, on the applicable Settlement Date, Party B will pay to Party A an additional amount in USD (the "Early Call Premium") as part of the Bond Payment, calculated in accordance with the following formula:

"Early Call Premium" means [Spread]% x Days/360 x Notional Amount where,

Days = the number of days from and including the Settlement Date to but excluding [Effective Date + [] Months]

"Notional Amount" has the value given to it in Appendix A hereto.

5.   Related Bond Transaction:

Option Buyer sells [] stated principal amount of the Bonds to [Party A] at a [clean/dirty] price of [   ]% on Trade Date, for value Effective Date.

6.   Account Details:

In respect of the Option:

Payments to Party A: To be advised.

Deliveries to Party B: To be advised.

7.   Notices:

Contact details (as at the Trade Date) for any notice required to be given hereunder are set out below:

[Party A]

Attn: Convertible Arbitrage Desk

Trading

Tel: +44 20 7888 4900

Ref: TCN Number []

Bond Settlements:

Tel: +44 20 7888 2510

Fax: +44 20 7883 7592

[Counterparty]

Attn: Please advise

Tel: Please advise

Fax: Please advise

Confirmation queries:

Asset Trading and Credit Derivatives Documentation Group

Tel: +44 20 7888 2493/3186

Fax: +44 20 7888 2725

[Party A] is regulated by The Securities and Futures Authority and has entered into this Transaction as principal. The time at which the above Transaction was executed will be notified to Party B on request.

Please confirm that the foregoing correctly sets forth the terms of our agreement by signing and returning this Confirmation.

Yours faithfully,

[Party]

By:_____

Name:

Title:

Confirmed as of the date first written above:

[COUNTERPARTY]

By:_____

Name:

Title:

Source: Credit Suisse First Boston LLC, used with permission.

APPENDIX A

TO CONFIRMATION BETWEEN [PARTY A] AND [COUNTERPARTY] (REFERENCE NO.: [])

SWAP TRANSACTION

Effective Date:	Settlement Date (as defined in Section 3 of this Confirmation)
Termination Date:	DD/MM/YYYY
Notional Amount:	USD 10,000,000
Calculation Agent:	Party A
Business Days:	London and New York
Fixed Amount(s):	
Fixed Amount Payer:	Party A
Fixed Amount Payer Payment Date(s):	Each DD/MM and DD/MM, commencing on the next scheduled Fixed Amount Payer Payment Date after the Effective Date and ending on the Termination Date (inclusive), all such dates subject to the Following Business Day Convention.
Fixed Amount(s):	USD xxx, on each Fixed Amount Payer Payment Date.
Floating Amounts:	
Floating Rate Payer:	Party B
Floating Rate Payer Payment Dates:	Each xx March, xx June, xx September and xx December, commencing on the next scheduled Floating Rate Payer Payment Date after the Effective Date and ending on the Termination Date, inclusive, subject to adjustment in accordance with the Following Business Day Convention.
Floating Rate Option:	USD-LIBOR-BBA
Designated Maturity:	Three months
Spread:	Plus [Spread] %
Floating Rate Day Count Fraction:	Actual/360
Reset Dates:	The first day of each Calculation Period.
Compounding:	Inapplicable

APPENDIX II CREDIT DEFAULT SWAP TERM SHEET

REFERENCE ENTITY NAME

PHYSICALLY SETTLED CREDIT PROTECTION TRANSACTION

INDICATIVE SUMMARY TERMS

The definitions and provisions contained in the 1999 ISDA Credit Derivatives Definitions, as supplemented by the Supplement Relating to Convertible, Exchangeable or Accreting Obligations dated November 9, 2001 and the Supplement Relating to Successor and Credit Events dated November 28, 2001 (the "Credit Derivatives Definitions"), as published by the International Swaps and Derivatives Association, Inc., are incorporated into this Indicative Summary Termsheet (the "Termsheet") and any subsequent Confirmation. In the event of any inconsistency between the Definitions and this Termsheet, this Termsheet will govern.

For the avoidance of doubt, where any term or condition is not set out in this Termsheet, the fallback or term or condition set out in the Definitions shall be deemed to apply.

1. General Terms

Trade Date:	DD/MM/YYYY
Effective Date:	DD/MM/YYYY
Scheduled Termination Date:	DD/MM/YYYY
Floating Rate Payer:	(the "Seller")
Fixed Rate Payer:	COUNTER-PARTY BANK (the "Buyer")
Calculation Agent:	Seller
Calculation Agent City:	London
Business Day:	New York & London
Business Day Convention:	Modified Following
Reference Entity:	REFERENCE ENTITY NAME

2. Fixed Payments

Fixed Rate Payer Calculation Amount:	USD 5,000,000
Fixed Rate Payer Payment	Each xx January, xx April, xx July, xx October, commencing on
Dates:	xx April YYYY
Fixed Rate:	x.xx% per annum
Fixed Rate Day Count Fraction:	Actual/360

3. Floating Payment

Floating Rate Payer Calculation
Amount:

USD 5,000,000

Conditions to Payment:

1. Credit Event Notice
   Notifying Party: Buyer or Seller

2. Notice of Publicly Available Information Applicable

3. Notice of Intended Physical Settlement

4. Credit Events

Credit Events:

The following Credit Event(s) shall apply to this Transaction:

- Bankruptcy
- Failure to Pay
- Obligation Acceleration
- Repudiation/Moratorium
- Restructuring

Grace Period Extension:

Not Applicable

Payment Requirement:

USD 1,000,000 or its equivalent in the relevant Obligation Currency

Default Requirement:

USD 10,000,000 or its equivalent in the relevant Obligation Currency

Obligations:

Obligation Category:

- Borrowed Money

Obligation Characteristics:

- None

5. Settlement Terms

Settlement Method:

Physical Settlement

Physical Settlement Period:

30 Business Days

Portfolio:

Exclude Accrued Interest

**Deliverable Obligation
Category:**

- Bond or Loan

**Deliverable Obligation
Characteristics:**

- Pari Passu Ranking
- Specified Currencies: Standard Specified Currencies
- Assignable Loan
- Consent Required Loan
- Transferable
- Not Contingent
- Maximum Maturity: 30 years
- Not Bearer

Excluded Deliverable
Obligations: Not Applicable

Escrow: Applicable

6. Dispute Resolution   Section 10.2 of the Credit Derivatives Definitions shall apply/is applicable.

7. Other Terms

Documentation: ISDA Confirmation to be provided by: [Party A]

Offices: [Party A]

                                Counterparty: London

Governing Law: The Governing Law of the applicable ISDA Master Agreement between the parties or, if no such agreement has been executed by the parties as of the Trade Date, English law.

By entering into a transaction with [Party A], you acknowledge that you have read and understood the following terms: [Party A] is acting solely as an arm's length contractual counterparty and not as your financial adviser or fiduciary unless it has agreed to so act in writing. Before entering into any transaction you should ensure that you fully understand its potential risks and rewards and independently determine that it is appropriate for you given your objectives, experience, financial and operational resources, and other relevant circumstances. You should consult with such advisers as you deem necessary to assist you in making these determinations. You should also understand that [Party A] or its affiliates may provide banking, credit and other financial services to any company or issuer of securities or financial instruments referred to herein, underwrite, make a market in, have positions in, or otherwise buy and sell securities or financial instruments which may be identical or economically similar to any transaction entered into with you. If we make a market in any security or financial instrument, it should not be assumed that we will continue to do so. Any indicative terms provided to you are provided for your information and do not constitute an offer, a solicitation of an offer, or any advice or recommendation to conclude any transaction (whether on the indicative terms or otherwise). Any indicative price quotations, disclosure materials or analyses provided to you have been prepared on assumptions and parameters that reflect good faith determinations by us or that have been expressly specified by you and do not constitute advice by us. The assumptions and parameters used are not the only ones that might reasonably have been selected and therefore no guarantee is given as to the accuracy, completeness, or reasonableness of any such quotations, disclosure or analyses. No representation or warranty is made that any indicative performance or return indicated will be achieved in the future. None of the employees or agents of [Party A] or its affiliates is authorised to amend or supplement the terms of this notice, other than in the form of a written instrument, duly executed by an appropriately authorised signatory and countersigned by you.

Source: Credit Suisse First Boston LLC, used with permission.

CHAPTER 9

Non-traditional Hedges

Markets can remain irrational longer than you can remain solvent.

—J.M. Keynes

Hedge fund managers employ a number of arbitrage strategies, variations of which can be applied to the convertible marketplace. The strategies include fixed-income arbitrage, relative-value arbitrage, and risk arbitrage, all of which can utilize convertible securities to create hedge opportunities. Arbitrageurs may use a combination of the positions discussed in this chapter to augment the traditional market-neutral, gamma, and option overlay strategies in their portfolios.

THE REVERSE HEDGE

This non-traditional but effective hedge aims to capture the temporary overvaluation of a convertible security. Sometimes called a "Chinese hedge," the reverse hedge is the opposite of a typical delta-neutral convertible/stock hedge. In this setup, the arbitrageur sells short the convertible while purchasing long the underlying common stock; in effect, the position is short volatility. This hedge opportunity often arises as a result of several situations: low liquidity in a popular convertible issue, high implied volatility that appears to be unsustainable, or simply the combination of a favorite issue in a currently favored industry. At times, the convertible market may experience excess demand for certain issues because of their size, quality, underlying stock, or industry, causing the bonds to become overvalued. In fact, it is not uncommon to find issues pushed to between 5 percent and 10 percent overvaluation, creating ample opportunities for the reverse hedge to prove profitable.

In fact, the practice of frequently establishing reverse hedge positions by hedge funds and trading desks provides liquidity to the convertible market.

At times the desired convertible security is either not immediately available in inventory or an outright seller has not been identified. In order to still facilitate a trade, the sell side may sell short the bonds to provide the buyer with the sought-after bonds.

To establish a successful reverse hedge, the arbitrageur must determine the appropriate hedge ratio between the short convertible position and the long position in the underlying stock. A neutral hedge may be desirable, as the hedge is established to take advantage of temporary convertible overvaluation and the intent would be to quickly cover the short position. The time risk is important, since most reverse hedges create a negative cash flow carry (due to the convertible's yield being much higher than that of the underlying stock) and as time passes the negative yield carry and theta can consume the valuation opportunity. Another risk to be considered stems from the inverse relationship between volatility and stock price: For example, were a reverse hedge established with a stock whose price then declined, volatility would likely increase, causing the option component of the convertible to increase in value, preventing the planned capture of the overvaluation. But declining stock prices and increasing volatility are also often associated with widening credit spreads, which have the opposite effect on convertible valuations. The arbitrageur thus needs to understand the position's omicron risk as compared to its vega risk to ensure that the hedge will pay off on the downside from one or both of these factors. Part of this consideration is to understand and set expectations regarding the extent of credit spread widening should the stock price weaken, and vice versa.

Although we noted above that the reverse hedge position appears to be short volatility, it is also indirectly long volatility through the short bond's exposure to credit spreads widening as a result of increasing volatility and a declining stock price. See Table 9.1. Because of this, the reverse stock hedge position may be set up with greater exposure to omicron risk than to vega, and still provide good returns. It should be noted, though, that the omicron payoff generated by increased volatility would not be as high as the directly correlated vega payoff because the correlation between volatility and credit spreads is not always high. This factor further distinguishes reverse hedges

TABLE 9.1   Hedge Profile Volatility and Spread Effects

	Stock Price	$\rightarrow$	Volatility	$\rightarrow$	OAS
Long convertible	Negative		Positive		Negative
Hedged convertible	No effect		Positive		Negative
Reverse hedge	No effect		Negative		Positive

from long convertible hedges, which are typically established with positions whose vegas are much higher than their omicrons. (The traditional convertible delta hedge with a high vega and low omicron is net long vega but, through the omicron exposure, the net vega is reduced, especially as the stock price declines.)

Characteristics to Identify the Opportunity

- Theoretically overvalued convertible that has historically traded near fair value or has a very volatile underlying stock that allows for extreme price convergence in the money or in the "busted" range.
- If shorting a convertible preferred, the dividend payment should not be due soon.
- The reason the convertible is expensive should be apparent and temporary, such as because of supply and demand shifts or recent "hot" underlying stock.
- The short bond position should be available to cover in a reasonably short time period.
- A positive trend in the underlying stock based on technical or fundamental analysis.
- High vega with high gamma or omicron.
- Upside convergence with high degree of certainty—make whole issues should be avoided because if provision is triggered the negative cash flow amount would be substantially larger.

Risks to Consider

- The convertible may remain overvalued, causing negative cash flow to eat away at the position's return profile.
- The short issue may be called in and the position must be delivered, forcing the hedge to be unwound at an inopportune time.
- The implied volatility may continue to increase, pushing the bond up in value.
- Credit improvement may occur, pushing the bond to trade on a higher price track.
- For issues with such features, extended put may be offered or make whole provision may be exercised.
- Underlying stock's dividend may be significantly reduced or eliminated, causing a stock price decline, higher volatility, and a commensurate increase in the convertible's value.
- Take-over may occur near current stock price but by an acquirer that has significantly better credit, or take-over put may be exercised.

The reverse hedge position is established when the convertible is overvalued and the ability to capture all or some of this overvaluation is likely. For example, let's assume the Texas Instruments 4.25 percent convertible bond due 2/15/2007 became very overvalued as a result of the high quality rating (S&P rated A–) in an industry group with very few issues of high quality, especially with some gamma. The demand for the issue pushed it to 7 percent overvalued, and a reverse hedge was established in the following manner. The common stock was trading at $36.60, while the convertible traded at $1,190 with a conversion premium of 44.5 percent. See Table 9.2. Fair value

TABLE 9.2   Long Stock and Short Convertible

Short Convertible	*Common Stock*				
		Symbol	TXN		
		Price $	36.60	Dividend $	—
		Volatility %	50	Yield	0.000%
	Convertible	Floor Yield	5.00	Quantity	100
		Symbol	TXN-X	Maturity	2/15/2007
		Price $	119.000	Coupon	4.25%
		Yield	3.57%	Conversion Ratio	22.4972
		Adj Strike $	14.093		
Profit & Loss Information	Hedge ratio: 48%	Holding period: *0.5* Months			
	% Change 1 Std. Deviation	–9.8%	Current	10.8%	
	Assumed Stock Px	33.02	36.60	40.56	
	Est Convertible Px	105.5	110.00	116.70	
	Convertible Px % Moves	–11.5%	–7.6%	–1.9%	
	Profit/Loss Long Stock	–3,902	0	4,316	
	Profit/Loss Short Convertible	13,500	9,000	2,300	
	P&L before Cash Flow	9,598	9,000	6,616	
	Short Income Due	–177	–177	–177	
	Total Profit/Loss	9,421	8,823	6,439	
	ROI	23.62%	22.12%	16.14%	
	Cost of Carry	–$57.55	–$57.55	–$57.55	
	Levered AROI	46.94%	43.96%	32.08%	

for the convertible issue was approximately $1,100. The arbitrageur shorts the bonds to willing buyers at this high price level while purchasing TXN stock long. The long position is purchased at a delta neutral hedge ratio of .48 with 1,090 shares long against 100M bond short. The reverse hedge generates a negative cash carry position, so either the price convergence must occur quickly or wide swings in the stock price must occur in order to generate a double-digit return on investment. The arbitrageur sets up this reverse hedge with the expectation that the valuation premium will bleed with reasonable moves in the stock price over the next week. As Table 9.2 indicates, if the stock declines one standard deviation over the next two weeks to $33 per share, the loss on the long position is $3,902, while the full potential gain on the short convertible position is $13,500, assuming the convertible reverts to fair value. The wide spread between the loss on the long position and the gain on the short position allows for a large margin of error should the implied volatility decline slightly. The opposite scenario is equally important: Should the stock price increase one standard deviation over the next two weeks to $40.56 per share, the gain on the long position is $4,316 while the short position gains a lesser amount at $2,300.

The long investment of 1,090 shares at $36.6 per share is $39,894, but, as seen in Figure 9.1, 2-to-1 leverage applied to this hedge would provide an even more attractive low-risk high return. What's more, this can be achieved over a very short holding period.

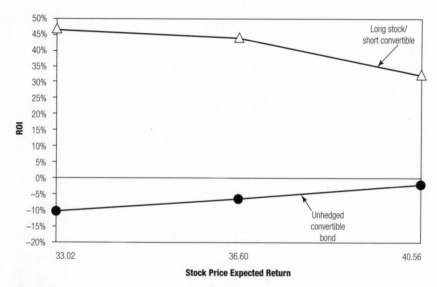

FIGURE 9.1 Convertible Reverse Hedge.

CALL OPTION HEDGE: MONETIZATION OF A CHEAP EMBEDDED CALL OPTION

Another non-traditional hedge opportunity that is sometimes available in the convertible marketplace involves a busted convertible with a call write overlay. That is to say, the call-option hedge requires identifying convertibles whose underlying stocks are undervalued to the extent that the convertible's embedded call option is no longer valued, while a corresponding listed call option is available, and with a reasonable amount of premium. In effect, the arbitrageur purchases the convertible's embedded call option for nothing—or nearly nothing—and sells a similar call option against it. Ideally, the call option or leap that is sold against the convertible should have a strike price at or very near the convertible's strike price, and may have a term as long as the call protection on the convertible. It gets a little tenuous to write a call option with a longer term than the convertible's call protected time frame because the option will have premium left even if the convertible is called. This type of hedge should be considered a long-term hedge because the option premium decay will take some time to realize. The hedge should also be looked at as a fixed-income alternative because the full return is expected to come from the convertible yield and the option premium received. The convertible's yield should thus be the same or better than yields available for the same credit in the fixed-income market.

Characteristics to Identify the Opportunity

- The convertible's price ignores the embedded option value.
- Availability of short-term listed option that decays quicker than the embedded convertible option.
- The stock exhibits some technical or fundamental sign of medium-term recovery.
- The credit quality of the issue is not suspect.
- Convertible's implied volatility significantly less than option's implied volatility.
- Option premium level is large enough to provide high return.
- Call option strike should be reasonably close to strike on the convertible.

Risks to Consider

- Upside loss should the implied option volatility increase while convertible's decreases further.
- Strike mismatch in the event of a take-over may make convertible's option worthless and short call valuable.
- Time decay slowly eats away attractive annualized return.

The following example and worksheets demonstrate this type of opportunity, using a hedge of the Analog Device 4.75 percent convertible due 10/01/2005 and rated BBB by S&P. In this scenario, the underlying stock corrected sharply and the convertible built a 200 percent premium (with the stock at $38 and the convertible at $876). The convertible's exercise price of $120 made it unlikely that conversion would occur during the call protected time frame. (The issue had call protection for 2.6 years longer.) The market not only priced the convertible's embedded call option at zero, but it also discounted the credit at a rate that was higher than the going rate for a similar credit, meaning that the convertible was undervalued even if valued only as a straight fixed-income issue. The yield to maturity in 4.5 years was 8.12 percent, and the call write could enhance this yield another 6 percent over the following two years. The sideways yield thus equaled 11 percent per year for the next 2 years, with the possibility that some additional upside return could be realized were the stock price to increase and cause the convertible to rally, provided that the stock price still stayed below the call strike on the option sold.

In this case, a two-year leap was available with a strike of $90 for approximately $8 per contract. With the convertible converting into 7.705 shares per bond, the following position was established. See Table 9.3.

As discussed earlier, in just about every hedge example, the use of borrowed funds enhances the risk-reward payoff of the hedge. In this situation, the levered hedge can be seen in Table 9.4; the returns are improved significantly by borrowing half of the investment amount at a small premium over LIBOR. See Figure 9.2.

STOCK HEDGE TO CAPTURE CHEAP OR FREE PUT OPTIONS

With deep-in-the-money convertibles, a hedge may be established as a means of capturing the issue's downside gamma, which is a result of its synthetic put option once again gaining value. More specifically, the put option in this case is actually the convertible's fixed-income value but viewed from the underlying common stock perspective. As discussed in Chapter 1, this convertible valuation approach is known as the "long stock plus put model." Since the fixed-income value of a convertible acts as a put value on the underlying common stock price, the arbitrageur may value the convertible as a long stock, plus a put option, plus the present value of the issue's yield advantage over the stock. Convertibles that are deep-in-the-money often trade close to parity value and are thus often theoretically undervalued. There are a number of reasons such in-the-money issues get mispriced: Long

TABLE 9.3 Analog Devices—Monetization of a Cheap Embedded Call Option

Company: Analog Devices
Sector: Technology
Industry: Semiconductor

Common Stock/Convertible Bond

		Description: 4.75% Convertible notes due 10/1/05					
Stock symbol:	ADI						
Price:	38.00	Price:	87.60	Invt value yield:	8.20%	Current Yield:	5.42%
Yield:	0%	Put feature:	None	Impl. Vol.:	13.28%	S&P/Moodys	BBB/NA
Beta:	1.18	Call feature:	10/03*ABS	Over/Under:	-4.22%	Conv. Ratio	7.705
Volatility:	50%	Next call price:	101.90	Implied Yield:	9.76%	Issue date:	9/26/00
Mkt Cap(mill $)	$13,601.11	Issue (mill $)	1,200	Over/Under:	-0.02%		

Convertible Analysis

Parity:	29.281	Conv. Prm:	199.17	Invest. Value:	87.07	Invst. Prm	0.61%
PV Yield Adv.:	178.02	Yield to Maturity:	8.12%	Over/Under:	-5.53%	Duration:	5.33

Risk-Reward Analysis

Est. Stock Move: 22.4 mths			CURRENT		
% Change Underlying:	-49.76%	-38.53%	0.00%	62.70%	99.05%
Stock Price:	19.09	23.35	38.00	61.82	75.63
Convertible Fair Price Track:	88.12	88.81	92.44	93.57	92.83
Convertible % Change:	0.59%	1.38%	5.53%	6.82%	5.97%
Convertible Total Return:	10.72%	11.52%	15.66%	16.95%	16.10%
Conversion Premium:	499.00%	393.50%	215.71%	96.42%	59.27%
Conv. % Participation:	0.00%	0.00%	N/A	27.04%	16.26%

(continues)

TABLE 9.3 *(Continued)* Call Write Payoff at Expiration

Hedge Analysis

Convertible Px:	87.60	Direction:	Sell	Price:	7.75
# Bonds Long:	100.00	Expiration:	Jan-03	Option Amount:	($5,425)
Long Inv. $:	$87,600	Implied Volatility:	70%	Protection $:	6.19%
Conversion Ratio:	7.705	Strike Price:	90.00	Protection %:	90.84%
Option Type:	Call	Quantity:	7	Total Investment:	$82,175

Hedge Risk-Reward

% Change Underlying:	−49.76%	−38.53%	0.00%	62.70%	99.05%	136.84%
Stock Price:	19.09	23.35	38.00	61.82	75.63	90.00
Convertible Fair Price Track:	88.12	88.81	92.44	93.57	92.83	93.74
Convertible % Change:	0.59%	1.38%	5.53%	6.82%	5.97%	7.01%
Est. Option Price Call 90:	0.00	0.00	0.00	0.00	0.00	0.00
Total Return:	18.03%	18.87%	23.29%	24.67%	24.76%	24.87%
AROI	9.66%	10.11%	12.48%	13.21%	13.27%	13.32%

Hedge Profit/Loss

100 Analog Devices	Total Investment: $82,175		Stock Px: 38.00		Convertible Px: 87.60	
% Change Underlying:	−49.76%	−38.53%	0.00%	62.70%	99.05%	136.84%
Stock Price:	19.09	23.35	38.00	61.82	75.63	90.00
Convertible Fair Price Track:	88.12	88.81	92.44	93.57	93.65	93.74
Convertible % Change:	0.59%	1.38%	5.53%	6.82%	6.91%	7.01%
P&L Convertible:	$520	$1,216	$4,845	$5,978	$6,050	$6,142
Profit/Loss Call 90:	$5,425	$5,425	$5,425	$5,425	$5,425	$5,425
P&L before Income:	$5,945	$6,635	$10,265	$11,395	$11,475	$11,565
Return % w/o Income:	7.23	8.07	12.49	13.87	13.96	14.07
AROI before Income:	3.88	4.33	6.69	7.43	7.48	7.54
Convertible Income:	$8,875	$8,875	$8,875	$8,875	$8,875	$8,875
Total Profit/Loss:	$14,820	$15,510	$19,140	$20,270	$20,350	$20,440
Total Return:	18.03%	18.87%	23.29%	24.67%	24.76%	24.87%
AROI:	9.66%	10.11%	12.48%	13.21%	13.27%	13.32%

TABLE 9.4 Analog Device—Option Monetization Hedge on Leverage

Hedge w/50% Margin

Convertible Price:	87.60	Direction:	Sell	Price:	7.75
# of Bonds Long:	100.00	Expiration:	Jan-03	Option Amount:	($5,425)
Net Long Amount:	$43,800	Impl. Vol.:	70%	Protection $:	12.38%
Conversion Ratio:	7.705	Strike Price:	90.00	Protection %:	90.84%
Option Type:	Call	Quantity:	7	Total Investment:	$38,375

Hedge Risk-Reward

Est. Stock Move: 22.4 mths

			CURRENT			Call 90
% Change Underlying:	-49.76%	-38.53%	0.00%	62.70%	99.05%	136.84%
Stock Price:	19.09	23.35	38.00	61.82	75.63	90.00
Convertible Fair Price Track:	88.12	88.81	92.44	93.57	92.83	93.74
Convertible % Change:	0.59%	1.38%	5.53%	6.82%	5.97%	7.01%
Est. Option Price—Call 90:	0.00	0.00	0.00	0.00	0.00	0.00
Total Return:	24.14%	25.65%	34.70%	37.61%	37.77%	37.86%
AROI:	12.93%	13.74%	18.59%	20.15%	20.24%	20.28%

Hedge Profit/Loss

100 Analog Devices	Current					
	Investment: $38,375		Stock PX: 38.00		Convertible PX: 87.60	
% Change Underlying:	-49.76	-38.53	0.00	62.70	99.05	136.84
Stock Price:	19.09	23.35	38.00	61.82	75.63	90.00
Convertible Fair Price Track:	88.12	88.81	92.44	93.57	93.65	93.74
Convertible % Change:	0.59%	1.38%	5.53%	6.82%	5.97%	7.01%
P&L Convertible:	520	1,216	4,845	5,978	6,050	6,142
Profit/Loss Call 90:	5,425	5,425	5,425	5,425	5,425	5,425
P&L before Income:	5,945	6,641	10,270	11,403	11,475	11,567
Return % w/o Income:	15.5	17.3	26.8	29.7	29.9	30.1
AROI before Income:	8.3	9.3	14.3	15.9	16.0	16.1
Convertible Income:	8,875	8,875	8,875	8,875	8,875	8,875
Margin Interest Charge:	-5,557	-5,673	-5,830	-5,845	-5,854	-5,912
Total Profit/Loss:	$9,263	$9,843	$13,315	$14,433	$14,496	$14,530
Total Return:	24.14%	25.65%	34.70%	37.61%	37.77%	37.86%
AROI%:	12.93	13.74	18.59	20.15	20.24	20.28

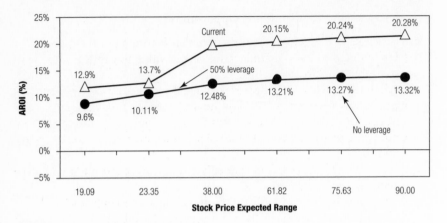

FIGURE 9.2   AROI Hedge Comparison: 50% Leverage versus No Leverage.

convertible buyers tend to buy convertibles with gamma and sell when the issue trades like stock, so they are natural sellers but not natural buyers of these issues. Also, undervaluation can stem from recent bad press or earnings announcements that cause excess selling, temporarily pushing an issue below fair value.

The capital requirements are low for in-the–money convertibles because of their high deltas and low conversion premiums. For this reason, they are very attractive to arbitrageurs as a means of capturing levered cash-flow returns or downside gamma (cheap puts). Because of their attractiveness, arbitrageurs may also set up issues even with a negative carry, as they expect to more than offset the loss through the capture of downside gamma. If, however, the position moves against them (going deeper in the money), they may attempt to effect a "flush-down." A "flush-down" is a convertible holder's creation of a coupon make-whole clause. In this scenario, the arbitrageur offers the issuing company the opportunity to repurchase the convertible and clean up its balance sheet. The company will typically offer the parity level in stock (in effect, converting the bond to stock), plus the present value of the remainder of the coupon payments through the period of call protection, discounted at an agreed-upon rate. This typically works out extremely well for the arbitrageur and, in many cases, for the issuing company as well.

Characteristics to Identify the Opportunity

- Theoretically undervalued convertible that is trading in-the-money.
- Close enough to fixed-income value or put value to capture value with reasonable stock price decline.
- Underlying stock with a bearish technical outlook or catalyst, such as weak relative strength, 200-day moving average break, negative EPS surprise, or declining EPS estimates.
- Underlying stock has potential for sharp price break based on excessive valuation.
- Balance sheet that is not in immediate question regarding liquidity or safety.
- Convertible with a yield advantage above the underlying stock.
- Call protection through at least the expected holding period.
- Downside stock price objective that offers convertible hedge total return well above target.

Risks to Consider

- Loss of call protection with no guarantee of last coupon or dividend payment.
- Credit deterioration as stock price declines—put strike moves down in this event.
- Stock short recall.
- Theta eats away yield advantage.

The in-the-money, theoretically inexpensive convertible does offer the bearish arbitrageur an appealing return potential. Arbitrageurs will set up positions in in-the-money convertible issues, provided they have a bearish opinion on them, and want to make this directional bet. To do so, the arbitrageur first purchases the in-the-money convertible and goes to a full delta hedge, one that is usually completely or very close to fully covered. If the underlying stock position moves up, the position trades dollars and the minimal cash flows provide some minor return. But since the put value is essentially not priced into the convertible's value, large profits can be made should the stock price decline significantly and the put option becomes valuable again. In effect, the convertible builds premium as the stock price declines and the premium represents profit potential.

Figure 9.3 demonstrates how the put-capture hedge works. Having set up the full delta neutral hedge at stock price A with the convertible at A1, when the stock price declines to price B, the convertible value declines to B1. As the convertible's value declines, it builds conversion premium as a result

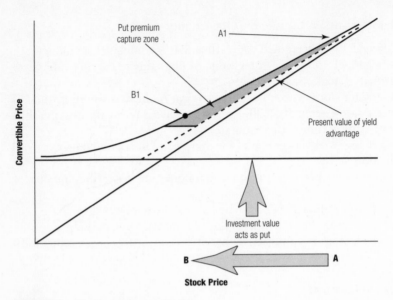

FIGURE 9.3   The Put-Capture Hedge.

of its price approaching the fixed-income component of the convertible. The convertible builds this premium on the downside because the probability of the issue being called for redemption or maturing at par value increases with lower stock prices. Of course, the convertible initially holds up at its fixed-income value even as the stock price continues to decline. The area marked "put premium capture" represents the return available to the arbitrageur.

Figure 9.4 tracks the convertible price, conversion parity level, and conversion premium as the underlying stock price declines. Let's assume that a 100 percent stock hedge was established when the convertible was in-the-money, at a price of 130 with a parity level of 128.5. Over the next month, as the stock price declined, the convertible declined in value to 109 and parity dropped to 95, providing a sizeable profit on the hedge as a result of the 13.5 percent premium expansion.

Once again, the directional bias needed to implement the "free put capture hedge" must be supported by fundamental, technical, and credit analysis. It is true, though, that the risk of loss on such a hedge is minimal, due to the fact that very little or no conversion premium is at risk and the hedge is completely or almost completely covered. In general, the risk of the non-leveraged "free put" hedge would be merely a low total return based only on the income flow from the long and short position that in many cases

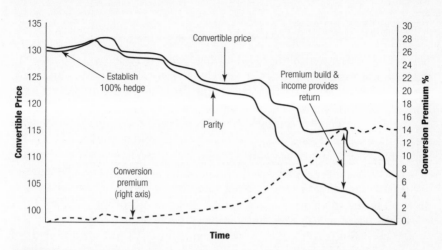

FIGURE 9.4 Convertible Price, Conversion Parity Level, and Conversion Premium as Stock Price Declines.

approaches the risk-free rate of return. Of course, some will say that if one is sure that the stock will decline in price, then one should just short the stock without the long convertible. The critical difference is that the naked short has unlimited upside risk, while the convertible hedge has nearly zero upside risk. If using leverage, it is important to note that the put capture hedge calls for the convertible to offer a yield advantage over the yield of the underlying stock, as a means of reducing the cost of the hedge.

Zero-coupon convertible securities (LYONs) are also good issues to use to demonstrate this hedge, since, in practice, they often present opportunities for the put capture hedge. Unlike a standard convertible's synthetic put option, the LYON has an actual put option and no current income flow. With no current income, the LYON is more sensitive to underlying stock price changes, and the in-the-money LYON can often quickly lose conversion premium and become very mispriced in the marketplace. Remember, a deep-in-the-money convertible can be priced at parity plus the present value of the yield advantage over the remaining period of call protection, plus a put option struck at the investment value of the convertible. Some zero coupons trading at low levels of implied volatility and that are deep-in-the-money, trade at parity because they have no yield advantage or even a negative carry and the put option is determined to be worthless over the call period with such a low implied volatility level.

CONVERGENCE HEDGES

The traditional convertible hedge involving long convertible and short the underlying stock is a convergence hedge on the upside because parity and theoretical value are certain to converge. As the stock price increases in value, the convertible's conversion premium declines because the option is deeper-in-the-money; ultimately, the two values converge. Two other convergence hedges that can be found occasionally in the convertible market take advantage of multiple convertibles issued by one company. Convergence opportunities between two convertibles from the same issuer may result because of differences in the two issues' implied volatility or because of significant differences in the credit spread assumptions for each. (See Appendix 9.1 for a partial listing of issuers with multiple convertibles outstanding.)

Many valid reasons exist for differences in OAS spreads and implied volatility spreads between two convertibles from the same issuer, and if the arbitrageur establishes a system to monitor "normal" relationships between them, he can identify divergences from the norm and discover new opportunities.

Implied Volatility Convergence

The implied volatility convergence hedge offers convergence without a directional bias. Purchasing long one convertible security and selling short another convertible security from the same company offers a low-risk way to take advantage of temporary market inefficiencies. In this strategy, the ideal hedge profile would be the purchase of an undervalued (below expected implied volatility) convertible and the simultaneous short sale of an overvalued (above expected implied volatility) convertible of the same issuer. But, more typically the arbitrageur will find the opportunity in which one security is fairly valued and the other is significantly mispriced. To identify the opportunity, the first step is to monitor the normal implied volatility relationship between two convertible issues from the same company, while making sure that the credit spread differences, call terms, and volatility skew are held constant or correctly accounted for. Once each issue is properly set up regarding issue-specific differences, the arbitrageur monitors the implied volatility spread between the two issues. Figure 9.5 shows a typical chart used to monitor the spreads. In this example, when a large divergence in implied volatility occurs between XYZ Co.'s A and B issues (vertical arrow), the hedge is established.

When setting up the hedge, the differences in equity sensitivity between the two issues must be neutralized. Matching the deltas of the issues by varying the amount of each issue owned neutralizes the equity sensitivity

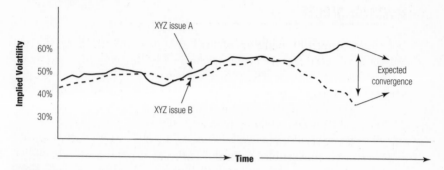

FIGURE 9.5 Chart Used to Monitor Spreads.

differences of the two issues. For example, the short bond position issue A has a .70 delta, while the long bond position issue B's delta is .60; therefore, shorting only 86 percent (delta of .60/delta of .70 = 85.7 percent) of issue A will neutralize the delta differences. The difference in the two issues' income flows is also critical because in some situations the position will have a negative carry. Theta differences can also cause some distress, so a rapid convergence to normal is generally necessary to avoid having to balance the different greeks between the two securities. The two major factors to consider with this type of hedge are first that the delta and gamma of the two issues will most likely be different and therefore the dollar amount long and short of each issue must be adjusted accordingly. Second, the position may create a negative cash carry as a result of shorting a bond with a higher yield or in a dollar amount large enough to offset the long position's income flow.

Characteristics to Identify the Opportunity

- Multiple issues from same company.
- Significant theoretical price discrepancies between two of the issues— break from the normal relationship.
- Vegas of each position and the expected move to normal for the spread creates a profit opportunity that meets or exceeds minimum return goals.
- Clear understanding of reason for mispricing and clear rationale for price convergence in near term.
- Current yields of the two issues not significantly different; preferably, the long candidate has a higher yield.
- Similar credit status or difference properly accounted for.
- Differences in greeks and drifts in greeks manageable to remain neutrally hedged.

Risks to Consider

- Credit risk may still remain, depending on long to short ratio.
- Convergence does not occur for a long period of time.
- Take-over occurs, with short rallying more than long.
- Significant greek mismatch allowing other risks to drive returns.

An example of a volatility convergence hedge can be seen in Table 9.5. XYZ Co. has two convertible issues outstanding. One issue is trading with an implied volatility of 25 percent, while the other is trading with an implied volatility of 45 percent. The expectation that the valuation between these two issues will converge provides the opportunity. It does not matter if the correct implied volatility is 25 percent, 45 percent, or somewhere in between, because it is the convergence to some normal spread or mean that creates the arbitrage profit. Since the convertible trading at an implied volatility of 45 percent is short and the convertible trading with an implied volatility is long, the amount of profit opportunity is based on the positions' vegas. If both issues converge to a 25 percent implied volatility, the short vega multiplied by the amount of bonds short and the 20-point move in volatility creates the return. Likewise, a convergence to 45 percent volatility creates a profit based on the long position's size multiplied by the long vega and the 20-point move in implied volatility. Of course for a convergence anywhere between the two, the return is a combination of the long and short vegas.

The return profile at each point of convergence is exceptional: Even if the two issues converge to a spread difference of as little as 10 percent, the annual return is still more than 12 percent with income and leverage.

An alternative to the convergence hedge is to set up two hedges from the same issuer, one a traditional hedge and the other a reverse hedge. The overvalued paper is established as a reverse hedge, while the fairly priced or inexpensive paper is set up as a normal delta neutral hedge. This may help matching the deltas a little easier, especially if the gammas are high, and rebalancing the hedge would also be easier. In the end, the convergence in valuation should achieve results similar to those for a single convergence hedge.

Credit Spread Convergence

The credit spread convergence hedge, like the implied volatility convergence hedge, seeks to exploit divergences from the normal relationship between two different convertible securities from the same issuing company. The OAS convergence hedges are similar to fixed-income arbitrage hedging that hedge funds and trading desks employ. There, fixed-income arbitrage requires identifying OAS spread differences that diverge from the normal be-

TABLE 9.5 Implied Volatility Convergence Hedge

	Security Description	Position Size	Price	Investment Amount	Delta	Vega	Implied Volatility	Current Yield
				Implied Volatility Convergence Hedge				
Short	XYZ Co. 5% due 3/15/07	(707)	1,150	($813,050)	0.75	0.3	0.45	4.35
Long	XYZ Co. 4.75% due 12/31/07	1,000	1,000	$1,000,000	0.61	0.25	0.25	4.75
	Net Investment—leverage 2 to 1			$500,000				

	Implied Volatility in 12 months						
	25%	30%	35%	40%	45%	50%	55%
Short Bond Return	$48,783	$36,587	$24,392	$12,196	$0	($12,196)	($24,392)
Long Bond Return	$0	$12,500	$25,000	$37,500	$50,000	$62,500	$75,000
Convergence Return	$48,783	$49,087	$49,392	$49,696	$50,000	$50,304	$50,609
Net bond interest	$12,150	$12,150	$12,150	$12,150	$12,150	$12,150	$12,150
Total Return	$60,933	$61,237	$61,542	$61,846	$62,150	$62,454	$62,759
AROI	12.19%	12.25%	12.31%	12.37%	12.43%	12.49%	12.55%

Note: P&L ignores changes in vega.

tween various debt issues from the same company. The convertible OAS convergence hedge seeks to exploit the same market anomaly. Like the volatility convergence hedge, the first step in identifying an opportunity to exploit is to set up a monitoring process.

By establishing a process to monitor the relationship between a company's various debt issues that adjusts for the security-specific (expected) differences, the arbitrageur can be quick to extract the inefficiencies when they occur. Figure 9.6 is an example of how monitoring can help in finding and understanding the OAS spread hedge opportunities.

The top chart shows the normal credit spread relationship between two of ABC Co.'s convertible issues, relative to the level of implied volatility. The issues have different terms to call, and because ABC #2 is subordinate to ABC

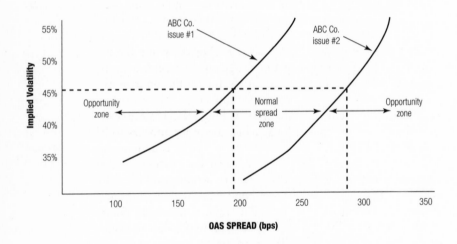

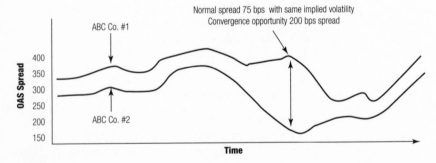

FIGURE 9.6   Normal Credit Spread Relationship.

#1 in the company's capital structure, a spread of 75 basis points is warranted. Also note that as implied volatility increases, the credit spreads increase and vice versa. The issues' implied volatility levels are both at 45 percent, meaning that the credit spread differences account for the anomaly if the spreads are wider than the normal. The opportunity to establish a convergence hedge occurs in the zones outside the normal OAS/ volatility curves. The lower chart in Figure 9.6 is used to monitor the spread relationship over time. This chart shows the spread widening from the normal 75 basis points to over 200 basis points and then converging back to the normal 75 basis points. The arbitrageur establishes a hedge when the spread is outside the normal range and attempts to capture the omicron in the positions.

The worksheet in Table 9.6 details the OAS spread convergence hedge. In this example, the current spread between ABC's two convertibles is 125 bps compared to the normal 75 bps, with an implied volatility of 45 percent for each issue. ABC #1 bond is trading at its normal OAS spread of 200 bps, while ABC #2 is trading at a wider 325 bps spread, 50 bps higher than its normal 275 bps. The ABC #1 bond is shorted, while the #2 bond is purchased with the appropriate amount to create a delta neutral dollar investment. As the table's bottom line shows, the profit opportunity is exceptional if the spread between the two issues converges close to the normal 75 bps. Since the arbitrageur is betting that the long bond is temporarily inefficiently priced and was purchased long, while the other appears to be fairly priced and shorted, the risk is that the mispriced bond is actually the short bond. On the worksheet above, the last column shows the risks that can occur if in fact the company's credit risk was deteriorating and the ABC #2 bond was reflecting this while the ABC #1 bond was lagging. Although both are expected to trade wider than normal if credit worsens, #2 bond's subordinate status will cause the spread between the two issues to widen to 125 bps, resulting in a loss. Like any hedge, an understanding of the creditworthiness and market-implied prices is critical to the success of this hedge, too. OAS convergence hedging can also be established by monitoring spreads in the CDS market relative to the convertible spreads, and setting up a similar convergence hedge between the CDS and convertible.

Characteristics to Identify the Opportunity

- Company has multiple convertible issues.
- The OAS spread between the two issues is abnormally wide or narrow.
- The omicron of each position is high enough to extract profits from the spread changes.
- The yield differential does not create a negative cash flow position.

TABLE 9.6 OAS Spread Convergence Hedge over Time

OAS Spread Convergence Hedge

	Security Description	Position Size	Price	Investment Amount	Delta	Omicron	Implied Volatility	Current OAS Spread	Current Yield
Short	ABC #1 5% due 1/15/07	1,045	850	($888,250)	0.45	0.20	0.45	200	5.88
Long	ABC #2 4.75% due 12/31/06	1,250	800	$1,000,000	0.40	0.23	0.45	325	5.94
	Net Investment			$500,000				125	

OAS Spread in 3 Months ABC #1

	185	190	195	200	210	220	230	240
Short Bond Return	($26,648)	($17,765)	($8,883)	$0	$17,765	$35,530	$53,295	$71,060

OAS Spread in 3 Months ABC #2

	260	265	270	275	285	295	305	365
Long Bond Return	$149,500	$138,000	$126,500	$115,000	$92,000	$69,000	$46,000	($92,000)
ABC #1 & #2 Spread bps	75	75	75	75	75	75	75	125
Convergence Return	$122,853	$120,235	$117,618	$115,000	$109,765	$104,530	$99,295	($20,940)
Net bond interest	$7,125	$7,125	$7,125	$7,125	$7,125	$7,125	$7,125	$7,125
Total Return	$129,978	$127,360	$124,743	$122,125	$116,890	$111,655	$106,420	($13,815)
AROI	26.00%	25.47%	24.95%	24.43%	23.38%	22.33%	21.28%	-2.76%

- The differences in bond covenants, subordination, call terms, put protection, and so on are understood and modeled correctly.
- The differences in greeks are manageable.

Risks to Consider

- Credit exposure may still remain.
- Take-over occurs and the price impact works against the hedge.
- Short bond has take-over put while long bond does not.
- Relative greeks are unstable, causing unintentional bleed.

The OAS convergence hedge can boost the performance of a convertible arbitrage shop with a strong credit support staff or with fixed-income arbitrage experience. Both types of convergence hedging will add to the opportunity set of the arbitrageur with a market neutral investment mandate.

MERGER AND ACQUISITION RISK ARBITRAGE TRADES

Typically, M&A arbitrage involves purchasing long the stock of the target company and shorting the stock of the acquiring company in order to capture the price move of the to-be-acquired company's stock up to the deal level and to benefit from further weakness in the acquiring company's stock.

The convertible arbitrageur can similarly participate in M&A activity via the convertible marketplace. Purchasing long the target company's convertible and shorting the stock of the acquirer at a delta neutral hedge ratio may offer an interesting hedge opportunity. The long convertible position is a lower risk alternative than using stock, as it offers better downside support if the deal falls through, plus some cash flow as you wait for the deal to be finalized. Upon completion of the deal, the hedge may continue to be held if the convertible converts into the new entity, or maybe closed if the deal was all or part cash. Convertible arbitrage shops with in-house M&A expertise can leverage the knowledge of the various deals and consider the profit potential in the convertible hedge. One specific risk with hedging M&A deals in the convertible market, however, is if an acquisition offer triggers a take-over put and the bond trades up near par while parity remains below par, and an offer at a higher price occurs. In this scenario, the higher price offer will push parity higher, but if it does not push it above the par put value, the convertible will not participate any further, thus capping the upside return potential. Once again, the arbitrageur must decide if their in-house expertise is adequate to evaluate the M&A deal, its probability of occurring, time horizon, and impact on the convertible hedge before considering this technique as an addition to the opportunity set.

RESET CONVERTIBLES (OR DEATH SPIRAL CONVERTIBLES)

Some publicly traded convertibles and many privately placed convertibles offer the buyer a series of conversion ratio resets to protect the purchaser in the event that the stock price declines. The reset is generally triggered at predetermined dates if the underlying stock price declines below some predetermined levels. The long buyer therefore has the conversion rate increased as the stock price drops below the threshold and this reset keeps the convertible from declining significantly. In the mid-1990s, many of the large banks in Japan issued very substantial convertible issues with reset features because most long investors were not interested in the convertibles, but the inducements made them attractive to the hedge community. To offer such a potentially diluting feature, the issuing company obviously is in need of capital and believes that this infusion will get the company back on track to profitability, making the reset worth the price.

As you might expect, the reset feature can have a very costly, negative impact on a company whose creditworthiness and stock price are under severe pressure. As the stock price declines, the hedge calls for shorting additional shares as the reset kicks in, or is expected to kick in. The stock shorting puts additional pressure on the stock price, pushing it farther down in value and calling for additional shares to be shorted as the conversion rate ratchets up again. As the process repeats itself, each time at lower stock prices, it becomes clear how the nickname "death spiral convertible" arose. Unfortunately for the issuer, the arbitrageur may not care if the company survives due to the shorts being so highly profitable all the way down.

CAPITAL STRUCTURE HEDGE

Opportunities arise among the various forms of capital employed by a firm. Identifying relative price discrepancies among the securities in a firm's capital structure and hedging one against the other is a technique often employed in hedge portfolios. Arbitraging relative price discrepancies between the convertible and the company's other debt is the most common capital structure trade engaged in convertible arbitrage portfolios. For example, purchasing a long convertible and shorting the high yield debt of the same company essentially creates a free option and neutralizes the credit risk. In other cases, the short high yield position serves as a convergence hedge and money can be made on both sides of the hedge. But typically, the primary objective of the short debt position in the capital structure hedge is to eliminate or reduce the credit risk in a traditional convertible hedge position.

Another type of capital structure hedge is done by purchasing long straight debt and short selling an overvalued convertible preferred stock. This has the benefit of locking in a positive yield spread, lowering the time to maturity, and moving up in the capital structure pecking order. Often the equity and debt markets are at odds with the total value of a firm. In some instances, the equity markets place a high (low) market value on the company, while the debt market places a low (high) value on the company. For example, the Pan Am Airlines convertible and straight bonds sold at very depressed levels for many months during the waning years of their existence, while the company's equity market cap appeared relatively large. This presented a good opportunity to purchase the bonds (trading flat) and short the stock at a delta near one. Many alternative scenarios using the full spectrum of capital markets are available. Similarly, many of the Internet and telecom convertibles issued during the late 1990s boom also presented opportunities because many of the companies' stocks were priced at very high market caps, while much of the debt remained very low grade.

Characteristics to Identify the Opportunity

- Market values one piece of capital structure significantly different from another piece (discount rates).
- Minor differences in credit standing understood but credit analysis indicates spreads are not properly priced.
- Securities move away from their normal historical relationship.
- Liquidity differences alone do not account for the anomaly.

Risks to Consider

- Bankruptcy causes pieces to be priced significantly different.
- Negative cash carry becomes burdensome.
- Merger or acquisition negatively impacts one or both sides of hedge.
- Greeks are unstable or become too costly to protect (other greeks bleed into return).

The Amazon convertible combined with Amazon's straight high yield security offered an interesting capital structure hedge. In mid-March 2000, the Amazon 4.75 percent convertible due 2009 was trading at 40 percent of par with a yield to maturity of over 19 percent, but with very little value assigned to the embedded call option. At the same time, Amazon's 10 percent straight bond due 2008 was trading at 58 percent of par with a yield to maturity around 15 percent. Also, the latter bond did not actually pay a coupon of 10 percent, since it was a zero coupon with a clause to start paying a cash interest payment on May 1, 2003. Purchasing 145 convertibles long at 40 and shorting 100 Amazon high yield at 58 creates an equal offsetting dollar investment netting to zero. By mid-July 2000 the Amazon convertible traded at 54, while realizing a net gain before income of $20,300. The Amazon high yield bond traded at 66 for a net loss of $8,000 on the short position. The combined hedge realized a net gain of $12,300 on a net investment close to zero. One risk in this type of hedge is that the long position is larger than the short position, leaving the credit exposure in the position net long. Although many applications of capital structure hedges are designed to remove all credit exposure from a traditional convertible hedge, this hedge was not set up to remove all credit exposure but instead to take advantage of some of the expected convergence in capital structure pricing.

DISTRESSED CONVERTIBLE HEDGE OR NEGATIVE GAMMA HEDGE OPPORTUNITIES

Convertibles that decline in price and fall into the distressed credit category often exhibit negative gamma as a result of the high correlation between their companies' plunging equity values and the corresponding credit spread widening (see Chapters 3 and 4). When this happens, the convertible arbitrageur loses the ability to cover some of the short position and lock in a profit from the decline because the convertible declines in value, too, often with the stock on a delta of 1.0 or higher. In fact, the arbitrageur will even need to add to the short side of the hedge in order to stem the losses from the declining long position, the opposite of what a traditional hedge would call for.

Figure 9.7 demonstrates the long convertible and short stock adjustments along the convertible price track. Establishing a traditional hedge in the hybrid range requires either adding to the stock hedge as convertible and stock price rises cause the delta to increase, or covering some of the short position as price declines cause the delta to decrease. But, when convertible prices fall into the distressed zone, the short position must actually be increased as the delta rises and the gamma turns negative.

Negative Gamma Bankruptcy Valuation or Prediction

Convertibles trading in the negative gamma distressed zone can also offer opportunities to the astute credit-aware arbitrageur. Arbitrage shops with

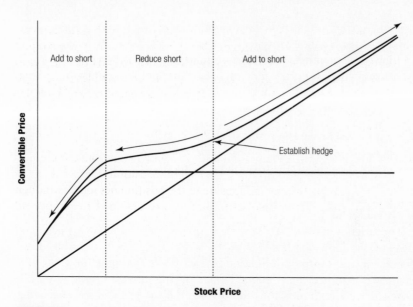

FIGURE 9.7 Long Convertible and Short Stock Adjustments.

strong distressed credit analysts will take advantage of the distressed convertible market just as they do the distressed high yield and private debt markets. Should the arbitrageur and/or analyst staff identify a convertible issuer that in all probability will go bankrupt, a convertible hedge can be established to create a net short position in hopes the company does not survive. A full dollar hedge will offer significant returns if the liquidation value of the bankrupt convertible (recovery rate) is above zero, which is often the case (distressed high yield issues have historically paid off 30 cents on the dollar).

Characteristics to Identify the Opportunity

- Busted convertible trading in distressed zone (delta near or greater than 1.0).
- Credit analysis determines that the company has a very slim chance of remaining a going concern.
- Ample stock-borrows and listed options available.
- Asset recovery rate for bondholder in bankruptcy well above zero.

Risks to Consider

- Wrong directional bet on the credit: stock and convertible move up sharply.

- Asset recovery rate is below estimate.
- Stock hedge is called away.
- Company is acquired prior to re-organization or bankruptcy.
- The following greeks are high and may be unstable—omicron, gamma, upsilon, and rho.
- Any other positive credit event.

The profit in this hedge is a result of the convertible bond value bottoming out near the expected recovery rate while the stock goes to zero, or very close to zero. It is thus imperative that the "predicted" bankruptcy hedge is established only after the convertible reflects extreme credit duress, otherwise the convertible may drop in value more than the equity (delta > 1.0). The worksheet in Table 9.7 shows how this hedge works on the downside. The stock is shorted at a rate that equates to a dollar hedge near 100 percent of the long bond value. In the worksheet, the convertible drops 62.9 percent over a 6-month holding period, while the equity declines 97.5 percent. It is assumed that the bond stops paying interest on the downside and the stock short ratio is constant throughout. As you can see, this hedge is not a market neutral hedge profile but a directional hedge with substantial upside risk. To mitigate the risk, the arbitrageur must actively reduce the hedge ratio as the stock price appreciates and/or purchase long-out-of-the-money call options at a strike price that protects enough of the capital to move the risk-reward to a more neutral profile (see Chapter 7 for examples). The risk-reward in Figure 9.8 becomes a worst case scenario on the upside with no hedge adjustments and no long call protection (we will discuss this later in this section).

The bankruptcy hedge is in most cases a highly specialized hedge. Every so often, a more neutral hedge can be established with the use of long call options and some active rebalancing on the upside. It would be uncommon to ever have a significant portion of any convertible arbitrage portfolio in this type of hedge without active rebalancing and some sort of option protection. See Figure 9.8.

Negative Gamma Bull Hedge

The other convertible hedge opportunity in the distressed credit zone occurs when the arbitrageur determines that the market has over-reacted to an issue's credit concerns. In this situation, the arbitrageur hedges at the delta neutral hedge ratio determined from the credit assessment he has made. The expected credit improvement pushes the convertible back up into positive gamma territory. Should the hedge work out on the upside, the entire credit spread narrowing will accrue to the arbitrageur, while the loss on the short side of the position is minimal.

TABLE 9.7 Negative Gamma Hedge—Bankruptcy—XYZ Company

Convertible	*Common Stock*						
		Symbol	XYZ				
		Price $	3.96	Dividend $			—
		Volatility %	77	Yield			0.000%
	Convertible	OAS spread 975		Quantity			100
		Symbol	XYZ-X	Maturity			11/15/06
		Price $	51.375	Conv. Prem.			471.65 %
		Yield	9.73%	Coupon			5.00 %
				Conversion Ratio			22.6950

Short Stock	*Short Stock*						
	Symbol	XYZ	Quantity	12,500	Hedge $ near 100% but ratio hedge much higher		
	Price $	3.96	Hedge $	96.34%			
	Fed Fund Rate	3.00%	Hedge %	550.78%			

Profit & Loss Information	% Change 1 std. Deviation	−97.5%	−30.3%	Current	43.4%	66.4%	102.0%
	Assumed Stock Px	0.10	2.76	3.96	5.68	6.59	8.00
	Est Convertible Px	19.05	36.25	51.38	57.00	65.00	79.00
	Convertible Px % Moves	−62.9%	−29.4%	0.0%	10.9%	26.5%	53.8%
	Est *Short* Stock Px	0.10	2.76	3.96	5.68	6.59	8.00
	Short Px % Moves	97.5%	30.3%	0.0%	−43.4%	−66.4%	−102.0%
	Profit/Loss Convertible	−32,330	−15,130	0	5,620	13,625	27,620
	Income/Dividend/ Short Interest	−133	58	2,729	1,445	2,975	3,107
	Profit/Loss *Short Stock*	48,250	15,000	0	−21,500	−32,875	−50,500
	Total Profit/Loss	15,787	−72	2,729	−14,435	−16,280	−19,773
	ROI 2 to 1 Leverage	61.45%	−0.28%	10.62%	−59.19%	−63.37%	−76.97%

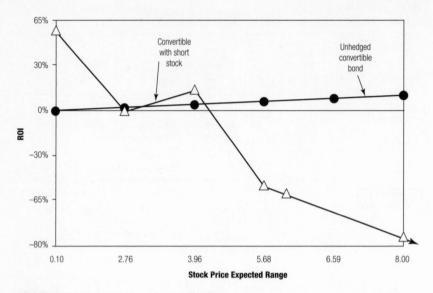

FIGURE 9.8   Negative Gamma—Bankruptcy.

Characteristics to Identify the Opportunity

- Busted convertible trading at a delta close to 1.0.
- Credit that offers a high probability of improving.
- Negative gamma position that should move to a positive gamma on the upside.
- Put options available for additional downside coverage.

Risks to Consider

- Wrong directional bet on the credit causing hedge ratio to be light.
- Take-over from a company with a lower credit quality and bond does not offer take-over put protection.
- High and potentially unstable greeks, including omicron, gamma, upsilon, and rho.
- Any negative credit event.

The negative gamma bull hedge worksheet example in Table 9.8 can be seen below. The return profile at the bottom of the worksheet looks much like a long equity position, offering the same upside positive return as it does

TABLE 9.8 Negative Gamma Bull Hedge—XYZ Company

Convertible	*Common Stock*						
		Symbol	XYZ				
		Price $	3.96	Dividend $		—	
		Volatility %	77	Yield		0.000%	
	Convertible	OAS spread 975		Quantity		100	
		Symbol	XYZ-X	Maturity		11/15/06	
		Price $	51.375	Conv. Prem.		471.65 %	
		Yield	9.73%	Coupon		5.00 %	
				Conversion Ratio		22.6950	

Short Stock	*Short Stock*					
	Symbol	XYZ	Quantity	1,500	Hedge ratio at expected upside delta & poor downside coverage	
	Price $	3.96	Hedge $	11.56%		
	Fed Fund Rate	3.00%	Hedge %	66.09%		

Profit & Loss Information							
% Change 1 Std. Deviation	−97.5%	−30.3%	Current	43.4%	66.4%	102.0%	
Assumed Stock Px	0.10	2.76	3.96	5.68	6.59	8.00	
Est Convertible Px	19.05	36.25	51.38	57.00	65.00	79.00	
Convertible Px % Moves	−62.9%	−29.4%	0.0%	10.9%	26.5%	53.8%	
Est *Short* Stock Px	0.10	2.76	3.96	5.68	6.59	8.00	
Short Px % Moves	97.5%	30.3%	0.0%	−43.4%	−66.4%	−102.0%	
Profit/Loss Convertible	−32,330	−15,130	0	5,620	13,620	27,620	
Income/Dividend/ Short Interest	−468	−219	2,075	1,047	2,105	2,121	
Profit/Loss *Short Stock*	5,790	1,800	0	−2,580	−3,945	−6,060	
Total Profit/Loss	−27,008	−13,549	2,075	4,087	11,780	23,681	
ROI	−105.13%	−52.74%	8.08%	15.91%	45.85%	92.18%	

downside negative returns. Once again, the downside protection of the hedge can be improved by purchasing long put options on the underlying stock and/or adding to the stock short as the stock price declines. The hedge is established with an upside move in mind and clearly does not provide protection on the downside. The dollar protection of the short position is only

11.56 percent of the long, while the hedge ratio is 66 percent, offering no meaningful protection if stock prices decline. Of course, correctly determining the credit improvement and subsequent upside move in the convertible can be very profitable. Like the bankruptcy hedge, in practice a hedge like this would be rare without some form of downside protection and active rebalancing. See Figure 9.9.

Active Rebalancing of the Negative Gamma Hedge

The two gamma hedge examples shown previously are highly unrealistic in that they assume that the arbitrageur establishes a passive hedge. The risk-reward profile of a passive negative gamma hedge is unattractive if not ugly, but the active gamma hedge provides some exceptional opportunities. In the worksheet in Table 9.9 the arbitrageur identifies that the original hedge assuming bankruptcy is wrong (96 percent dollar hedge and 550 percent ratio hedge) and adjusts the hedge to the bull gamma ratio (12 percent dollar hedge and 66 percent ratio hedge) as the stock price appreciates. Assuming the company's stock moves up as it gains access to capital or some other positive credit event occurs, the arbitrageur adjusts the hedge ratio to reflect the "bull case" on the upside and the hedge can again become profitable. If a negative credit event occurs, the hedge ratio would again need to be increased to the bankruptcy ratio. The risk-reward graph in Figure 9.10 starts to look more neutral with active hedging; with option hedge overlays, one can easily achieve a neutral hedge.

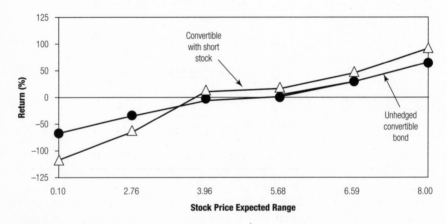

FIGURE 9.9   Negative Gamma—Bull Hedge.

TABLE 9.9 Negative Gamma Hedge—Rebalancing Hedge Ratio—XYZ Company

Convertible	*Common Stock*						
		Symbol	XYZ				
		Price $	3.96	Dividend $			—
		Volatility %	77	Yield		0.000%	
	Convertible	OAS spread 975		Quantity		100	
		Symbol	XYZ-X	Maturity		11/15/06	
		Price $	51.375	Conv. Prem.		471.65 %	
		Yield	9.73%	Coupon		5.00 %	
				Conversion Ratio		22.6950	

Short Stock	*Short Stock*						
	Symbol	XYZ	Quantity	−12,500			
	Price $	3.96	Hedge $	−96.34%	Adjust stock hedge on upside		
	Fed Fund Rate	3.00%	Hedge %	−550.78%			

Profit & Loss Information	# of Shares short	12,500	12,500	12,500	1,500	1,500	1,200
	% Change 1 Std. Deviation	−97.5%	−30.3%	Current	43.4%	66.4%	102.0%
	Assumed Stock Px	0.10	2.76	3.96	5.68	6.59	8.00
	Est Convertible Px	19.05	36.25	51.38	57.00	65.00	79.00
	Convertible Px % Moves	−62.9%	−29.4%	0.0%	10.9%	26.5%	53.8%
	Est *Short* Stock Px	0.10	2.76	3.96	5.68	6.59	8.00
	Short Px % Moves	97.5%	30.3%	0.0%	−43.4%	−66.4%	−102.0%
	Profit/Loss Convertible	−32,330	−15,130	0	5,620	13,620	27,620
	Income/Dividend/ Short Interest	−133	58	2,729	1,246	2,105	2,107
	Profit/Loss *Short* Stock	48,250	15,000	0	−12,040	−3,945	−5,454
	Total Profit/Loss	15,787	−72	2,729	−5,174	11,780	24,273
	ROI 2 to 1 Leverage	61.45%	−0.28%	10.62%	−20.14%	45.85%	94.49%

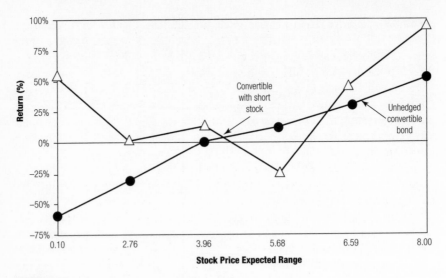

FIGURE 9.10 Negative Gamma—Rebalancing.

Hedge opportunities in the negative gamma range of the convertible price track should be considered opportunistic and the options market may be considered as catastrophic insurance to protect the extremes. With active rebalancing in this highly volatile portion of the convertible marketplace, the arbitrageur can achieve some exceptional returns, albeit with slightly more risk. The credit spread risk, recovery rate risk, gamma risks, and event risks are all very high, offering high returns for the astute arbitrageur. Because event risks are very high in this segment of the market, the delta/hedge ratio mismatch is also a major concern due to "jumps" in the equity price in one direction or another. In some jump price move situations that move against the initial hedge, the re-adjustment of the hedge can keep losses manageable. In situations in which the rebalance will lock in too large a loss, then the appropriate option overlay (long put or long call) should be considered. If the cost of the option overlay is too high, then the arbitrageur should pass on this hedge opportunity.

Hedging Mandatory Issues

Stock hedging with mandatory issues offers some unique advantages and problems. The mandatory convertible market offers high dividend yields on the long side of the hedge and when combined with the short interest rebate, they may offer the best total yields available in the marketplace. Unfortunately, these high yields come with a hedge that offers very little gamma trading opportunities and can be subject to a high degree of premium decay in the last few quarters of the security's life. As discussed in Chapter 3, the gamma of DECS structure will turn negative on the downside because of the increasing delta, causing the arbitrageur to add to the short position when a stock price declines, while doing the opposite when a stock price increases. Trading profits will be very hard to come by due to the downside's increasing delta and negative gamma, and the upside's decreasing delta. Therefore, arbitrageurs must find mandatory issues that are significantly undervalued, while also avoiding a high degree of theta that could eat away the income from the dividend.

The DECS' embedded long and short call options should both be evaluated. Finding an issue with a low-implied volatility level for the embedded long call and a high-implied volatility for the embedded short call option offers the best chance of realizing some profit from under-valuation. The DECS structure has embedded long vega risk as a result of the embedded long call, but also short vega risk as a result of the embedded short call option. Since the short call option has a higher conversion rate than the long call option, the structure will be net short vega if the stock price is between the two conversion trigger prices. The closest option to the current price will have additional influence on the pricing of the security with respect to volatility. Finding opportunities around ex-dates for the mandatory convertible is also preferred.

Characteristics to Identify the Opportunity

- Embedded call option closest to current stock price is mispriced.
- Both embedded options mispriced.
- Mandatory dividend yields significantly larger than underlying stock dividend yield.
- Present value of mandatory dividend discounted at a higher rate than appropriate.
- During periods of high volatility, opportunity to hedge DECS with stock prices near the lower trigger, with the expectations of selling the volatility in the short call at a high level.
- During periods of low volatility, look for hedge opportunities with DECS trading near the upper strike price, where the long call may be purchased cheaply.

Risks to Consider

- Credit rating is compromised and discount rate for dividend increases.
- Volatility shifts, leaving the long vega or short vega.
- Theta risk eats away yield—stand still yield much lower than current yield.

The hedge worksheet in Table 9.10 demonstrates a stock hedge with a DECS convertible that is undervalued and offers a significant yield advantage to capture. The convertible yields 11.57 percent, while the stock yields only 0.38 percent. In this example, the DECS is 2.3 percent undervalued: Should it move back to the expected valuation level, the three-month return is significant. The position consists of long 3,400 shares of the convertible and short 2,100 shares of the underlying stock. The hedge ratio need only be 80 percent because the convertible is expected to decline only half as much as

TABLE 9.10   Stock Hedge with a DECS Convertible

Capital One Financial		DECS Hedge Worksheet			
Common Stock	COF				
Stock Price	27.87	Dividend			$ 0.0267
Stock Volatility	41	Yield			0.383%
DECS Terms					
Symbol	COFPRC	Expiration			12/16/04
Price	$ 27.000	Life to Exp. (yrs)			2.2739
Yield	11.57%	Qtrly Div			0.7813
Lower Strike	$ 63.910	Upper Strike			$ 78.610
Lwr Cnv Ratio	0.7824	Upper Cnv Ratio			0.6361
Lower Px	$ 1.712	Upper Px			$ 0.997
Implied Vol	41	Implied Vol.			41
% Change 0.25 years	−20.5%	−14.5%	Current	14.5%	20.5%
Assumed Stk Px	22.157	23.829	27.870	31.911	33.583
Est DECS Px	24.182	25.467	27.612	31.181	32.222
DECS Px Moves %	−10.44%	−5.68%	2.30%	15.49%	19.34%
Total Return	−7.54%	−4.23%	5.19%	16.94%	22.23%
DECS Shares	3400	$82,219	$86,588	$91,800	$106,015	$109,555
Stock Shares	2100	$46,529	$50,041	$58,527	$67,013	$70,525
P/L DECS ($)	−$9,581	−$5,212	$2,111	$14,215	$17,755
P/L Short Stock ($)	$11,998	$8,486	$0	−$8,486	−$11,998
Stock Div ($)	−$56	$0	−$56	$0	−$56
DECS Div ($)	$2,656	$0	$2,656	$0	$2,656
Short Int ($)	$174	$94	$219	$126	$264
Total P/L ($)	$5,192	$3,368	$4,931	$5,855	$8,622
ROI (%)	5.66%	3.67%	5.37%	6.38%	9.39%
AROI (%)	22.94%	29.76%	21.78%	51.73%	38.09%

the stock on the downside, allowing for very good protection without giving up upside return. Because the stock price is below the lower strike, the position will offer a relatively reliable tracking with the stock price. Indeed, as the worksheet shows, should the stock price increase from the current price of $27.87 to $33.58, the convertible moves from its current price of $27 to $32.22, tracking closely with the stock price move. But, by capturing the slight under-valuation and the high dividend yield using only a partial hedge, the 3-month return is 9.39 percent and the annual return would be 38 percent. A move to the downside stock price of $22.16 produces a 3-month return of 5.66 percent with an annual return of 22.94 percent. Obviously, using leverage will significantly enhance the return profile of this position. Should the position not return to the expected valuation track, the combination of the high dividend yield, the short interest rebate, and some dynamic trading opportunities should still provide an annual return in the mid-teens.

BASKET HEDGING EQUITY DELTA

In some situations, creating a basket of long convertible issues that are highly correlated with each other and /or an index offers the arbitrageur better liquidity and even the ability to hedge issues with no stock borrow or very limited borrow. For example, the South East Asian convertible market offers many convertibles, but with poor access to stock borrow. Also, in some countries it is illegal to short stock, making convertible arbitrage difficult. The basket hedge approach can be less costly and less time consuming to monitor and rebalance than would be the individual hedges in the basket. The increase in exchange traded funds, derivatives on industry indexes, and closed end funds have also expanded the opportunity set for basket hedging.

The drawbacks to hedging with a highly correlated, but not 100 percent correlated, position is that the correlation for one or more positions moves counter to the arbitrageur's expectations for a significant period of time or to a significant amount. The risk of a company-specific event (fraud, loss of significant client, etc.) that causes a sharp drop in the underlying stock and convertible that is counter to the rest of the industry group will negatively impact the hedge. There are a few obvious ways to minimize this risk: diversification and additional hedge overlay. One should diversify the long holdings to the extent that any one position will not cause a catastrophic result, or utilize out-of-the-money put options to hedge each position against catastrophic events.

Characteristics to Identify the Opportunity

■ Attractive convertibles with difficult stock borrow that have (1) under-valued long vega, (2) high gamma—high volatility, (3) good cash-flow capture opportunity.
■ Less expensive or less time-consuming means to hedge a portion of the portfolio.
■ Large sector or industry exposure in market that is trading below expected implied volatility.
■ Futures or funds available to short.
■ Large inflow of capital that needs to be invested quickly.
■ Rebalancing existing stock hedge with an overlay.

Risks to Consider

■ Correlation between index and long basket may not be stable.
■ Imprecise hedge with delta drift—risk neutrality may be difficult to achieve.
■ Active trading of long side and changes in fund or index constituents reduces correlation.
■ Company-specific risk of a long position may not be hedged properly.

To establish the basket hedge, the arbitrageur combines a number of long convertibles that are highly correlated with the intended index that offers futures, mutual funds, or exchange traded funds (ETFs). The underlying stocks from the long basket should offer a high degree of historical correlation with the chosen index over various time periods. A correlation matrix needs to be constructed and the basket weights of the long securities optimized to improve the index correlation. The correlation should be stress tested to ensure that a significant move in the underlying or the changes in the convertibles' deltas do not significantly distort the correlation of the hedge. One method of improving the accuracy of the hedge is to establish baskets of stocks within an industry. Most of a stock's return and variance (about 85 percent, according to the academic literature) can be explained by the general market move and industry. By constructing industry or sector baskets of 6 to 12 stocks, the correlation of the issues to the basket and the sustainability of the correlation is readily improved.

The correlation matrix in Table 9.11 demonstrates the stress testing and the optimization table that can easily be constructed with an Excel spreadsheet. Combining the stock price histories of the potential basket issues and the index intended to provide the hedge, the arbitrageur can determine the degree of confidence in the hedge and the potential risks. The underlying

TABLE 9.11 Stress Testing and Optimization Table

Basket Correlation to Index Future

Stress Test 20% Move

Underlying Stock	Equal Weight	Optimized Weight	Issue Delta	From Equal Weight				
Issue A	1.00	0.70	1.00	1.20	1.00	1.00	1.00	1.00
Issue B	1.00	1.03	0.93	1.00	1.20	1.00	1.00	1.00
Issue C	1.00	0.87	0.62	1.00	1.00	1.20	1.00	1.00
Issue D	1.00	1.23	0.68	1.00	1.00	1.00	1.20	1.00
Issue E	1.00	1.17	0.43	1.00	1.00	1.00	1.00	1.20
Average Correlation	94.00	98.00		94.40	95.10	94.90	95.30	95.20

Underlying Stock	Position Amount	Discount to Theoretical	Issue Delta	Delta Adj. Exposure	Gamma
Issue A	$17,500	(2.4)	1.00	$17,500	0.04
Issue B	$25,750	(2.6)	0.93	$23,948	0.05
Issue C	$21,750	(3.4)	0.62	$13,485	0.25
Issue D	$30,750	(1.5)	0.68	$20,910	0.20
Issue E	$29,250	(1.1)	0.43	$12,578	0.15
Investment $	$125,000			$88,420	

Index level	215	Future:	215.4

Hedge → sell (88,420/215) = 411 contracts

stocks' correlation history should be compared over various time horizons from as long as three years but, most importantly, during the last twelve and three months. The various time horizons will help the arbitrageur to understand the instability and potential drift of the correlation over time. Using the optimizer in Excel, the correlation or R^2 of the long positions can be improved, in this example moving from an equally weighted portfolio to an optimized weighting, which improves the correlation from .94 to .98. Each position's drift in correlation from the index is also measured, to ensure that the overall diversification is adequate. In this example, a 20 percent move from the equal weighting still results in a relatively high and stable combined correlation to the index. The long portfolio should have near zero delta exposure when hedged with the short future or ETF. The long basket's weighted dollar delta exposure is hedged by selling futures in an amount that dollar neutralizes the long delta. In this case, 411 contracts are sold to hedge $88,420, with each contract representing $215 dollars or the index level. The rebalancing of the hedge occurs just like any other delta neutral hedge, with changes in delta exposure that can be anticipated based on the weighted-average gamma exposure.

The basket hedges can be constructed for sectors or industries when the ability to short an index fund, sector fund, or ETFs is available. Although the U.S. market does offer very good liquidity to borrow stock, the basket hedge offers the ability to quickly establish a hedge or to employ a large degree of capital in a short period of time. The basket hedge can also be established against an existing stock hedge sector as a means of providing a quick overlay to reduce risk in a rapidly eroding sector or industry. The non-U.S. convertible markets are also prime candidates for basket hedging because of the higher degree of liquidity with shorting futures instead of stocks. Thanks to its versatility and potential for a speedy implementation, the basket hedge is another important addition to the arbitrageur's toolbox.

SYNTHETIC WORKSHEET HEDGE

Convertible arbitrageurs may also construct or create their own convertible structure to fill holes in the portfolio or to exploit inefficiencies in the warrant or options markets. The arbitrageur may purchase a long-term option or warrant and also attach a bond to the position to create an undervalued convertible. In this situation, the bond is not actually attached or usable instead of cash for exercise, but instead is carried on the trade books as part of the position that provides cash flow and risk reduction, if necessary. The bond may be from a completely different issuer or even a government issuer and therefore is not correlated to the option and will reduce the downside company-specific risks. Some arbitrageurs may choose to only establish the option hedge without the bond position, thereby reducing capital and levering the returns. But, a significant portion of convertible arbitrages' uncorrelated returns is a result of the levered cash flows from the bond side of the position. The cash flows also act as a means of providing consistent returns, while the volatility convergence may take time to unfold, making the bond portion important to many hedge positions. The synthetic may also be established with a bond that is trading at an OAS much wider than the arbitrageur's credit assessment determines is appropriate, and it may again attach a correlated or uncorrelated undervalued option to it.

The other synthetic convertible opportunity that arbitrageurs can incorporate into their portfolios is *structured convertible notes*. These synthetics are created by the large brokerage firms' derivative desks at the request of the arbitrageur. The arbitrageur may identify options that are trading below the long-term implied volatility but cannot establish a reasonably sized position because of the lack of meaningful liquidity in the options market. The derivative desk can create over-the-counter options and convertibles. The convertibles typically have a medium-term note backed by the brokerage house's credit; the strike price, expiration, call terms, yield, or conversion premium can be requested. Of course, the conversion premium and delta tradeoff compared to the coupon payment must be within the context of the market. The derivative desk traders are experts in pricing and structuring this type of paper, so exceptional opportunities are rare unless the arbitrageur is more knowledgeable than the traders regarding a company's financial structure, business environment, and resulting expected changes in volatility. The arbitrageur should also have three or four derivative desks compete on price for the structure of the deal because this slightly improves the valuation odds in his favor. Of course, any combination of options, warrants, index options, high-yield bonds, corporate bonds, busted convertibles, and government bonds can be used to create the position.

Characteristics to Identify the Opportunity

- Undervalued option or warrant.
- Undervalued bond.
- Need for additional portfolio credit diversification in a sector with few convertibles.
- Change the risk exposure in the portfolio. (For example, increase the delta and decrease omicron.)

Risks to Consider

- Uncorrelated hedge—may lose on both sides still.
- May be less liquid if structured via brokerage firm.
- Same risks as other delta neutral.
- Counterparty—contractual risks.

Table 9.12 demonstrates the market-neutral hedge created by purchasing an undervalued long-term option or LEAP and also purchasing the discounted bonds from the same issuer. The underlying stock is shorted, creating a market-neutral hedge opportunity. The hedge, even without leverage and without the benefits of credit improvement, provides a competitive return.

TABLE 9.12 Synthetic Hedge—XYZ Company

Stock	*Common Stock*					
		Symbol	XYZ			
		Price $	26.00	Dividend		$0.00
		Volatility	50%	Yield		0.00%
Corporate	*Corporate*					
		Symbol	XYZ-RA			
		Price $	100.00	Quantity		100
		Coupon	7.80%	Spread over Treasuries		563 bps
		Yield to Maturity	7.80%	Maturity		1/30/05
Long Call	*LEAP*			Quantity		40
		Symbol	XYZAB	Expiration		1/22/05
		Strike $	10.00	Time to Expiration		2.26 years
		Market Price $	6.00	Implied Volatility		45.25%
		Fair Value $	6.72	Historical Volatility		50.00%
		Under/Over Valued	–12%	Delta		0.5957
				Gamma		0.0198
				Vega		0.1504

	Hedge Ratio: 59%	**Holding period: 3 Months**		**Short Stock 2,375**	
Profit & Loss Information	% Change 1 Std. Deviation	–22.1%	–16.2%	Current	19.3%	28.4%
	Assumed Stock Px	20.25	21.79	26.00	31.03	33.37
	Est Corporate Px	100.00	100.00	100.00	100.00	100.00
	Est LEAP Px	3.29	4.20	6.72	9.69	11.06
	Call Px % Moves	–45.2%	–30.0%	12.0%	61.5%	84.3%
	Profit/Loss Corporate	0	0	0	0	0
	Bond Income/Short Rebate	2,040	2,137	2,182	2,204	2,237
	Profit/Loss Short Stock	13,647	10,004	0	–11,918	–17,537
	Profit/Loss LEAP	–10,840	–7,200	2,880	14,760	20,240
	Total Profit/Loss	4,847	4,941	5,062	5,046	4,940
	ROI	3.91%	3.98%	4.08%	4.07%	3.98%
	AROI	15.64%	15.94%	16.33%	16.28%	15.93%

DIVIDEND REDUCTION CONVERTIBLE HEDGE

The arbitrageur uses his understanding of all aspects of convertible valuation to identify potential opportunities. As described in Chapter 3, a convertible valuation moves inversely to changes in the underlying stock's dividend rate.

The arbitrageur must be aware of significant increases in dividend payout ratios for individual holdings because of the negative impact on the convertible valuation and the higher dividend due on the short stock. But, opportunities may also arise when a convertible with a high degree of sensitivity to changes in the underlying stock dividend (phi), undergoes a dividend reduction or elimination. The arbitrageur of course needs to anticipate this occurrence and move before the valuation starts to discount the probability of a rate cut. The article in Figure 9.11 from *The Wall Street Journal* provides an example of this maneuver; it highlights the speculation in the convertible arbitrage community regarding the auto companies cutting their dividend rates and the opportunity to make money on this hedge.

Characteristics to Identify the Opportunity

- Access to capital for the company has tightened, while capital needs remain high.
- Recent earnings and cash flow insufficient to continue to pay dividend.
- High phi convertible.
- Credit properly discounted in convertible valuation, while dividend reduction not discounted.

Risks to Consider

- Credit continues to weaken and access to capital worsens.
- Dividend cut timing—cut takes much longer than anticipated and the hedge, excluding the dividend reduction play, is mediocre.
- Hedged at a lower delta because dividend reduction results in a target delta lower than current. Decline in stock price without corresponding dividend cut results in under-hedged position and lower returns on investment.
- The same risks as any market neutral hedge.

The most difficult aspects of this hedge are timing when the dividend cut occurs and measuring the accompanying credit deterioration. Most often, dividend cuts occur when a company must conserve cash as a result of poor operating results and/or capital access becomes too costly. The company most likely is undergoing credit pressures and the stock is also under pressure. The arbitrageur must evaluate the extent of the decline in credit quality to properly hedge the position. The opportunity of the hedge is derived from the convertible valuation increasing while at the same time the dividend due decreases, improving the cash flow from the hedge.

Table 9.13 is an example of the profit opportunity from Ford's potential stock dividend elimination and the price and ROI impact on the Ford

THE WALL STREET JOURNAL.   FRIDAY, OCTOBER 18, 2002

Hedge Funds Buy Convertibles, Bet on Ford, GM Dividend Cut

Speculators Hope to Profit If Auto Companies Trim Payouts to Save Money

By Tom Barkley
Dow Jones Newswires

NEW YORK—Convertible securities of **Ford Motor** Co. and **General Motors** Corp. have been hit by a double whammy, as the auto makers' share and bond prices have fallen.

But some hedge funds are buying convertibles issued by the auto makers in hopes the companies cut their dividends. The strategy is based on speculation, and Ford and GM say they plan to maintain current dividends.

The hedge funds—which have latitude to make big wagers in the markets—concluded one or both of the companies might trim dividends to conserve cash after credit-rating agency Standard & Poor's Corp. on Wednesday downgraded GM a notch to triple-B and warned it may cut Ford's triple-B-plus rating.

"The idea growing in people's heads is that we may see a dividend cut for one or both of the two majors, and that gives them pause for thought," said Jeremy Howard, head of U.S. convertible research at Deutsche Bank. "If they do, the bonds will pop."

Convertibles are bond/stock hybrids: They are fixed-income securities, but can convert into common shares. Hedge funds typically play off the underlying volatility of the stock by buying the convertible and shorting the stock, essentially selling borrowed shares.

When a company pays a dividend on its stock, hedge funds essentially have to pay that out. So, the interest hedge funds make on convertibles must be more than enough to compensate for the dividend to be attractive.

If Ford or GM were to lower its common dividend, the yield differential on the convertibles would improve.

GM spokesman Jerry Dubrowski said the Detroit company has no plans to cut its annual dividend of $2 a share. He reiterated what the company's chief financial officer, John Devine, said in a conference call Tuesday: "We feel the dividend rate we have right now is sustainable."

David Reuter, a Ford spokesman, dismissed talk about the Dearborn, Mich., company's 40 cent annual dividend, saying, "At this point in time, our dividend has remained consistent every quarter this year, and we have no plans to change it at present."

But Jeff Devers, president of the convertible-arbitrage firm Palladin Group LP, said he believes there is an "excellent" chance one of the companies will cut its dividend. He thinks buying the convertibles of the auto companies would be a good trade, though it isn't one he is making.

FIGURE 9.11   Convertible Arbitrageur's Hedge Dividend Cut Expectation.
Source: "Hedge Funds Buy Convertibles, Bet on Ford, GM Dividend Cut" by Tom Barkley. *The Wall Street Journal*, October 18, 2002. Reprinted by permission of *The Wall Street Journal* via the Copyright Clearance Center.

TABLE 9.13   Dividend Reduction Convertible Hedge

Initial Hedge with 50% Margin

	Per share Dividend	Quantity	Price	Investment	Cash Flow
Convertible	$3.50	100,000	50	$5,000,000	$350,000
Stock	$0.40	(141,200)	14	($1,976,800)	($56,480)
Capital initial				$5,000,000	$293,520
Margin				$2,500,000	
LIBOR @ 2.5% short					$0
credit equal to borrow cost					
Net Capital				$2,500,000	
Levered ROI				**11.74%**	Annual cash flow

After Dividend Is Eliminated

	Per share Dividend	Quantity	Price	Investment	Cash Flow
Convertible	$3.50	100,000	53.5	$5,350,000	$350,000
Stock	$0.00	(141,200)	14	($1,976,800)	$0
Capital initial				$5,000,000	$350,000
Margin				$2,500,000	
LIBOR @ 2.5%				$0	
Net Capital				$2,500,000	New annual cash flow
Gain on Convertible				$350,000	
Levered ROI	Convertible price increase with change in dividend			**28%**	

Motor Capital 6.5 percent convertible trust preferred due 1/15/2032. Establishing a neutral stock hedge with 50 percent borrowed capital offers a relatively attractive return without any change in the stock's dividend. The elimination of the dividend increases the convertible value from $50 to $53.50, assuming no change in the equity value. The total return (cash flow and capital gain) from the hedge equals 28 percent, should the dividend be eliminated.

TRADING DESK VALUE ADDED

Bid-Ask Spread Arbitrage

Convertible hedge funds utilize many techniques to build and maintain the portfolio. Trading opportunities occur that offer the arbitrageur the opportunity to step in between the spreads of the buyer and seller and facilitate the trade while never risking any capital. For example, a buyer of 500 Clear Channel bonds at 102 appears while a seller for 500 Clear Channel bonds at 101 is also active. The arbitrageur steps in and almost simultaneously purchases the bonds at 101 and resells them at 102 for a risk-free profit. The bid-ask-spread arbitrage is available in all market environments but generally only in smaller trade sizes (up to $5 million).

Hot New Issues

Another source of very low risk profits is the new issue convertible market. It is no coincidence that some of convertible hedge funds' best-performing quarters are the same quarters during which new issues are abundant. The source of the low-risk profit comes in the form of new issues that trade at a premium to the new issue price (hence, the "hot issue" categorization) for the first few hours of trading. Convertible hedge funds are active in the new issue convertible marketplace and will usually participate in any deal that looks like it will trade at a premium initially. If a new issue is priced at par, but the first trade is 103 percent of par, the arbitrageur that participated in the new issue may then short the stock, locking in the 3 percent return, and establish a delta neutral hedge at that point. Or, if the new issue is not a very attractive hedge candidate, the hedge fund will simply unload the issue and book the risk-free profit. The position may have only been held for minutes.

A riskier means to benefit from a hot new issue is to short the stock of the issuer on the announcement of the deal. The short is based on the premise that new convertible issues have a negative impact on the underlying stock price due to dilution, as well as the hedge community's participation in shorting the stock against the convertible. The arbitrageur estimates how many bonds they will receive from the new issue allocation and then takes a conservative delta neutral hedge profile with the short stock against the anticipated allocation. When successful, the hedge pays off on the short stock side and also on the long side of the hedge. Both sides of the hedge make money, and the position can be quickly reversed to net a handsome short-term profit. Of course, if the deal is canceled, the short stock would likely rally, leaving the arbitrageur with a naked short position—and a loss. Many of the underwriters attempt to stem some of the front running on the short side by announcing deals before the market opens for trading at the open.

TRADE EXECUTION

Trade execution can significantly contribute to or detract from the performance of the hedge position. Traders must understand both sides of the trade and evaluate and plan a strategy for execution for each trade. Time to execute, price, and market impact are the measures of success or failure. Convertible arbitrage involves trades that cross many markets, including equity, convertible, high yield, international equity, international convertible, swap market, derivatives market, options market, and currency market. Traders need to employ many tools that have been discussed in this book but also all of the trade systems and technical analysis systems that may improve trade timing and execution.

Example Trade

The arbitrageur wants to purchase $5 million of XYZ convertible and short stock at a .70 delta hedge rate. The arbitrageur finds on outright seller that will execute both sides of the hedge but for only $2 million worth, with the caveat that the other $3 million be worked versus stock at an .80 delta with 3/8 stock price move discretion. How do you determine if this is reasonable, and how long should the trader allow the trade to work?

The first step is to understand if the other side of the trade is providing liquidity by shorting the bonds, selling from inventory, or stepping between another client selling the bonds. In two of these situations, the selling trader will be purchasing stock to facilitate the trade. Of course, as the stock price increases, the price of the convertible increases. Therefore, the mere fact that the trade is being worked will cause upward pressure on the arbitrageur's position—and cost. Accordingly, the expected trading impact should be measured and negotiated up front. Further, the liquidity of both the convertible and the stock needs to be assessed. The convertible liquidity is a function of the absolute size of the issue, the issue size relative to the issuing companies' capital structure, the trading volume in the stock, the uniqueness of the issue, and the ease of hedging the issue. The ease of hedging the issue relates to the cost of the hedge, the stability of the greeks, and the complexity of protecting the position.

Once the convertible's liquidity is determined, the price impact of the trade from the equity perspective should also be measured. For example, the $5 million long purchase is accompanied by a $3.5 million dollar stock short that translates into 175,000 shares of stock at $20 each. Based on the average daily trading volume of the stock of 1,000,000 shares, this trade represents 17.5 percent of the average trading volume. If the stock trades in relatively small blocks, this trade may take more than an hour to execute and subject the trade to additional volatility. The arbitrageur may decide to execute immediately by giving the other side of the trade one hour's worth of normal volatility in the price. More specifically, this means that if the stock has on average an hourly volatility of 1.2 percent, then the arbitrageur dollar neutralizes the delta at the negotiated delta and pays up for the full execution (0.012 * delta * bond price). If the trade was very large and represented 50 percent of the stock's average trading volume, the arbitrageur may pay one half-day's volatility to get immediate execution or accept the price volatility risk that may be above normal and ask to execute the stock versus the Volume Weighted Average Price (VWAP).

APPENDIX 9.1   PARTIAL LISTING OF COMPANIES WITH MULTIPLE CONVERTIBLE ISSUES OUTSTANDING AS OF DECEMBER 10, 2002

TABLE 9.14   Partial Listing of Companies with Multiple Convertible Issues Outstanding

Issuer	Stock Ticker	Coupon	Maturity	Market Value ($MM)	Delta	Rating
American Intl Group	AIG	0%	11/09/31	$968.83	0.19	AAA
American Intl Group	AIG	0.50%	5/15/07	$196.88	0.18	AAA
American Online	AOL	0%	12/06/19	$1,274.82	0.00	BBB
Tribune/AOL (PHONES)	AOL	2.00%	—	$574.50	0.24	A–
Centerpoint Energy /AOL Exch	AOL	2.00%	—	$282.12	0.94	BBB–
Best Buy	BBY	2.25%	1/15/22	$337.60	0.13	BB+
Best Buy	BBY	0.68%	6/27/21	$333.29	0.03	BBB–
Computer Assoc	CA	5.00%	3/15/07	$658.35	0.23	BBB+
Computer Assoc	CA	1.63%	12/15/09	$384.00	0.49	BBB+
Carnival Cruise	CCL	2.00%	4/15/21	$634.50	0.33	A
Carnival Cruise	CCL	0%	10/24/21	$614.94	0.45	A
Clear Channel	CCU	2.63%	4/01/03	$570.68	0.01	BBB–
Clear Channel (Jacor)	CCU	0%	2/09/18	$210.24	0.00	BBB–
Cendant	CD	3.88%	11/27/11	$1,189.50	0.10	BBB
Cendant	CD	0%	5/04/21	$986.10	0.01	BBB
Cendant (Mandatory)	CD	7.75%	—	$592.00	0.70	BBB
Cendant	CD	0%	2/13/21	$418.66	0.12	BBB
CenturyTel (Mandatory)	CTL	6.88%	—	$504.80	0.75	BBB+
CenturyTel	CTL	4.75%	8/01/32	$170.44	0.37	BBB+
Echostar Comm	DISH	5.75%	5/15/08	$836.25	0.30	B–
Echostar Comm	DISH	4.88%	1/01/07	$826.25	0.21	B–
Loews Corp/DO	DO	3.13%	9/15/07	$1,019.19	0.05	A

TABLE 9.14 *(Continued)*

Issuer	Stock Ticker	Coupon	Maturity	Market Value ($MM)	Delta	Rating
Diamond Offshore	DO	0%	6/06/20	$440.74	0.04	A
Diamond Offshore	DO	1.50%	4/15/31	$417.74	0.22	A
Electronic Data Sys	EDS	0%	10/10/21	$745.56	0.00	A–
Electronic Data Sys (Mandatory)	EDS	7.63%	—	$638.20	0.63	NR
General Motors	GM	5.25%	3/06/32	$2,310.88	0.30	BBB
Fiat/GM	GM	3.25%	1/09/07	$1,844.49	0.10	Baa3
General Motors	GM	4.50%	3/06/32	$1,095.72	0.16	BBB
Health Mgmt Assoc	HMA	0.25%	8/16/20	$330.52	0.34	BBB+
Health Mgmt Assoc	HMA	0%	1/28/22	$285.66	0.35	BBB+
Intl. Paper	IP	0%	6/20/21	$1,099.86	0.23	BBB
Intl. Paper	IP	5.25%	—	$416.18	0.36	BB+
Interpublic Group	IPG	0%	12/14/21	$532.61	0.01	BBB–
Interpublic Group	IPG	1.87%	6/01/06	$259.47	0.03	BB+
Interpublic Group	IPG	1.80%	9/15/04	$210.94	0.01	NA
Ivax Corp.	IVX	4.50%	5/15/08	$536.84	0.11	NR
Ivax Corp.	IVX	5.50%	5/15/07	$217.81	0.11	NR
L-3 Comm	LLL	4.00%	9/15/11	$458.32	0.53	BB–
L-3 Comm	LLL	5.25%	6/01/09	$373.50	0.62	BB–
Lowes Companies	LOW	0%	2/16/21	$769.45	0.51	A
Lowes Companies	LOW	0.86%	10/19/21	$557.83	0.37	A
LSI Logic	LSI	4.00%	11/01/06	$393.84	0.07	B
LSI Logic	LSI	4.00%	2/15/05	$364.47	0.00	B
LSI Logic	LSI	4.25%	3/15/04	$328.34	0.02	B
Motorola (Mandatory)	MOT	7.00%	—	$813.60	0.66	Baa2
Liberty Media/MOT	MOT	3.50%	1/15/31	$387.75	0.41	BBB–
Motorola	MOT	0%	9/27/13	$77.13	0.02	BBB–
Inco Ltd.	N	5.50%	—	$476.58	0.08	BB
Inco Ltd.	N	0%	3/29/21	$277.21	0.54	BBB–
Inco Ltd.	N	5.75%	7/01/04	$170.78	0.06	BBB–
Inco Ltd.	N	7.75%	3/15/16	$158.31	0.04	BBB–
Northrop Grumman (Mandatory)	NOC	7.25%	—	$726.98	0.81	NA
Northrop Grumman (Mandatory)	NOC	7.00%	—	$432.14	0.57	BB
Nextel Comm	NXTL	6.00%	6/01/11	$528.96	0.32	B
Nextel Comm	NXTL	5.25%	1/15/10	$508.61	0.04	B
Nextel Comm	NXTL	4.75%	7/01/07	$235.37	0.14	B
Nextel Comm (Mandatory)	NXTL	0%	—	$70.45	0.46	CCC+

(continues)

TABLE 9.14 *(Continued)*

Issuer	Stock Ticker	Coupon	Maturity	Market Value ($MM)	Delta	Rating
Roche	RHHBY	0%	5/06/12	$1,693.53	0.02	NA
Roche	RHHBY	0%	4/20/10	$1,320.27	0.01	NR
Roche	RHHBY	0%	7/25/21	$1,102.61	0.30	NA
Solectron	SLR	0%	11/20/20	$1,377.09	0.00	BB
Solectron	SLR	0%	5/08/20	$520.02	0.00	BB
Solectron (Mandatory)	SLR	7.25%	—	$456.40	0.72	B+
Teva Pharma	TEVA	1.50%	10/15/05	$543.75	0.00	BBB–
Teva Pharma Fin	TEVA	0.38%	11/15/22	$474.75	0.07	BBB–
Teva Pharma Fin	TEVA	0.75%	8/15/21	$385.65	0.01	BBB–
Tyco International	TYC	0%	11/17/20	$3,318.47	0.00	BBB–
Tyco International	TYC	0%	2/12/21	$2,276.25	0.00	BBB–
Veritas Software	VRTS	1.86%	8/13/06	$397.94	0.09	B+
Veritas Software	VRTS	5.25%	11/01/04	$115.70	0.98	B+

APPENDIX 9.2   CONVERTIBLE ARBITRAGE TAKE-OVER RISKS

Since one of the most significant event risks facing a convertible arbitrageur is the risk of a take-over, a separate discussion and example is included in this book.

TAKE-OVER RISKS—AN EXAMPLE

One of the more significant risks encountered when hedging convertible securities occurs when an acquisition or merger is announced regarding the convertible issuer. In many situations, an acquisition will benefit the convertible owner because generally acquisitions occur at premiums to the current stock market price and the convertible will participate to some extent through the convertible's link to the underlying stock. This is especially true for convertibles trading at a premium to par value. Generally, a convertible that is above par value has a lower conversion premium and therefore a better opportunity to participate in any stock price appreciation as a result of the acquisition bid. Should the acquisition occur at a price below the conversion price on the convertible, various outcomes exist.

Many convertibles issued since the mid- to late-1990s have some degree of "take-over protection." The degree of protection varies, according to factors such as the type of acquisition and whether it is considered hostile or not. Typically, the take-over protection in most prospectuses provides the owner of the convertible the right to put the bonds back to the issuer at par value in the event of a take-over.

Example: Mergers and High Premium Convertible Hedges without Take-Over Put Protection

A recent example of the dangers of M&A activity and convertible hedging can be understood with Heartland Industrial's acquisition of Mascotech Inc. On July 31, 2000, the Mascotech 4.5 percent convertible due 12/15/2003 was trading at 79 with a 5.69 percent current yield and a yield to maturity in 3 years of 12.94 percent. The convertible had a relatively high conversion premium of 113 percent, but with only 3 years to maturity the bond would rapidly accrete to par value and also offer good downside protection for the hedge. The delta neutral hedge called for shorting only 900 shares of stock against 100 bonds long for a 27.9 percent hedge. See Table 9.15.

On August 2, 2000, Heartland Industrial Partners offered $16.90 per share for Mascotech Inc. and as a result the stock climbed to $16, but the bond dropped to 69.5 because the acquiring company was offering a price well below the conversion price and the acquirer was also a private company. The convertible hedge lost money on both sides. With the 900 shares short and the difference between $11.50 and $16.00, the short stock lost $4,050. Unfortunately, the 100 long bonds value also declined from 79 to 69.5, or $9,500, for a total loss of $13,550, representing an immediate −17.15 percent drop in the hedge return.

Of course, if the acquiring company was a stronger credit, then the bond value may in fact increase in value and help to offset some of the short stock loss. In each case, an assessment should be made regarding the risk of take-overs. An arbitrageur may want to avoid high premium hedges in an industry that is currently in the consolidation phase and in which M&A activity is high. Arbitrageurs may still consider hedges in the active industry if put protection in the event of a take-over is present and not ambiguously written in the prospectus. In some situations, the management team of the company being acquired determines if the acquisition is hostile, thereby triggering the take-over put or, if it is not hostile, rendering the take-over put unexercisable. This type of "put protection" is generally protection for the management team and not for the bondholders. If the management team receives a golden parachute or guaranteed job protection, then the take-over

TABLE 9.15 M&A Hedge without Take-Over Put Protection

Hedge Analysis w/ Margin

Convertible Price:	79.00		Direction:	Short	Price:	11.50	LIBOR rate: 6%
# of Bonds Long:	100.00	50%	Expiration:	NA	Short Amount:	$10,350	Rebate: 75%
Long Amount:	$23,700		Implied Vol.:	NA	Protection $:	13.10%
Conversion Ratio:	32.258		Strike Price:	NA	Protection %:	27.90%
Option Type:	NA		Quantity:	900	Total Investment: $23,700

Hedge Risk/Reward Analysis

Est. Stock Move:	12 Months	1.0 year	.50 year	CURRENT	.50 year	1.0 year
% Change Underlying:		-28.91%	-21.44%	0.00%	27.29%	40.67%
Stock Price:		8.17	9.03	11.50	14.63	16.17
Convertible Fair Price Track:		76.73	77.06	78.58	81.87	84.01
Convertible % Change:		-2.86%	-2.45%	-0.52%	3.63%	6.35%
Total Return:		18.51%	8.84%	-1.75%	7.44%	17.69%
AROI:		18.51%	18.47%	N/A	15.44%	17.69%

is not considered hostile. The bondholders remain at the mercy of management's opinion and job security.

If the Mascotech bond had put protection that was triggered, the hedge would have worked very well because the bond would have traded to very near par and the hedge position would have resulted in a gain. If the bonds traded to 98, not quite par value until the acquisition was finalized, the long position would have netted a $19,000 gain with the same loss on the short of $4,050. The total hedge return without income would be $14,950 or 18.9%!

Of course, many variations of outcomes can occur with take-overs and convertible hedging. The arbitrageur should consider reasonable worst case situations, paying special attention to prospectus language regarding take-over "protection."

Risks to Consider with Acquisitions and Convertible Hedges

1. No take-over put protection or ambiguous protection. Read prospectus carefully.
2. Bond below par with high premium and take-over price well below conversion price. Weaker or equivalent credit acquiring convertible issuer. Results in loss on short with no gain and possible loss on long.
3. Bond below par with high premium and take-over price below conversion price. Stronger credit or acquiring convertible issuer. Results in loss on short with gain on long. The risk of the stock loss being greater than the bond appreciation still high.
4. Bond above par with the take-over bid below the conversion price. The convertible long may drop in value to a parity level below par. This "premium collapse" will occur in take-overs above par if the bonds will not remain outstanding. Results in loss on short and loss on long.
5. Take-over above par and above conversion price but parity on bond below current convertible price. Loss on short and loss on long with the potential to lose interest payment due also.
6. Take-over with bond near par with put protection but parity take-over bid below or at par. Results in loss on long or no gain with a loss on short.

CHAPTER 10

Portfolio Risk Management

Convertible arbitrage portfolio management includes the continual process of creating individual strategies to produce un-correlated, low-volatility alpha. See Figure 10.1. To achieve this on an ongoing basis, the overall portfolio must be taken into account regularly. Indeed, portfolio evaluation, rebalancing of active and passive risks, optimization, and monitoring all make up part of the daily discipline in an active convertible hedge portfolio, including the following factors to attend to: Each position's active risks require constant monitoring, as do any passive risks that may bleed into the risk-return profile; positions need review from both a performance expectation and liquidity standpoint; market-related, systematic risks need to be closely watched, along with the derivative hedge overlays and the costs of the protection. Last but not least, the arbitrageur also constantly monitors the new opportunities that present themselves with the changes in the market.

The complexity of a portfolio of hedged convertible positions with varied objectives and risk exposure makes it necessary to look at the net greek exposures and determine if additional hedging overlays are necessary. It is important to segregate the various types of hedge positions to ensure that the inefficiency that is exploited at the position level is not hedged away at the portfolio level. See Figure 10.2. Some risks, such as delta and specific credit (omicron), are best hedged at the position level because the risks are non-systematic, while other systematic risks should be hedged at the portfolio level. Examples of systematic risks include shifts in market volatility (vega), yield curve changes and related interest rate risk (rho), and general credit spread risk (omicron). The portfolio's primary risks, those that may contribute the most to failing to obtain the target returns, should be those first evaluated for further hedging. It is imperative that the arbitrageur identifies the primary and secondary risks at the portfolio level and monitors their potential impact on the overall P&L.

Diversification is addressed at the portfolio level. This includes industry and sector exposure, credit exposure, and even the exposure to the various types of convertible hedges. If a portfolio has excess concentration in a spe-

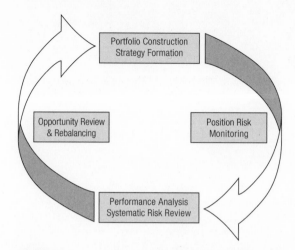

FIGURE 10.1   Process of Portfolio Risk Management.

cific industry or sector, the arbitrageur may overlay an industry/sector option or futures contracts to reduce event risks. In some circumstances, shorting a closed-end sector fund will also provide the necessary protection.
Within the convertible arbitrage universe, many different hedge strategies
and profiles exist, and it is important to diversify these strategies as well as
segregate them when overlaying any systematic risk hedges. For example,
bull gamma hedges are long small amounts of delta, gamma, and vega, while
reverse hedges are short vega and gamma. Option overlays at the position
level may be used to short vega, reduce omicron, increase vega, increase
gamma, offset theta, and just about any other combination. However, the
critical portfolio level hedge overlay and risk management should not eliminate a risk that is otherwise actively accepted at the position level.

Portfolio risk management practices include scenario analysis that
measures the portfolio returns under various investment environments.
Value at Risk (VAR) tools are commonly used by risk managers because of
their ease of use. VAR models can quickly assess how changes in volatility
or correlation changes will impact the portfolio. Unfortunately, with less-
liquid assets or with those whose distributions are skewed and non-normal,
the results will be suspect. VAR models are not very effective with portfolios
with optionality and they are also not very useful for the convertible arbitrageur. Convertible arbitrage portfolios may be best suited for scenario
analysis with extreme "shock" scenarios included. Risk managers may also
include Monte Carlo simulations in their review process. Monte Carlo simulations are an excellent choice for convertible arbitrage risk management

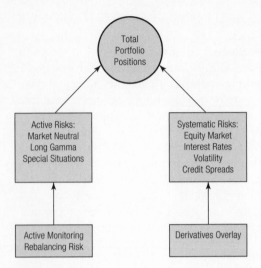

FIGURE 10.2   Risk Management—Active and Systematic Risks.

because of the non-linear payout functions of the varied embedded options and hedges. Importantly, the convertible arbitrageur needs details to properly assess risk and opportunities, but the VAR models are high-level models that lack enough information to be valuable to the arbitrageur. This chapter is intended to provide examples of the systematic risks that should be addressed and the hedge techniques that can reduce or eliminate them. It concludes with a discussion of troubles encountered by convertible arbitrageurs in the past, particularly during "shock" scenarios, to serve as examples of what can go wrong when systematic risks are inadequately or incorrectly addressed.

BALANCE SHEET LEVERAGE

The degree of financial leverage employed in the portfolio should be the first risk measurement addressed. Financial leverage can be defined as the ratio of total assets to net worth. The prime broker regulates the extent of the leverage in the hedge fund ever since the Federal Reserve changed Regulation T in 1996. Trading partners and counter-parties may also impose some limitations on the degree of leverage in the portfolio. The arbitrageur must balance the leverage in the portfolio with respect to the overall credit quality, liquidity risks, greek risks, financial market risks, and costs of the funds. It is important to remember that a doubling of leverage doubles the risk without doubling of returns, because of the cost of the funds borrowed. Of course, within the convertible hedge portfolio some positions represent higher risks than others and therefore should not use as much leverage. It may be helpful to segregate a portfolio into sub-accounts, with the prime broker based on the degree of leverage appropriate for the individual positions. The prime broker will regulate borrowing on a position, taking into consideration the credit quality, structure of the issue, equity sensitivity of the position, and the hedge ratio. Still, the arbitrageur has a significant amount of room to operate within, even with the leverage restrictions imposed by the prime broker or other counter-parties.

The levered convertible hedge fund offers exceptional returns with a low standard deviation, as discussed in Chapters 1 and 5, but still retains a somewhat higher degree of risk exposure. Although the levered convertible fund may demonstrate a lower standard deviation of returns and beta in "normal" markets, as compared to an un-levered convertible portfolio, the story can be much different during extreme conditions. The levered portfolio can produce higher returns with less gamma bleed and equity sensitivity than the un-levered portfolio, because the un-levered portfolio needs to enhance the return, and this is generally accomplished through some more gamma hedging and equity market bleed. The un-levered portfolio will appear riskier at first glance, but the leveraged portfolio is subject to a higher degree of liquidity risk and market shock. As we have seen, financial market shocks do cause damage to the convertible arbitrage community, and especially the highly levered funds. Levered funds will have a higher vega risk and rho2 risk (increase in the cost of borrowing via higher short-term interest rates) that can be difficult to offset during a crisis. The de-leveraging of hedge funds may occur in a very short time frame, putting significant liquidity and price risk on the portfolio. In effect, the levered convertible arbitrage portfolio has no catastrophic insurance protection, while the un-levered portfolio can generally weather the storm and survive.

One additional means of determining how much to leverage a position and, ultimately, the total portfolio, is to consider the individual position's "model error" or actual price drift from the theoretical valuation. For example, convertibles that are deep-in-the-money and convertible into a liquid stock are very easy to price theoretically, and therefore the potential error or the standard deviation of the actual price differences around the theoretical value should be very small. Conversely, a low-grade, out-of-the-money convertible is subject to a significant degree of volatility in valuation, and therefore not a good candidate to use a high degree of leverage to set up the position.

Figure 10.3 shows the degree of the accuracy of convertible models at various points along the convertible price track. The difficulty in estimating

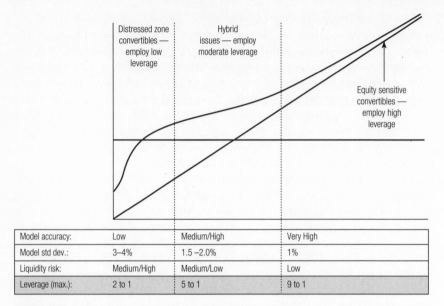

Model accuracy:	Low	Medium/High	Very High	
Model std dev.:	3–4%	1.5–2.0%	1%	
Liquidity risk:	Medium/High	Medium/Low	Low	
Leverage (max.):	2 to 1	5 to 1	9 to 1	

FIGURE 10.3   Theoretical Model Valuation Risks and Balance Sheet Leverage.

inputs becomes higher as the convertible drops below the conversion price or as the credit quality declines. Convertibles that are deep-in-the-money can be valued as long stock plus the present value of the yield advantage over the time period remaining for call protection. This is a very easy calculation with no controversy or subjectivity in valuation. On the other hand, a low-grade convertible that is out-of-the-money is subject to a wide degree of differences in opinion regarding credit quality, implied volatility, expected life of the issue, and default recovery rates. Clearly, the valuation error is larger for the low-grade busted issue and the risk of convergence to theoretical value is much higher. The arbitrageur in each hedge profile assesses the predictability and confidence level for each position, levering the issues with a high degree of confidence or low modeling risk, while using no or low leverage for hedges with a lower degree of confidence or high degree of modeling error.

SCENARIO ANALYSIS

Most prime brokers will offer a comprehensive accounting and portfolio risk analysis package to hedge fund clients. One important tool included in the package is the scenario analysis worksheet, as seen in the worksheet in Table 10.1. Worksheets such as this one look at the portfolio's sensitivity to changes in equity price moves for a given time horizon or for a fixed market move (holding all other factors constant). The overall positions' P&L can be assessed as well as the portfolio level P&L. This equity price movement scenario captured in the worksheet assumes 1 and 2 standard deviations in the stock price movements over a 3-month period.

Scenario #2 introduces changes in interest rates and the effect on the portfolio for the same stock price movements. See Table 10.2. The yield curve is shifted up and down 100 basis points, with the total impact at each equity market move indicated. Note that in this example, regardless of the change in equity price movements, even with the change in the yield curve, the portfolio still maintains a relatively neutral portfolio profile.

The third scenario in the worksheet shifts volatility levels in the marketplace plus and minus 5 points. With this tool, the volatility skew can be changed or the entire curve can be moved. The portfolio's sensitivity to volatility shifts and equity market changes is totaled for each equity price move, and then the entire portfolio impact is again registered for each column.

The scenario analysis worksheet can include changes in interest rates, changes in the term structure of rates, changes in volatility or the skew, changes in credit spreads and/or changes for each credit rating, or changes in currency rates. Even more complex models can be built to allow for changes in all of the above at the same time. In general, the arbitrageur is concerned about one or two major factors from the macro perspective and this analysis can improve his or her understanding of the risks and trade-off involved.

Finally, major market move stress testing should be run to understand the impact of large significant shifts in the financial markets and the likely impact on the portfolio. An example of this might be an immediate 20 percent decline in equity prices combined with a 200 basis point increase in credit spreads and a 20-point increase in volatility and convertibles fall to 4 percent undervalued. Of course, the liquidity squeeze that would be associated with this type of market environment cannot be easily modeled, but it is sufficient to assume that a dramatic decrease in liquidity would result, and the convertible under-valuation attempts to account for some of the liquidity drain. Not surprisingly, most portfolios would be subject to a loss under these extreme conditions.

The portfolio that demonstrated a relatively good neutral profile under the scenario analysis in the worksheet in Table 10.1 shows some major weakness under the extreme condition scenario, i.e., downside market shock in Table 10.2. An upside extreme conditions environment is also calculated to

TABLE 10.1 Scenario Analysis

Security Description	Holdings	Price	Theoretical Value	P&L for Range of Stock Price Movement				
				−2 s.d.	−1 s.d.	Current	+1 s.d.	+2 s.d.
L KJC Co. 5.0%—6/15/06	1,000,000	98.000	99.625	−$137,200	−$34,300	$16,250	$45,962	$164,640
S KJC short stock	34,300	20.000		$153,664	$48,020	$0	−$44,590	−$142,688
L ZNC Inc. 4.50%—9/15/07	1,200,000	112.750	114.000	−$216,480	−$54,120	$15,000	$72,521	$259,776
S ZNC short stock	30,926	35.000		$311,731	$97,416	$0	−$70,356	−$225,139
L KayJo Co. 0%—12/15/12	1,500,000	47.800	48.125	−$78,870	−$19,718	$4,875	$26,421	$94,644
S KayJo short stock	9,859	40.000		$63,096	$19,718	$0	−$25,633	−$82,025
L Cole Inc. 5.25%—6/01/04	1,000,000	101.500	102.250	−$131,950	−$32,988	$7,500	$44,203	$158,340
S Cole short stock	26,390	25.000		$137,228	$42,884	$0	−$39,585	−$126,672
L Justice Inc. 3.5%—3/15/09	975,000	94.625	95.000	−$92,259	−$23,065	$3,656	$30,907	$110,711
S Justice short stock	30,753	15.000		$95,950	$29,984	$0	−$27,678	−$88,569
Total P&L →				$104,910	$73,832	$47,281	$12,173	$123,018

Scenario #2

Interest Rate Changes

				−2 s.d.	−1 s.d.	Current	+1 s.d.	+2 s.d.
+100 Basis Pts				$98,615	$71,248	$45,863	$11,869	$121,296
−100 Basis Pts				$109,631	$76,342	$48,700	$12,517	$125,725

Scenario #3

Volatility Shifts

				−2 s.d.	−1 s.d.	Current	+1 s.d.	+2 s.d.
−5 Volatility Pts				$97,566	$70,140	$45,390	$11,808	$119,697
+5 Volatility Pts				$108,057	$76,785	$49,031	$12,599	$127,939

TABLE 10.2 Scenario Analysis—Extreme

Security Description	Holdings	Price	Theoretical Value	Downside Market Shock	Upside Market Shock
L KJC Co. 5.0%—					
6/15/06	1,000,000	98.000	99.625	−$171,500	$198.940
S KJC short stock	34,300	20.000		$153,664	−$156,065
L ZNC Inc. 4.50%—					
9/15/07	1,200,000	112.750	114.000	−$313,896	$346,368
S ZNC short stock	30,926	35.000		$311,731	−$330,673
L KayJo Co. 0%—					
12/15/12	1,500,000	47.800	48.125	−$110,418	$122,249
S KayJo short stock	9,859	40.000		$82,814	−$99,968
L Cole Inc. 5.25%—					
6/01/04	1,000,000	101.500	102.250	−$184,730	$211,120
S Cole short stock	26,390	25.000		$137,228	−$155,173
L Justice Inc. 3.5%—					
3/15/09	975,000	94.625	95.000	−$147,615	$161,454
S Justice short stock	30,753	15.000		$107,943	−$109,881
	Total P&L →			−$134,779	$188,370

understand the impact of a positive surge in financial markets. The reverse of the negative conditions is used for this scenario. Under the extreme negative scenario, the non-levered portfolio would be subject to nearly an 8 percent loss and of course leverage would magnify this. The arbitrageur may choose to hedge against these extreme conditions, although the likelihood of this occurrence is small. The choice of hedging includes purchasing out-of-the-money index put options, purchasing volatility swaps, or hedging the credit spreads via swaps. Later in this chapter, we will discuss swaps to hedge the systematic risks.

HEDGING SYSTEMATIC RISKS WITH INDEX OPTIONS

One means to protect the portfolio against systematic market breaks is to purchase index option puts that are out-of-the-money. These put options can be purchased on indexes that best represent the portfolio's holdings, or even sector put options can be used to reduce the exposure in a sector that may be prone to event risk. For the portfolio discussed above in the extreme

TABLE 10.3 Determining the Number of Index Option Puts Needed to Protect the Portfolio

---

Index option contracts index current level = 1092
June 2003 with strike 950 (–13% out-of-the-money)

$$\text{Contracts to purchase} = \frac{(\text{Market value of portfolio * adjusted beta})}{(\text{Contract strike * 100})}$$

$$18 \text{ contracts} = \frac{\$1,703,797 * (1.2*.83)}{(950 * 100)}$$

20% market correction
Put value = 950 – 873 = 77
Dollar value of hedge at expiration = $138,600

---

market conditions scenario, S&P 500 put options were selected for the hedge. The put insurance is a fixed cost policy that pays off in extreme events. Table 10.3 indicates the number of contracts needed to protect the portfolio. The puts selected are the S&P 500 index June 950 currently 13 percent out-of-the-money with an implied volatility of 20 percent and 3 months to expiration. To determine the number of put option contracts to purchase, the portfolio's market value is multiplied by the adjusted beta, and this sum is divided by the index strike price multiplied by 100. The adjusted beta represents the weighted average beta for the underlying stocks (1.20) against the S&P 500 and then the underlying beta is multiplied by the convertible's expected delta in the extreme conditions (0.83). We saw in the worksheet in Table 10.2 that in extreme conditions, the convertible hedge portfolio is expected to decline by nearly 8 percent or $134,779. The hedge could offset this by providing an additional $130,000 were the same 20 percent market decline to occur. Each put option cost $379 per contract for three months of protection. Therefore, the total cost of the portfolio protection is $6,822, or 0.4 percent of the portfolio value (1.6 percent annual cost), slightly reducing the dollar protection to $123,178 for a 20 percent correction.

The use of index put options can have a significant impact on the negative return portion of the portfolio's return distribution. Figure 10.4 shows the portfolio's return distribution without additional index put protection, as well as the distribution with index put protection (dashed distribution). Properly hedged the distribution's left tail is cut off before the negative return area, while the cost of the hedge can be seen in the slightly lower distribution in the positive return area of the distribution.

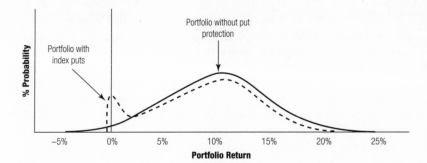

FIGURE 10.4 Portfolio Return Distribution without Additional Index Put Protection.

HEDGING INTEREST RATE RISK—YIELD CURVE SHIFTS

Changes in interest rates can cause unintended gains and losses in the convertible hedge portfolio, and they can be substantial. Shifts in the yield curve produced some severe price declines in the convertible arbitrage community in 1987 and 1994 for those who did not hedge interest rate risks. U.S. Treasury futures contracts are listed; they are standardized contracts that also offer a liquid means to hedge interest rate risk in the convertible portfolio. The U.S. Treasury futures hedge, discussed below, does not hedge against credit spread risk (omicron), only changes in the yield curve.

It is advantageous to hedge interest rate risk (rho) at the portfolio level because an individual position's rho can move quickly should a stock price move dramatically up or down. But at the portfolio level, these moves are mitigated by the moves of other issues, providing a much more stable portfolio rho. Generally, any macro or systematic event should be hedged at the portfolio level and monitored at the portfolio level in order to simplify the process and avoid excess rebalancing. Short-term interest rate risk (rho2), or the cost of borrowing with respect to the leverage in the portfolio, can also be hedged at the portfolio level with LIBOR futures or exchanged for a fixed rate in the swap market.

In the portfolio summary analysis, a rho should be calculated for each position based on the expected move in interest rates between adjustments to the hedge. This may be for as little as 1 basis point move or as much as 50 basis points, depending on the size of the portfolio, the convexity, and the amount of rho bleed acceptable to the arbitrageur. Although rate changes may not be occurring quickly, the portfolio's rho must be monitored actively because changes in the underlying equity prices will cause changes in the convertible values and their corresponding rho, duration, and convexity. Changes in volatility (vega) and the passage of time (theta) will also impact the rho risk, but generally more slowly. To determine the number of contracts to short for the interest rate hedge, calculate a point rho for each position, including option hedges if appropriate. Then, determine the dollar change in the position for a given change in interest rates. Table 10.4 shows how the hedge works in practice.

The rho point move based on a one-basis-point move in interest rates is calculated for each convertible's theoretical value. The change should only include changes in theoretical value, not the change in actual value, because the under- or overvaluation of the issue and its move to theoretical value is not dependent on interest rate changes. The objective in the analysis is to isolate the rho and avoid bleed from the other greeks. The position point move is multiplied by the position size to get the dollar loss for each individual holding. The sum of the portfolio's dollar loss for a one-basis-point move in interest rates is divided by the U.S. Treasury futures dollar loss, for each one-basis-point increase in interest rates. The U.S. Treasury note future that is selected to short should have a duration that is close to the convertible portfolio's duration.

$$\text{Number of future contracts} = \frac{\text{\$ Change in convertible portfolio for a 1 bps move}}{\text{\$ Change in UST futures contract for a 1 bps}}$$

In the example in Table 10.4, the portfolio is expected to lose $4,201.75 for a 1-basis-point increase in interest rates. The 5-year U.S. Treasury future contract is expected to lose $34.50 for each 1-basis-point increase in interest rates. Therefore, the arbitrageur must short 122 U.S. Treasury futures contracts to hedge the rho risk, as the gain on the short future position will offset the loss in the portfolio. Of course, this is a dynamic hedge that needs to be adjusted to keep the rho risk at bay.

HEDGING VOLATILITY WITH VOLATILITY SWAPS

The convertible hedge portfolio is also subject to the risks of implied volatility shifts. In general, the portfolio is long-volatility. As discussed in earlier chapters, delta neutral hedges are considered long-volatility hedges, making the convertible hedge portfolio exposed to volatility risk in almost every hedge position. Most positions are established with the convertible trading below the expected implied volatility level, and therefore an increase in volatility should cause many of the positions to increase in value, the objective

TABLE 10.4 Interest Rate Protection for the Portfolio

Security Description	Holdings	Price	Theoretical Value	Rho Pts	Duration	Change in Theoretical Value 1 bps Move	$ Loss 1 bps
ABC Co. 5.5%—6/01/05	1,000	98.500	99.625	0.300	3.400	0.301	3,000.00
XYZ Inc. 4.0%—3/15/07	1,200	112.000	114.000	0.014	2.890	0.012	168.00
Big Dog Co. 0%—12/15/12	1,500	47.750	48.125	0.040	6.100	0.083	600.00
MMX Inc. 4.75%—6/01/04	1,000	101.500	102.250	0.019	3.300	0.019	190.00
Top Shelf 3.75%—3/15/09	975	94.250	95.000	0.025	3.500	0.026	243.75
					$ RHO Exposure →		4,201.75

Interest Rate Hedge	Contract Size	Price		Rho-1bps			
U.S. Treasury Future 5-year Dec-03	100	103.250		0.345		0.334	34.500
Contracts Short →	122						

of many of the hedges. The overall market's implied volatility level shifts would thus have some impact on the portfolio's valuation, holding all other factors constant.

Volatility or vega risk can be managed at the position level by selling call options against a position when the high volatility level is unsustainable. Buying put options can also reduce this vega risk to the extent that volatility and equity prices move inversely to each other. Variance and volatility swaps are an excellent means to hedge volatility at the portfolio level. The volatility swap allows arbitrageurs a direct means to gain long or short exposure to market volatility. The swaps will not only allow risk reduction, but also provide a means to dynamically rebalance the delta-neutral hedge profile. Volatility or variance swap contracts are similar to other negotiated swaps, and can be tailored for the specific needs of the arbitrageur.

An Example to Hedging the Portfolio's Vega via a Volatility Swap

The convertible portfolio summary page includes the individual position's vega (in points) for each one-point change in implied volatility. See Table 10.5. Each position vega in points is multiplied by the position size to come up with the dollar exposure to vega. The position dollar exposure is then summed to determine the entire portfolio's dollar exposure to a 1-point change in implied volatility. In this example, the arbitrageur believes that overall market volatility levels are unsustainable at the current level and would like to provide protection against a volatility decline. The arbitrageur enters into a swap contract with J.P. Morgan's derivative banking unit to short volatility at the current level of 65 percent for the remainder of the year. The contract is based on the NDX 100 index because the arbitrageur feels it offers the best hedge for the portfolio. Each contract unit pays $250 for every 1 point in NDX volatility. Since the portfolio has a combined dollar vega exposure of $24,137, the arbitrageur purchases 97 contracts (24,137/250 = 97). The volatility swap will also need to be actively rebalanced to maintain the hedge's neutrality.

As seen in the volatility swap's payoff structure in Table 10.6, the portfolio can be effectively hedged against volatility declining, but at the expense of giving up further gains from volatility increasing. In reality, volatility changes are highly correlated with other factors that must be addressed before a hedge is established. Increasing volatility typically is associated with increasing risk aversion in the financial markets, resulting in changes in the fixed-income and equity-linked greeks. Volatility is often positively correlated with credit spreads (see Figure 10.5) and negatively correlated with the

TABLE 10.5 Hedging Vega with Volatility Swaps

Security Description	Holdings	Price	Theoretical Value	Vega Pts	Implied Volatility	Change in Theoretical Value 1 bps Move	$ Loss 1 bps
ABC Co. 5.5%—6/01/05	1,000	98.500	99.625	0.540	39.000	0.542	5,400.00
XYZ Inc. 4.0%—3/15/07	1,200	112.000	114.000	0.600	46.000	0.526	7,200.00
Big Dog Co. 0%—12/15/12	1,500	47.750	48.125	0.250	32.000	0.519	3,750.00
MMX Inc. 4.75%—6/01/04	1,000	101.500	102.250	0.340	65.000	0.333	3,400,00
Top Shelf 3.75%—3/15/09	975	94.250	95.000	0.450	53.000	0.474	4,387.50
					$ Vega Exposure →		24,137.50

Volatility Swap Index & Terms	Contract Unit	Volatility Strike Price
NDX 100 INDEX Dec. 03	$250/1 Pt	65.000

Swap payer: J.P. Morgan
Maturity date: 12/15/2003
Trade date: 01/01/2003

Units purchased →   97

261

TABLE 10.6   Volatility Swap's Payoff Structure

Realized Volatility	Volatility Swap	Portfolio Impact
35%	30	$727,500
40%	25	$606,250
45%	20	$485,000
50%	15	$363,750
55%	10	$242,500
60%	5	$121,250
65%	0	$0
70%	−5	−$121,250
75%	−10	−$242,500
80%	−20	−$485,000
85%	−25	−$606,250
90%	−30	−$727,500

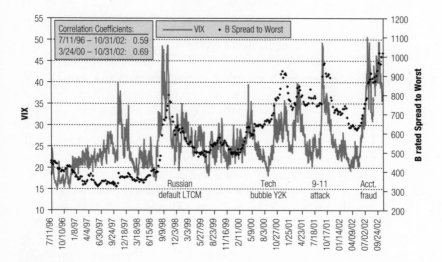

FIGURE 10.5   Volatility (VIX) and Spread to Worst Comparison. (From July 11, 1996 to October 31, 2002.)

equity market indexes, offering additional portfolio hedge complications and overlay opportunities.

As Figure 10.5 indicates, volatility measured by the S&P VIX index and credit spreads measured by the CSFB single B rated bond index are relatively highly correlated. Because of this high correlation at the macro level, volatility swaps can also be used to hedge credit-spread risks and also hedge against equity market directional moves. The behavioral stability and correlation between credit spreads and volatility also increases when a shock or perceived financial market risk increases, making the swap hedge more valuable. For example, in the chart opposite, the equity market declined, credit spreads widened, and volatility spiked during the Russian default and Long-term Capital Management crises in 1998, the Tech/Y2K bubble bursting, the terrorist attacks on 09/11/01, and the crisis in accounting confidence during 2002. During each of these periods, the arbitrageur would have benefited from a volatility swap to hedge any or all three risks (credit spread, equity market, or volatility shift). The bursting of the technology/Y2K bubble in early 2000 was associated with some slight increase in spreads and volatility earlier in the year. But, by late 2000/early 2001, the market recognized that the correction was a full-blown bubble burst, and that recession was likely pushing volatility and credit spreads higher. Volatility swaps offer triple correction protection during extreme conditions.

HEDGING OMICRON WITH VOLATILITY SWAPS

Similar to hedging vega with volatility swaps, omicron risk can also be hedged with swaps. Under this scenario, the positive correlation between credit spreads and volatility is expected to hold. The arbitrageur calculates the dollar exposure to a credit spread widening and then overlays a volatility swap to protect the portfolio from spreads widening further. But, unlike the vega hedge, the arbitrageur needs long exposure to volatility to hedge the credit risk. Also, since the hedge is not a direct credit-spread hedge but a "correlation" hedge, the expected correlation should to some extent drive the multiplier used. If the portfolio already has a swap with short exposure to volatility, then adding in a long swap exposure to volatility will reduce the overall exposure, while hopefully protecting against rising volatility and/or the credit-spread risks. If volatility instead declines, the swaps should still protect the convertible position's valuation. It is more common that the volatility swap is either used to hedge vega when volatility is already high and credit spreads are wide, or to hedge credit-spread risk when volatility is low and credit spreads are narrow; rarely would the tactic be used to achieve both types of protection simultaneously.

The portfolio hedge with volatility swaps to protect against a credit spread widening can be seen in Table 10.7. Once again, the portfolio summary page calculates each position's exposure to omicron for a 1 basis point

TABLE 10.7 Hedging Omicron with Volatility Swaps

Security Description	Holdings	Price	Theoretical Value	Omicron Pts	Credit Rating	OAS Spread	Change in Theoretical Value 1 bps Move	$ Loss 1 bps
ABC Co. 5.5%—6/01/05	1,000	98.500	99.625	0.210	b	400.000	0.211	2,100.00
XYZ Inc. 4.0%—3/15/07	1,200	112.000	114.000	0.330	b1	650.000	0.289	3,960.00
Big Dog Co. 0%—12/15/12	1,500	47.750	48.125	0.150	ba3	220.000	0.312	2,250.00
MMX Inc. 4.75%—6/01/04	1,000	101.500	102.250	0.250	b	575.000	0.244	2,500.00
Top Shelf 3.75%—3/15/09	975	94.250	95.000	0.240	ba3	350.000	0.253	2,340.00

$ Omicron Exposure → 13,150.00

Volatility swap Index & terms	Contract Unit	Volatility Strike Price
NDX 100 INDEX Dec. 03	$500/1 PT	25

Change unit value to align with historical spread and volatility relationship

Swap payer: J.P. Morgan
Maturity date: 12/15/2003
Trade date: 01/01/2003
Long volatility exposure
Units purchased → 26

Expected correlation with Volatility = .50% to .60%

increase in spreads and then multiplies this by the position size to get the dollar exposure. The total dollar exposure to 1 basis point increase in credit spreads is then divided by the swap's unit value exposure to volatility to determine the approximate number of long volatility swap units that are necessary to hedge omicron. But, it is also necessary to estimate the correlation between credit spreads and volatility to fine-tune the hedge further. In this example, since the recent past few credit spread widening occurrences have translated into roughly a 2 basis point move in credit spreads for every 1-point increase in volatility, the hedge is established with twice as many units as a volatility swap vega hedge would call for. Doubling the contract amount or changing the contract unit value for each 1-point move in volatility can accomplish this.

In the portfolio summary above, the volatility level of the equity market is considered very low and credit spreads may be subject to further widening should volatility increase above the current level of 25 percent. The portfolio's dollar exposure to omicron is $13,150 and it is determined that a long volatility swap with a $500/1-point move in volatility contract is to be purchased to hedge omicron. Although this is not a direct hedge, it may be preferable to a credit default swap (CDS) basket hedge because of the cost difference and/or liquidity differences.

HEDGING OMICRON WITH CREDIT DEFAULT SWAP BASKET OR SHORT CLOSED END FUNDS

Omicron can also be more directly hedged with a credit default swap (CDS) basket if it has characteristics that are very similar to the long portfolio. Characteristics such as credit quality, duration, convexity, and sector exposure are particularly important to compare between the basket and the portfolio. Since a convertible hedge portfolio's fixed-income characteristics are very dynamic because of the hybrid nature of the security, CDS basket swaps must be monitored closely to ensure that the swap remains relevant to the portfolio's holdings. The basket CDS works the same way as the individual company CDS discussed in Chapter 8, but instead of a single issue, a basket of issues is constructed to replicate as closely as possible the credit risk and characteristics of the portfolio. Arbitrageurs may also consider shorting a high-yield closed end fund against the portfolio, but this will typically bring additional duration, convexity, and credit rating mis-matches into the hedge. Each hedge alternative should be considered on both a cost basis and potential error basis to determine which one offers the best current opportunity to reduce omicron risks.

ROUGH SPOTS FOR CONVERTIBLE ARBITRAGE

Utilizing the full range of convertible arbitrage techniques and anticipating when to emphasize one over another separates the experienced arbitrageur from the soon-to-be-unemployed. The market can be very unforgiving at times (see Figures 10.6 and 10.7), even for the hedged portfolio. *The convertible market is also subject to "liquidity holes" that for a short time suspend the theoretical valuation equilibrium mechanics, causing individual issues to become significantly undervalued.* But an artful utilization of the full range of hedge techniques, employed at opportune times, can result in smooth, consistent, double-digit returns.

The 1987 Stock Market Crash

In essence, the crash was an equity market collapse after months of rising interest rates and a dollar reversal. Liquidity evaporated and convertible spreads widened. The now maligned "Portfolio Insurance" hedging technique fueled the market correction because it was based on the premise to buy on the way up and sell on the way down. Like all dynamic hedging practices, the portfolio insurance technique required liquidity, which the market suddenly did not supply. The convertible arbitrage techniques that worked

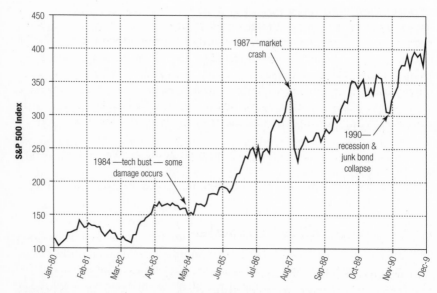

FIGURE 10.6 S&P 500 Index and Shocks to Convertible Hedge Industry. (Monthly from January 1980 to December 1991.)

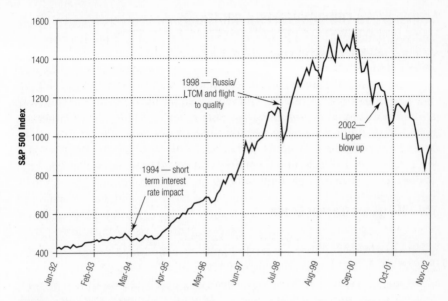

FIGURE 10.7 S&P 500 Index and Shocks to Convertible Hedge Industry. (Monthly from January 1992 to November 2002.)

in this panic environment included buying index option puts, bear gamma hedges, and high-quality market neutral hedges. Low-grade convertible hedges did not provide the protection expected as a result of the sharp increase in credit spreads. The most damage, of course, was done with highly leveraged portfolios. Credit spreads widened, liquidity evaporated, and conversion premiums collapsed, subjecting the highly levered convertible arbitrageur to margin calls and portfolio liquidation at precisely the wrong time.

> **What worked**—bear gamma hedges, high-grade market neutral, index option puts.
>
> **What did not work**—leverage, low-grade market-neutral, bull gamma, cash flow capture.

The 1990 Recession and Junk Bond Market Collapse

A clear sign of the difficulty that convertible hedge funds had during this period is seen in how few convertible hedge track records pre-date this period. Of course, convertible hedge funds did exist beforehand, but opted to start over rather than to include this rough period in their track records. The problems started when the government threatened to tax leveraged buyouts and the United Airlines LBO failed. The low-grade bond market was also coming under a significant amount of pressure as the government went after Michael Milken and Drexel Burnham and blamed part of the Savings & Loan crises on the junk bond market. Many S&Ls were forced to sell their low-grade credits and spreads widened sharply. In addition, the first war with Iraq was looming and energy prices also spiked. The equity market declined as a flight to quality occurred, and low-grade convertible credit spreads widened excessively. The CDS market was not in existence, so hedging credit spread risk was very difficult. High-grade neutral hedges and bear hedges worked best by generally trading dollars but avoiding losses. Obviously, having a low degree of leverage was also instrumental in the ability to preserve principal during this rough spot. Hedging interest rates helped a small amount, but not enough to offset the spread risk. Many convertibles were pushed in excess of 10 percent down below theoretical fair value levels, and demonstrated negative gamma.

> **What worked**—investment grade bear-gamma and neutral hedges, in-the-money cash flow capture and cheap put capture hedges, covered call write/stock hedge, index puts, and interest rate swap/futures.
>
> **What did not work**—Leverage, below investment grade delta neutral and bull-gamma hedges, credit sensitive low-grade hedges (due to negative gamma).

The Bond Market Decline of 1994

The Fed raised interest rates while issuing a warning to highly leveraged bond markets and hedge funds. Although the yield curve shifted up, mainly on the short end, credit spreads remained approximately the same. Equity sensitive convertibles held up well because the equity markets remained stable. Interest rate sensitive convertibles, especially the lower duration issues, declined. The 144A market was relatively new and the issues were not marginable, causing hedge funds to unload the issues as the costs of borrowing went up.

Most stock hedges that were in-the-money performed fine but the interest rate sensitive hedges were subject to convertible price declines even though the underlying stocks may not have gone down. The leverage in the convertible arbitrage community declined as the cost of borrowing increased, causing some negative push below theoretical fair value for interest rate sensitive convertibles. Funds that hedged interest rates with swaps or futures held up well, while those without the interest rate hedge were subject to rho and rho2 risk as well as convertible valuation risks, causing some large losses in the convertible arbitrage community.

What worked—Equity sensitive cash flow capture, put capture, hedging interest rate risk via swaps or futures, covered call writing, and stock hedge covered call writing,

What did not work—Any interest rate sensitive hedges including delta neutral, bear gamma, or bull gamma, 144A issues used on hedges that were pushed well below fair value, index option puts, individual security put buying, hedging spread risk, and leverage, if interest rate risk was not hedged.

Russian Default and LTCM in 1998

During the second quarter of 1998, Smith Barney closed its proprietary bond trading operations, putting some pressure on the bond and convertible markets, while at the same time, the hedge fund run by Long-term Capital Management realized the crisis facing their hedge portfolio; then, in September, Russia nearly defaulted on its sovereign debts and obligations. Together, these events precipitated a flight to quality in the financial markets, causing credit spreads and volatility to spike, as the world equity markets declined sharply. For one quarter, the liquidity in the convertible market for low-grade issues became very poor. Investors sold low-credit quality convertibles, pushing these issues to large discounts from theoretical value and significantly widening spreads. Hedge funds and trading desk liquidations further exacerbated the market. Unlike 1994, when interest rate hedging also provided protection, only credit spread hedging worked this time around. Put buying offered some protection, but the correction in equity prices was short-lived and timing was extremely important in entering and exiting the hedge with any level of success.

What worked—investment grade gamma bear hedge, investment grade delta neutral, and in-the-money cash flow capture in mid- and high-grade credits, hedging spread risk, hedging volatility, put buying, and some call overwriting.

What did not work—low-grade bull gamma, low-grade delta neutral and credit sensitive issues, interest rate swaps or futures, leverage without credit hedge.

Lipper Convertible Arbitrage Fund 2002

Despite it being the third year in the equity bear market, and a treacherous corporate bankruptcy environment, most convertible hedge funds managed to avoid complete disaster during this period. But, Lipper & Co. had two hedge funds that made the news, and sent a chill through the convertible hedge fund market (see *The Wall Street Journal* reprint, Figure 10.8).

Sudden Impact: Kenneth Lipper Hedge Funds Slash Valuations

By Charles Gasparino
And Gregory Zuckerman
Staff Reporters of The Wall Street Journal

Two hedge funds run by prominent money manager Kenneth Lipper were forced to slash the value of their portfolios by about $315 million, following heavy losses in the convertible-bond market.

The losses, representing a decline of as much as 40% in one of the funds since the end of November, sparked selling in both the stock and bond markets yesterday as investors worried that Mr. Lipper would be forced to dump investments to raise money.

Mr. Lipper, chairman of Lipper & Co., declined to comment. (Lipper & Co. and Mr. Lipper are unrelated to Lipper Inc., the mutual-fund data company.) A former aide to ex-New York City Mayor Ed Koch, Mr. Lipper attracted a high-profile clientele that included Hollywood producers and deal makers, as well as institutional clients like big pension funds. He was a consultant on the 1987 Oliver Stone movie "Wall Street." Mr. Lipper co-produced an Oscar-winning documentary on the Holocaust, "The Last Days."

In a letter to investors sent Wednesday, Mr. Lipper blamed the funds' sudden decline on "the extraordinary combined severity of 2001 events," including the fallout from the California energy crisis, the decline in telecom stocks, the September terrorist attacks and the market uncertainty amid the war on terrorism. "These events have had the most profound impact on the current market value of our portfolio securities in the airline, hotel, leisure, tourism, energy and electric generating industries," Mr. Lipper wrote.

The firm said it was forced to slash the value of its holdings after concluding that the value of its securities had tumbled and wouldn't recover anytime soon. That problem was made worse by the fact that the firm focused on riskier and relatively illiquid securities that were difficult to price accurately, and didn't fully protect its investments with other trades.

Still, people in the hedge-fund world wondered why it took so long for these factors to force Mr. Lipper to begin to cut the value of his portfolio to more realistic levels. Many of the securities in his portfolio—largely risky convertible bonds, such as telecom bonds—have been sinking for months.

At the end of November, Lipper told investors that the two funds now in the spotlight were up about 7% in 2001. Now, the firm is saying that its biggest fund, Lipper Convertibles LP, which caters to U.S. investors, is down 33% in 2001, and down more than 40% since November. The fund now has $400 million in equity, with holdings of $1.76 billion.

Abraham Biderman, a managing director at Mr. Lipper's money-management firm, says the fund decided to "become more conservative" in how it values its holdings and he said there was "no fraud" involved in the earlier pricing. He said the investments in the Lipper funds included illiquid securities that can be hard to price on a regular basis.

In the letter to investors, the firm said that on Jan. 14, its convertible-portfolio manager and its research director "departed unexpectedly." (Neither of those managers, Edward Strafaci and Mike Visowsky, could be reached for comment yesterday.)

Mr. Biderman said both executives—who were directly responsible for pricing the securities in the funds—left their jobs for other positions in the hedge-fund world. After their departure, the firm launched a "bottoms-up review" of its portfolio that resulted in the decision to cut the value of the funds' holdings.

The move to cut the value of the funds is likely to attract attention from securities regulators given the sharp decline in value. Officials at the firm said yesterday that they knew of no investigation by the Securities and Exchange Commission. However, Mr. Biderman said the regulatory filings that Lipper has made in recent months regarding pricing were inaccurate, and would have to be corrected.

Hedge funds, which are lightly regulated, are investment vehicles for wealthy individuals and institutions. They can use leverage, or borrowed money, to boost returns.

The convertible market, meantime, is among the hottest on Wall Street. As stocks have tumbled, investors in the past year have fled to the relative safety of convertibles, which pay interest like bonds but can be converted into stocks.

Hedge-fund managers have responded by loading up their portfolios with convertible bonds. Still, second-tier companies have flooded into the convertible market in the past year, making it much riskier than in the past, according to analysts. And with so many new hedge funds chasing returns, the temptation has grown to shift to more volatile, but higher yielding, convertible investments.

Overall, the return for the average convertible-bond hedge funds is about zero this year, and was positive last year.

But Mr. Lipper focused on the riskiest part of the market, illiquid convertibles with long-term maturities, and these securities have done much worse. While it's not hard to find accurate pricing for much of the bonds in the market, a segment of the riskiest investments trade infrequently, making it harder to obtain up-to-date pricing.

The biggest markdown in Mr. Lipper's hedge funds involved the convertible bonds of energy company Calpine Corp., which has seen the price of its convertible bonds fall by more than 50% since November. But the price of the securities has been falling for months, and some traders said Mr. Lipper's firm should have marked down its position long ago.

The markdowns are certainly a big blow to Mr. Lipper, 60 years old, and his company, which has built into a sizable player in the hedge-fund world by specializing in various fixed-income investments.

Overall, the firm manages about $5 billion of assets, with about $3 billion of equity invested in the firm.

The firm allows investors to exit from funds every quarter, and few withdrew their money at the end of September, the most recent opportunity to take money out of the funds, suggesting that few knew of any problems before their disclosure this week.

Yesterday, as the firm was scrambling to prevent investors from yanking their money out, it released a statement that said it had retained the Wall Street firm Bear Stearns Cos. "in an advisory role to manage" the convertible funds.

Mr. Biderman said he didn't believe the losses threaten the firm's survival, noting that Lipper's high-yield bond investments and other holdings, are doing fine.

FIGURE 10.8   Lipper Slashes Value of Its Holdings.

Source: "Sudden Impact: Kenneth Lipper Hedge Funds Slash Valuations" by Charles Gasparino and Gregory Zuckerman. *The Wall Street Journal*, February 22, 2002. Reprinted by permission of *The Wall Street Journal* via the Copyright Clearance Center.

The firm's largest fund, Lipper Convertibles LP was down 33 percent in 2001 and was down an additional 40 percent from November 2001 through January 2002. The convertible fund's problems not only highlight the troubles that a convertible arbitrageur can get into in a rough environment, but also the importance of how positions are marked to the market and how "theoretical value" for some distressed issues is a moving target.

MANAGING THE CONVERTIBLE ARBITRAGE MANAGER

This book would be incomplete without some final words on how to apply some of the techniques and risk analysis if you are not a practitioner, but instead hire the convertible hedge fund manager. The due diligence that is applied to any money manager who is hired is equally applicable to the hedge fund manager. The quality of the research staff, experience, research tools, pay incentives, and communication are equally important to hedge fund manager reviews. It is essential to understand the hedge fund shop's strengths and weaknesses and to align the portfolio risks with them. If the convertible arbitrage shop starts taking outsized risks in an area identified as a potential weakness, a discussion should be forthcoming. This book should prove to be a reference guide for convertible arbitrage due diligence and risk management. Chapters 3 through 10 should help in the understanding of the position risks, various techniques, and portfolio risks that face the arbitrageur.

The ongoing due diligence of a hedge fund manager should stress communication of active and passive portfolio risks above all. Some transparency is necessary but complete understanding of the key risks overshadows any amount of detail. Convertible arbitrage transparency is misleading in that any greeks supplied by the arbitrageur are subject to his or her interpretation of implied volatility, credit spreads, call provisions, interest rate volatility, convergence, time to convergence, and a host of other variables that impact the meaning and true transparency of the information. Of course, a third party could supply this information but this would also prove to be unhelpful, because the differences in the variables and opinions is often the value added that the hedge fund manager brings to the table, and how the alpha is created. Instead, the due diligence should stress the risks addressed in Chapter 10, with an understanding of what risks are actively hedged and which ones are passively accepted. It is useful to understand when a passive portfolio risk may be actively hedged and when an active risk may become passively accepted. Every portfolio review should also check the shock scenario risk and leverage of the portfolio along with a brief review or sample of a few position-specific hedges. The individual position hedges may be discussed after they are closed—a kind of "what worked" or "did not work" and why approach. This serves to keep the understanding of the product at a detail enough level for the proper level of risk management, as well as a de facto analysis of the types of security-specific risks that the manager has made. Finally, the breadth of the types of convertible securities and the creative financial engineering that is going on in the convertible securities and derivatives markets makes any book dated as soon as it is published. The intent of this book is to present an intermediate level of understanding to the convertible arbitrage hedging techniques that can be easily adapted to the new twists in convertible terms, types of securities, or derivative hedge products.

Glossary*

144A. Indicates that the convertible security was issued under SEC rule 144A and was not registered by the Securities and Exchange Commission. 144A securities can only be purchased by Qualified Institutional Buyers (QIBs).

ACES. Automatically Convertible Equity Securities. Mandatory conversion preferred with ratio determined by stock price at maturity.

ACTS. Adjustable Convertible Trust Securities. PRIDES-type preferred consisting of trust preferred plus a stock purchase contract.

Arbitrage. The simultaneous purchase and sale of securities to take advantage of pricing differentials created by market conditions.

Arch Volatility Model. Autoregressive Conditional Heteroskedaticity—Estimating volatility using time series models.

Asset Swap. An exchange of two assets, such as the replacement of one debt obligation with another.

Beta. A measure of a stock's relative volatility in relation to the market. A beta of 1.0 represents average market volatility. A beta of 2.0 would reflect twice the market's volatility.

Binomial Option Model. A model that uses a lattice, or tree, approach to value an option, thereby providing a more flexible pricing model.

Black-Scholes Option-Pricing Model. A model used to calculate the value of an option by considering the stock price, strike price and expiration date, risk-free return, and the standard deviation of the stock's return.

---

*This glossary was compiled from the following sources: Convertbond.com, a division of Morgan Stanley and Company, Inc. with permission of Morgan Stanley; Convertible Special Report and Convertible Monthly Report with permission of Merrill Lynch Convertible Research; and Calamos, John P., *Convertible Securities, The Latest Instruments, Portfolio Strategies, and Valuation Analysis,* New York: McGraw-Hill, 1998, with permission of The McGraw-Hill Companies.

Bleed. Change in the "greeks" with the passage of time or the propensity for one greek's return to be impacted by the changes in other greeks.

Bond Value. See Investment Value.

Break-Even Time. Bond yields typically are greater than dividend returns on the underlying common stock. The break even measures the time it would take for the added return on the bonds to equal the conversion premium. This is also known as the payback period. Possible redemption of the bonds could invalidate the calculation.

Busted Convert. A convertible selling essentially as a straight bond. Assuming the issuer is "money good"-that is, can continue to meet interest obligations-such issues have very little equity participation.

Call Date. The next date, or the first date, the convertible security may be repurchased from the holders at the option of the issuer.

Call Feature. A right to redeem debentures prior to maturity at a stated price, which usually begins at a premium to par (100 percent) and declines annually. Of late, new convertible issues are non-callable for at least three years, except under very limited circumstances.

Calls and Call Protection. Most bond issuers retain the right to redeem their bonds before the maturity date. This is known as a call. However, most bonds have call protection for a period of time. This call protection enhances the convertible's attractiveness because it ensures that the income advantage the convertible offers over the common stock may be enjoyed for a definite period of time. Issuers usually redeem convertibles in order to force conversion into their underlying stock. For this to occur, parity must be well above the call price. If the underlying stock advances rapidly, and the issue is immediately callable, a convertible may be called before its income advantage has kicked in. Issuers also call convertibles when they have an opportunity to refinance at a lower interest cost.

Call protection usually takes one of two forms: (1) unconditional call protection in which the issue cannot be called prior to a certain date and, (2), conditional call protection in which an issue cannot be called before a certain date unless certain conditions have been met, usually the underlying stock must trade at a premium for a specified period. Generally this is 130 percent (or some multiple) of the conversion price. The period of unconditional call protection is also known as the "hard no call" period.

Call Terms and Provisions. The call terms typically indicate under what circumstances the security can be called, and often involve date and price considerations. Convertible securities often have provisions that are subject to the underlying stock's price. For example, the convertible security cannot be called for three years from issuance unless the stock price exceeds 150 percent of the conversion price for 30 consecutive days. Call terms and provisions are outlined in the securities indenture and are determined at or prior to issuance.

Capital Asset Pricing Model (CAPM). An economic model for valuing stocks by relating risk and expected return, based on the idea that investors demand additional expected return (risk premium) if asked to accept additional risk.

Capital Market Line. A graph used to demonstrate the risk premium assumed in the Capital Asset Pricing Model, illustrating the expected rates of return of a particular investment based on its beta and in relation to the risk-free rate of return.

Cash-Plus Convertible. Convertible security that requires payment of cash upon exercise.

Change-of-Control-Feature. Certain options available to the holder in the event of a controlling-stake change by the issuer. This usually includes the right to sell the convertible back to the issuer.

Chi. A measure of the rate of change in the fair value of a convertible security with respect to a change in the spot exchange rate.

CHIPS. Common-linked Higher Income Participating debt Securities. Mandatory conversion preferred with limited upside participation.

Conditional Call. Circumstances under which a company can affect an earlier call. Usually stated as a percentage of a stock's trading price during a particular period, such as 140 percent of the exercise price during a 40-day trading span. Also known as a "provisional call."

Conversion Parity. The value of a bond or convertible preferred based solely on the market value of the underlying equity. Also known as "conversion value."

Conversion Premium. The amount by which the market price of a convertible bond or convertible preferred exceeds conversion value, expressed as a percentage. It is a gauge of equity participation.

Conversion Price. Stated at the time of issue, the price at which conversion can be exercised. It is usually expressed as a dollar value.

Conversion Ratio. The conversion ratio determines the number of shares of common stock for which a convertible can be exchanged. The conversion ratio is determined upon issuance of the security and is typically protected against dilution from stock splits, but not from secondary offerings. To determine conversion ratio, divide $1,000 par value by the conversion price.

Conversion Value (Stock Value). The equity portion of the convertible bond. It is based on the conversion price set by the company at the time the bond is issued. This price in turn determines the number of shares of stock into which each bond can be converted. This can be determined by multiplying the common stock price by the conversion ratio. Conversion value represents the intrinsic value or equity value of the bond in stock.

Convertible Asset Swap. A process by which a convertible's fixed-income component is synthetically separated from the embedded equity-option component to allow the two components to be managed separately.

Convertible Bond. A convertible bond provides the performance attributes of common stock and a bond. These securities typically pay a semi-annual coupon. The security is typically a subordinated debenture with a fixed principal amount and time to maturity with a right to convert into common stock based on its conversion ratio. The upside of the convertible comes from its common stock component, while the downside protection comes from the cash coupon, fixed maturity, and status in the capital structure, which is senior to common and preferred stock.

Convertible Debenture. A general debt of obligation of a corporation that can be converted into common stock under the conditions set forth in the indenture.

Convertible Debt Spread. The difference between the convertible and the non-convertible debt yields of similar-quality securities.

Convertible Preferred Stock. A preferred stock that is also convertible into common stock. It is similar to a convertible bond, except that it represents equity in the corporation. Unlike the interest payments made on a convertible bond, the dividend income paid by the convertible preferred stock is not a pretax income item for the issuing corporations. Corporations holding convertible preferreds are entitled to a 70 percent exclusion of dividends.

Convertible Price. The current approximate market price for the convertible security, typically quoted as a percentage of par for bonds and an actual dollar price for preferred stocks. This price will change as the common stock changes depending on the relationship between the convertible price and its equity value.

Convertible Security. A bond or preferred stock that can be exchanged, hence converted, into the common stock of the issuing corporation.

Credit Default Swap. A specific kind of counterparty agreement in which one party transfers third party credit risk to the other.

Credit Risk. The degree of probability that a bond's issuer will default in the payment of either principal or interest.

Credit Spread. The spread reflects investor perception relating to how likely the issuing company will be able to make timely interest payments and pay off the principal at maturity. The larger, or wider, the spread, the more concern investors have regarding the issuing company's ability to make timely interest payments. The smaller, or tighter, the spread, the less concern investors have. The credit spread assumption is used to calculate the investment value.

CRESTS. Convertible Redeemable Equity Structured Trust Securities. Unit consisting of a trust preferred and a stock purchase contract.

Currency Risk. The risk that an investment's value will be affected by changes in exchange rates. Also called "exchange rate risk."

Current Yield. Stated interest or dividend rate, expressed as a percentage of the market price of the convertible security.

DARTS. Derivative Adjustable Ratio Securities. Mandatory exchangeable with ratio determined by stock price at maturity.

DECS. Debt Exchangeable for Common Stock; See definition of PRIDES.

Delta. A measure of the change in the convertible's price with respect to the change in the underlying common-stock price.

Dollar Premium. The difference between the market price and the conversion value, expressed in number of dollars or points.

ELKS. Equity Linked Debt Securities. Mandatory conversion preferred with limited upside participation, exchangeable into stock other than that of issuer (synthetic).

ENHANCED PRIDES. PRIDES-type preferred consisting of Treasury securities plus a stock purchase contract.

Eurodollar Convertibles. U.S. Dollar-denominated convertible bonds that are not registered with the SEC and are traded outside the U.S. These bonds are issued in bearer form and may be sold to U.S. investors after a seasoning period, usually 40 days.

EXCAPS. Exchangeable Capital Units. Units consisting of a perpetual capital security and a stock purchase contract. Issued by a capital subsidiary of the company.

Exchangeable Convertible Bond. Similar to a convertible bond or convertible preferred stock, but exchangeable into the common stock of a different public corporation.

Exchangeable Convertible Preferred Stock. A convertible preferred stock that can be exchanged for a convertible bond with the same terms at the option of the issuer.

Exercise Price. Price at which the underlying stock is either purchased or sold. Exercise prices are stated in option contracts, convertible securities, and warrants.

Expiration Date. Last date on which an option, warrant, or right of convertibility can be exercised.

EYES. Enhanced Yield Equity Securities. Mandatory conversion preferred with limited upside participation.

Face Value. The stated value, or par value, of a convertible security when issued and when it is redeemed at maturity. Bonds are typically issued at a par value of $1,000 and the interest on bonds is stated as a percentage of its par value. Preferred stocks have par values, typically $50 or $25, and the dividends are expressed as a percentage of the respective par values.

Fair Value. The theoretical value of the convertible as determined by a convertible pricing model.

Feline PRIDES. From a holder's perspective, Feline PRIDES have an investment profile similar to standard PRIDES. Specifically, Feline PRIDES incorporate a stock forward purchase contract and a fixed income security. Feline PRIDES may be broken into their component securities. The basic unit is an Income PRIDES, which is similar to a standard PRIDES except that it can be split into a Growth PRIDES and a TOPrS. The Growth PRIDES security has a stock forward contract identical to that of the Income PRIDES, however, the forward contract is combined with a Treasury security, not the company's own debt.

Flex-Caps. Preferred shares that mandatorily convert into at most one share of common stock at maturity. A Flex-Cap participates in 100% of the stock's rise up to the partial cap, then 50% of any additional appreciation.

Forced Conversion. To call a debenture. Companies usually will force conversion when the underlying stock is selling well above the conversion price.

In this way, they assure that the bonds will be retired without requiring any cash payment.

Gamma.   The change in delta with respect to change in the common-stock price. Gamma is a second-order partial derivative of the convertible price.

Garch Volatility Model.   See Arch model—Incorporates both autoregressive time series models and moving averages to estimate volatility.

Hedge Ratio.   The number of underlying common shares sold short or represented by a put or call option divided by the number of shares into which the bonds are convertible.

Hedging.   A trading technique involving the sale of one security or option against a purchase of another related security. The object is to minimize risk in one position while attempting to profit from inefficiencies in the market's valuation of the various securities.

HIGH TIDES.   Unit consisting of a trust preferred and a stock purchase contract.

Interest Rate Risk.   The risk associated with investments relating to the sensitivity of price or value to fluctuation in the current level of interest rates.

Interest Rate Vega.   The change in price of a convertible with respect to a 1 percent change in the volatility of interest rates.

Investment-Grade Convertibles.   Those rated as investment-grade quality by Standard & Poor's (BBB– or better) or Moody's (Baa3 or better). Ratings by Standard & Poor's (BB+ or lower) or Moody's (Ba1 or lower) are considered non-investment grade.

Investment Premium.   The amount that the market price of the convertible is above its investment value, expressed as a percent of the investment value.

Investment Value (Bond Value).   The fixed-income component of the convertible. This is determined by calculating a bond value based on the assumption that the bond is not a convertible. The coupon rate and maturity date of an equivalent straight bond are used to decide this value. Over the short term, the investment value represents the investment floor.

Investment Value Yield.   Estimated yield to maturity utilized to calculate the straight bond portion of the convertible. This can be determined by evaluating any straight debt the company may have outstanding or yield to maturity of similar quality debt in the marketplace.

Issue. Convertible bonds are known by the name of the issuer, the coupon, and the maturity date, e.g., Hanson 9.5 percent 31/1/2006. Issuers may have a number of different issues outstanding.

Issue Call Protection. The difference in years between the issue date and the next call date.

Issuer. The company name under which the security trades. As some bonds can be exchanged into shares of different entities, the issuer name is not always the same as the underlying security name.

Issue Size. Indicates the size of the convertible issue in millions of dollars for bonds and millions of shares for preferreds. Issue size can be helpful in determining the liquidity of an issue.

Kurtosis. The extent of peakedness in the distribution.

Legal Provision and Prospectus Risk. Potential risks for issues, such as early call, takeover protection, special dividends, last interest rate payment in the even of call and so forth, as provided for in relevant documents.

Leverage. Using borrowed capital to increase investment return.

Liquidity Risk. The potential that an investor might not be able to sell an investment as and when desired.

LYONs. Liquid Yield Option Notes. Zero-coupon convertible bond with an embedded put option. These securities are designed to provide tax advantages to their issuers while simultaneously providing holders both equity participation and downside protection. Issued at a deep discount, these bonds accrue to face value and have no regular interest payments. Accretion is taxed as ordinary income.

Mandatory Conversion Ratio. At maturity PRIDES/DECS mandatorily convert into common stock. The number of shares received per PRIDES/DECS is determined by the stock price on the conversion date. There are three possibilities for the value of the PRIDES/DECS at maturity:

1. The common closes below the initial price. The PRIDES/DECS converts into one share of common.
2. The common closes between the initial price and the conversion price. The PRIDES/DECS converts into common according to a sliding scale designed to give the PRIDES/DECS holder common shares exactly equal in value to the initial issue price. The exact ratio is laid out in the prospectus, but will be between 1 and the minimum ratio.
3. The common price exceeds the conversion price at maturity. The PRIDES/DECS converts into the optional conversion number of common shares.

Mandatory Convertibles. A convertible that is automatically converted to stock at a specified time.

MARCS. Mandatory Adjustable Redeemable Convertible Securities. Mandatory conversion preferred with ratio determined by stock price at maturity.

Market Neutral. An investment strategy that aims to produce almost the same profit regardless of market circumstances, often by taking a combination of long and short positions.

MCPDPS. Mandatory Conversion Premium Dividend Preferred Stock. Mandatory conversion preferred with limited upside participation.

MIPS. Monthly Income Preferred Securities. MIPS are preferred securities issued through a limited partnership subsidiary. Holders of MIPS receive monthly payments, which may be deferred for up to 5 years. Return profiles are essentially the same as convertible trust preferreds. MIPS holders are required to file a schedule K-1 because of their limited partnership status.

Moody's Rating. Credit rating assigned by Moody's to the company's debt. The scale runs from Aaa1 the highest, to Ca3 the lowest non-defaulted rating. Ratings from Aaa1 to Baa3 are considered investment grade.

Next Call Price. Determined at or prior to issuance, this is the price at which the issuer may redeem the bond or preferred stock. The call price is usually above the par value of the security in order to compensate the holder for the loss of income prior to maturity. The earliest call price is most significant in evaluating a bond.

OID. Original Issue Discount bonds have below market coupon levels and are offered at a steep discount to par. Returns reflect both the coupon income and accretion of the discount. Accretion is paid only at maturity or earlier redemption, and is taxable as ordinary income.

Omicron. A measure of the change in the fair value of a convertible with respect to change in credit spread.

Option. A security that represents the right to buy or sell a specified amount of an underlying security at a specified price within a specified time.

Overvalued Convertibles. Since convertibles tend to trade on a fair value price track, convertibles that are overvalued, as determined by the convertible pricing model, should be avoided. Overvalued convertibles may decrease to their normal valuation without any change in the underlying stock price.

Parity. The conversion ratio times the current market value of the common stock. Parity is the stock value of the convertible security. Also called "conversion value."

Payback. The number of years it takes for the convertible's income advantage to offset the premium paid. In other words, payback is the premium recovery period. Although payback calculations give no credit to the time value of money, payback is still commonly used as a valuation benchmark. There are two methods of calculation: 1) Traditional Payback = (% Premium/1 + % Premium)/Cvt Current Yield – (Stock Div Yield/1 + % Premium) where % premium is expressed in decimal form. 2) Dollar for Dollar Payback = (% Premium/1 + % Premium)/Cvt Current Yield – Stock Div Yield.

PAY PHONES. Premium Accelerated Yield Participating Hybrid Option Note Exchangeable Securities. Thirty-year contingent unsecured subordinated exchangeable debt security with PRIDES-type ratio reset and income stepdown in year three.

PEPS. Participating Equity Preferred Shares, are a type of convertible security that is designed to provide investors with high current income along with high equity-like participation in the underlying stock. PEPS usually provide a coupon of 6.00 percent to 8.00 percent and are issued with relatively low premiums of 18 percent to 23 percent. The PEPS coupon is usually paid quarterly. These securities typically mature in 3 to 5 years, are typically listed, and are usually call protected for most of their lives.

PERCS. Preferred shares that offer limited upside participation with the underlying stock (generally 30 percent to 35 percent price cap) and mandatorily convert into common stock at maturity. PERCS offer investors higher yields in exchange for capped appreciation and downside risk. They are among the most equity-sensitive convertible structures. (a.k.a. MCPDPS, TARGETS, YES, CHIPS, ELKS, EYES, PERQS, or YEELDS.)

PERQS. Performance Equity-linked Redemption Quarterly-pay securities. Mandatory conversion preferred with limited upside participation; exchangeable into stock other than that of issuer (synthetic).

Phi. A measure of the change in the fair value of a convertible with respect to a change in the underlying stock dividend yield.

PHONES. Participating Hybrid Option Note Exchangeable Securities. Thirty-year contingent unsecured subordinated exchangeable debt security with fixed income advantage over reference shares.

PHONES, ZONES, and ZENS. These securities are usually issued at the same price as the common with an exchange premium of 5.26 percent. They typically have a yield that is 1.50 percent to 2.00 percent greater than the common dividend, and in most cases this coupon is subject to any additional common stock dividend distribution. PHONES typically have maturities of 30 years. These securities can be exchanged at any time into a cash value equal to 95 percent of an average price of the underlying common stock over a period of trading days. For taxable investors, these securities do have a negative phantom tax implication. These securities are typically callable at any time at a call price equal to the higher of the issue price or the market value of the underlying common stock, plus a coupon make whole that gives holders any unpaid coupons for the first three years of the security's term.

PIERS. Preferred Income Equity Redeemable Stock. Trust preferred, convertible at holder's option.

PIES. Premium Income Equity Securities. Mandatory conversion preferred with ratio determined by stock price at maturity.

Positive Yield Advantage. The convertible yields more than the underlying stock. The convertible should enjoy a yield advantage over its underlying common stock. The short sale of stock requires the seller to be responsible for paying the dividend. The difference between the convertible's yield and the yield of the underlying stock should represent a positive yield advantage.

PRIDES. Preferred shares that are exchangeable at a premium any time (at the holder's option) into common shares, but mandatorily convert at maturity to common stock. Conversion ratio is typically between 1.0 and 0.82, and is determined by the stock price at maturity. PRIDES are among the most equity-sensitive convertible structures.

Principal-Protected Convertible Structured Notes. A form of structured note that is arranged by an investment banker and has the credit risk of a third party.

PRIZES. Participating Redeemable Indexed Zero-premium Exchangeable Securities. Thirty-year contingent unsecured subordinated exchangeable debt security with fixed income advantage over reference shares; PRIDES-type ratio reset in year three.

Put Feature. The right to sell the convertible back to the issuer at a predetermined price. Typically, most zero-coupon convertibles have a put feature.

Qualified Institutional Buyer (QIB). A QIB is an institutional investor who owns or invests on a discretionary basis at least $100 million in eligible securities. Banks, savings and loan associations, and equivalent foreign institutions must also have a net worth of at least $25 million.

QUIPS.   Quarterly Income Preferred Securities. Trust preferred, with or without mandatory conversion.

RECONS.   Return Enhanced Convertible Securities. Mandatory conversion preferred with limited upside participation.

Registration/Registered.   Indicates that the convertible security has been registered with the SEC and may by purchased by the general public.

Reset-PRIDES.   Mandatory convertible preferred (usually 3 year maturity) that typically offers protection against the first 20 percent decline in the underlying stock, and roughly 80 percent participation in gains over 20 percent. Conversion ratio is between 1.25 and 0.833, and is determined by the stock price at maturity.

Resets.   Convertibles featuring a reset schedule that would increase the conversion ratio if the stock were to decline over a predetermined time frame.

Rho.   A measure of the change in a convertible security's value with respect to a change in interest rates.

Risk-Reward Ratio.   The ratio of the potential degree of downside risk to the upside potential displayed in a convertible security. It is determined by examining various possible future market scenarios as well as by analyzing projected price movements of the underlying common stock.

S&P Rating.   Credit rating assigned by S&P to this company's debt. The rating system runs from AAA+ the highest possible rating, down to C– the lowest. Ratings of AAA+ to BBB- are considered investment grade.

SAILS.   Stock Appreciation Income Linked Securities. Mandatory conversion preferred with ratio determined by stock price at maturity.

Screw Clause.   A prospectus provision in which a holder who voluntarily converts into common shares before the first call date forfeits income accrued since the last payment.

Share Price.   Bid price of the underlying security into which the convertible is exchangeable.

Sharpe ratio.   A risk-adjusted measure developed by William F. Sharpe, calculated using standard deviation and excess return to determine reward per unit of risk. The higher the Sharpe ratio, the better the historical risk-adjusted performance.

Skewness. The degree and direction (positive or negative) of departure from a normal symmetrical distribution.

Split Rated. Those convertibles that are rated investment grade by one ratings agency (for example, Moody's) but rated non-investment grade by another agency (for example, S&P).

SPURS. Shared Preference Redeemable Securities. Trust preferred, convertible at holder's option.

Step-Up Convertible. A convertible whose original coupon payment increases, or "steps up," on a designated date. The added cash flow gained upon the coupon's increase gives the convertible an extra degree of interest-rate protection, decreasing the downside risk.

Stock Dividend Yield. The annual yield on the common stock, i.e., the annual gross dividend / stock price.

Stock Vega. The change in price of a convertible with respect to a 1 percent change in the volatility of the underlying stock.

Stock Volatility. The standard deviation of the stock's return over a specific period of time. Volatility helps quantify the likelihood of a change in the price of the stock, but not direction. Prices of small companies tend to be more volatile than those of large corporations.

Straight Debt Yield. See **Investment Value Yield**.

STRYPES. Structured Yield Product Exchangeable for Stock. Trust preferred with mandatory conversion, backed by treasury securities.

Synthetic Convertibles. Combining a non-convertible debt instrument with a warrant or option to create the characteristics of a convertible issue.

Systematic Risk. The portion of a stock risk due to the general movement of stock prices.

TAPS. Threshold Appreciation Price Securities. Trust preferred with mandatory conversion, backed by treasury securities.

TARGETS. Targeted Growth Enhanced Term Securities. Mandatory conversion preferred with limited upside participation.

TECONS. Term Convertible Securities. Trust preferred, convertible at holder's option.

Theta. A measure of the change in the convertible's price with respect to changes in time.

TIDES. Term Income Deferrable Equity Securities. Trust preferred, convertible at holder's option.

TIMES. Trust Issued Mandatory Exchange Securities. Trust preferred with mandatory conversion.

TIPS. Trust Issued Preferred Securities. Trust preferred, convertible at holder's option.

TOPrS. Trust Originated Preferred Securities. These securities are designed to provide tax and rating advantages to the issuer, through the use of a Delaware statutory business trust. From a holder's standpoint, these securities are essentially the same as other convertible preferreds. Major differences: trust preferreds are nonperpetual (usually 30 year maturity), and issuers typically have the option to defer interest payments for up to 20 quarters. However, trust preferreds rank above other preferreds in the capital structure (roughly equivalent to subordinated debentures).

Trading Flat. Bonds trading flat are bought and sold without the payment of accrued interest. Income bonds and bonds in default trade flat.

TRACES. Trust Automatic Common Exchange Securities. Trust preferred with mandatory conversion, backed by treasury securities.

TrENDS. Trust Enhanced Dividend Securities. Trust preferred with mandatory conversion, backed by treasury securities.

Trust Structured Preferred. A preferred that is issued through a subsidiary trust to effectively turn the non-tax deductible dividend issued by the company into a deductible interest payment for the company.

Underwriter. The lead underwriter for the security who is useful to know because he or she often makes markets in the security and can provide information on the security and its issuer.

Unsystematic Risk. Risk of a stock specific to the company's financial condition or industry group.

Upside Beta/Downside Beta. This measure indicates the convertible's price sensitivity to changes in the overall stock market (not including the income portion of the convertible).

Upside Gamma/Downside Gamma. The change in delta with a specific upward/downward move in the underlying stock.

Upsilon. A measure of the change in the fair value of a convertible with respect to change in the credit recovery rate. The credit recovery rate is an estimation of the principal amount recovered in the event of default on the security.

Valuation. For equity oriented investors, convertibles can be viewed as either a stock plus put, or bond plus call. Stock plus put: A convertible security can be viewed as a stock plus a put. The upside of the convertible comes from the underlying stock. The higher the price of the underlying stock goes, the higher the convertible price should go. The downside protection of the convertible comes from its higher yield, fixed maturity value, and status in the capital structure, which all combine to give the security downside protection. Stock alternative: At very high prices, the convertible still should provide a higher current yield than its underlying common stock and have a low premium. The combination of the higher yield and low premium results in a low breakeven time. The breakeven time is the time it would take a buyer of a convertible to recover the premium paid for it. Low breakeven convertibles typically have the most equity sensitivity, and given the yield advantage, it is not unusual for a convertible with this characteristic to outperform the common on a total return basis. Bond plus call: A convertible can also be viewed as a bond plus a call. In this case the upside of the convertible comes from the call represented by the conversion feature. Moreover, the downside protection also comes from the bond attributes of the security, including the generally higher yield, fixed maturity value, and place in the capital structure.

Variance. A measure of the average distance between each of a set of data points and their mean value; equal to the sum of the squares of the deviation from the mean value.

Vega. A measure of the sensitivity of the convertible's price to changes in implied volatility.

Volatility. The relative rate at which the price of a security moves up and down. Volatility is found by calculating the annualized standard deviation of daily change in price. If the price of a stock moves up and down rapidly over short time periods, it has high volatility. If the price almost never changes, it has low volatility.

Warrant. Option to buy a stock at a stated price, extending up to 10 years. Warrants themselves bear no dividend and no voting rights.

Warrant Premium. The difference between the market value of the warrant and its exercise price expressed as a percentage.

Years to Call. The difference in years between now and next call date.

YEELDS.   Yield Enhanced Equity Linked Debt Securities. Mandatory conversion preferred with limited upside participation, exchangeable.

YES.   Yield Enhanced Stock. Mandatory conversion preferred with limited upside participation.

Yields to Put and Call.   The gross redemption yields that are calculated to the date of the earliest put or call.

Yield to Maturity.   The rate of return on a bond, which takes into account the market price, interest payments, and time until date of maturity.

ZENS.   Zero-premium Exchangeable Subordinated Notes. Thirty-year contingent unsecured subordinated exchangeable debt security with fixed income advantage over reference shares.

Zero Coupon Convertible.   A convertible that pays no interest. Rather, it trades at a deep discount from face value and may be redeemed at maturity for its full face value.

ZONES.   Zero-premium Option Note Exchangeable Securities. Thirty-year contingent unsecured subordinated exchangeable debt security with fixed-income advantage over reference shares.